Gender Matters in Educational Administration and Policy

Gender Matters in Educational Administration and Policy:
A Feminist Introduction

Edited by

Jill Blackmore and Jane Kenway

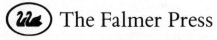 The Falmer Press

(A member of the Taylor & Francis Group)
London • Washington, D.C.

UK The Falmer Press, 4 John St., London WC1N 2ET
USA The Falmer Press, Taylor & Francis Inc., 1900 Frost Road, Suite 101, Bristol, PA 19007

First published 1993

A Catalogue Record for this book is available from the British Library

ISBN 0 75070 147 1
ISBN 0 75070 148 X pbk

Library of Congress Cataloging-in-Publication Data are available on request

Typeset in 9.5/11pt Bembo
by Graphicraft Typesetters Ltd., Hong Kong

Printed in Great Britain by Burgess Science Press, Basingstoke on paper which has a specified pH value on final paper manufacture of not less than 7.5 and is therefore 'acid free'.

Contents

Contents

Acknowledgments

We wish to express our appreciation to all the writers in this volume for their support of the project and their contributions. We also express our gratitude to Leonie Taylor and Renate Moles for their expert secretarial assistance.

Preface

The purpose of this introductory text is to bring the somewhat gender-blind fields of educational administration and policy into contact with feminism. More specifically, its purpose is to demonstrate the manner in which a range of feminist perspectives enhance the field with regard to theory, research and institutional practice. To this end, women academics/activists from various disciplines and theoretical positions, within and beyond education, were invited to contribute chapters taking up an issue of particular interest and concern to them. We thus have chapters which deal with a diverse but interrelated set of issues ranging from organization theory to theories of the state, from curriculum policy and administration to women and leadership, from science and subjectivity to evaluation and assessment. Collectively, these chapters demonstrate the considerable scope and potential of feminist scholarship in and for the field and provide many different points of departure for a variety of sets of interests and sorts of activity. Despite their diversity, all the authors are concerned to identify the forces which produce and confirm gender inequalities and injustices and those which have the potential to contribute to gender-just reform. As a result, they demonstrate the poverty of much of the male-stream work in the area which refuses to recognize the significance of gender and, just as importantly, they open up new possibilities for effecting gender justice in and through education. The collection begins with a telling tale.

Jill Blackmore
Jane Kenway

November 1992

A Telling Tale from the Field

Hester Eisenstein

I want to consider an area where theory and practice are in tension. The area of theory that interests me is feminist theory, and in particular theories of gender difference. The area of practice that interests me is reform of the promotions system in the Education Department of New South Wales, Australia. What I want to do here is raise some issues about the treatment of gender in feminist theory, using illustrative materials from my past experience in the Department of Education and more broadly my experience in Equal Employment Opportunity implementation in NSW since 1981. In particular, I want to introduce a concept that I call 'gender experience' as a way of finding a direction forward; to integrate, on the one hand, the lived experience of feminist political intervention with, on the other hand, an adequate and realistic theory of gender. I have developed these ideas further in *Gender Shock: Practising feminism on two continents* (1991).

I shall start by outlining some of the theories of gender with which I take issue and, in so doing, I shall comment in a very broad and oversimplified way. I shall then refer to a case study drawn from my experience of the introduction of reform of the teacher promotions system in the state education system of NSW. Rather than providing answers, I shall raise questions.

Let me first critique some mainstream theories of gender. Obviously the first one is the early model that we started out with: that of sex role socialization. It is necessary to go over this ground, as I think that in the current framework we are, as it were, living in a 'soup' of ideas about gender difference and sex role difference. It is almost as though there are archaeological layers of ideas about the nature of difference. One of the layers, of course, is the notion of sex role socialization. This has had significant impact as an explanatory model, both of the social structures we have inherited and for future action. Most readers will be aware of the work of Jean Blackburn and others in this area who first asked, 'Is this an adequate conceptualization?' In *Contemporary Feminist Thought* (1984), I critiqued the idea of sex roles and the concept of androgyny that follows from it. One variation on this is Rosabeth Moss Kanter's book, *Men and Women of the Corporation* (1977), which draws on sex role theory and adds to it the notion of tokenism. That book now seems perhaps rather oversimplified, as her model suggests that difference is only a function of proportion, if you like, and that if we get enough women in there somehow the differences will be erased. The situation is more complex than this.

Next, there is the theory of gender that has grown out of the success of women's studies internationally. I think of this as an 'élitist' model produced by women's studies practitioners: a kind of 'us' and 'them' model of gender difference. People such as Nancy Hartsock, the American political scientist who wrote *Money, Sex and Power: Towards a feminist historical materialism* (1983), write about the standpoint of women as a privileged epistemological location. The attitude towards gender difference embodied in standpoint theory seems to be that somehow, as Women's Studies practitioners, we write about most women and characterize how they are, and they are quite remarkably uniform in their characteristics. They are all extremely nurturant and affiliative and loving and good at interpersonal relations, reinforcing the old Parsonian division between instrumental and expressive. They are very expressive, but the implication is that they are not very rational. The only exceptions to this rule are the women in academic positions who are writing about other women. These academics are remarkably different in that they are all highly intellectual and rational and seem to have all those male characteristics (like tenure). What I find less than satisfying is the contrast between the élite of women who have the so-called male characteristics of being rational, instrumental, good at administration and politics, and then the mass of 'other' women, not feminist academics, who are nurturant and so on. This is the second model which emerged and which I equally believe not to be particularly useful to practitioners working for women in bureaucracies and schools.

The third is the model Carol Gilligan has put forward in *In a Different Voice: Psychological theory and women's development* (1982), which received much media play in the United States. Feminists found use for it in the Australian context, though it did not have the same sort of power there. Gilligan began her work on the moral development of women. She critiqued Lawrence Kohlberg, her former PhD supervisor, saying that Kohlberg's theory of moral development was based entirely on male subjects. She asked, what do we find about the stages of moral development in women? In her case study, she used attitudes of women to abortion. To me this is very skewed research, because to characterize abortion as a moral issue is to tip the scale absolutely in terms of the framework of the study (as did Kohlberg). Gilligan is now extremely trendy in the United States. Her work is being used by feminist legal scholars to critique the law as 'male'. Again, Gilligan's is a theory of women as virtually inherently 'other' and different. Although throughout the book she disavows that what she is saying is sex-linked, none the less there is no other alternative framework presented, except that men seem to approach moral and philosophical problems with an approach based on rights, obligations and contract. Women, by contrast, tend to approach moral problems from a quite different perspective, a standpoint which looks at linkages, affiliations and interpersonal relationships. As a theory of gender, it strikes me as an encapsulation of difference that we cannot really use in the bureaucratic context.

To recapitulate the three models that I am in effect critiquing. They are, first, the model of sex roles/androgyny (for example, Rosabeth Moss Kanter); second, the Women's Studies élitist model, which characterizes an élite group of women as rational and a mass of women as nurturant; and the third one is the Carol Gilligan model, which is talking about a difference of moral sense between men and women.

The reason I find all of them inadequate is that I experienced the 'politics of gender' in a very large, patriarchal and powerful organization, and none of those models seem to be functional and useful in my work. I therefore take a very empirical approach to it, and it is the theory/practice tension which underlies my critical stance. What I want, then, is a theory of gender that adequately looks to and theorizes the lived reality of gender difference that I experienced in an administrative and political context — a large state educational bureaucracy. What I experienced on a daily basis was that the gender experience of being female in that structure had enormous and powerful significance. The above accounts of gender difference are too static, and do not provide a theoretical framework to explain that gendered experience.

In order to make clear our experience in the Equal Opportunity Unit in NSW, I first offer brief details about the promotions system for teachers in the NSW Education Department before we brought in the reform. I then relate key aspects of the reform that was instituted, and illustrate some of its complexities by providing descriptions of random anecdotes and incidents which informed my sense of unease about gender theories of difference. I do not pretend to have done a finely tuned analysis; it is more just a series of vignettes, frames, or experiences, that I want to share.

Before 1986, the teacher promotion system in the Department of Education in NSW, particularly to the principalship, was one based strictly on seniority. I think we were probably the least reformed state system of education in the country. Before 1980, in each Australian state educational bureaucracy, it was standard practice to 'place' each teacher when they joined the teaching force on promotion lists. Each teacher's position on these lists was initially determined by her or his years of training, experience and qualifications, whether full or part time, permanent or temporary. Teachers 'rose' up the promotions list in each class automatically with years of service. Whether a teacher gained a particular advertised vacancy depended only upon whether a more 'senior' person applied. Our reform outlined below meant NSW would be midway between Western Australia with its phased merit system and Victoria, which followed a much more radical form of local selection of principals by a committee formed by the School Council and made up of representatives of teacher unions, School Council and the Ministry of Education. In the Victorian local selection process established in 1984, anyone from the senior teacher class who was deemed to be promotable (a matter determined by a school-based committee of principal, peers and ministry representatives) could apply and be appointed according to merit.

In NSW we introduced three elements of the promotion reform package in 1987. First, for principal positions (except for the little tiny primary schools that were too numerous to select on this basis), we went from a straight seniority system to a system of 'comparative assessment'. Rather than being appointed by order of seniority, principals' positions were filled by 'comparative assessment': namely, by application and interview among the people on the relevant promotions list (and after transfers were completed). This meant anyone on that list could be successful, and some people quite low down on the list were. Although the interviews were very centralized and highly controlled, it was still an opportunity for someone newly on the list to demonstrate a capacity for leadership. We were quite careful about setting out the criteria and process.

Second, if the change were only from seniority to a form of merit for selection of principals, the relevant lists for primary and secondary principals would exclude many women. This was because women were way, way down on the promotion lists for well-known and documented reasons, such as loss of seniority for child rearing. It was therefore decided to retain seniority for promotion positions below the level of principal and institute 40 per cent *limited* preference for women for principal positions. It was limited in two senses: first, in that it constitutes 40 per cent of promotion positions; and second, it was limited for a five-year period. Afterwards it was to be reviewed. The debate about the 40 per cent was one of the most interesting parts of this entire exercise. This procedure was put into operation before I became the leader of the EO Unit and after a great deal of statistical analysis. This work included an assessment of retirement patterns, because there were a number of senior women in the department who were retiring. If that rate were projected into the future the loss of female leadership was quite dramatic. When those figures were made public, a consensus began to emerge that something further needed to be done, Recognition of this as a problem was thus quite an important system-wide achievement (and we are talking about 46,000 plus teachers).

Third, the debate then narrowed to what was to be done. The decision was to give 40 per cent of the first offered positions to women. Again, the mechanism was very carefully worked out because, of course, the immediate concern was, 'Well, which jobs are you going to give them? You're only going to give them the good jobs, right?' We therefore worked out an elaborate method as the vacancies occurred. We would tag the positions as 1, 4, 7 and 10, and positions 1, 4, 7 and 10 would be *first* offered to women if they had that school on their promotion application. If not, we would revert to the seniority list and go down to the next most senior woman. It was a mechanical process which the Appointments Committee in Personnel put into operation in 1987. Ironically, the Department of Education is such a hierarchical and disciplined organization that, once Personnel were told to do this, they just did it! In fact, they had to be stopped, as they were about to just keep filling in positions. We had to tell them, 'Hang on, we said when we hit 40 per cent we should stop.' That fascinated me, because it was sort of like, 'This is the new system.' So patriarchal ideology is overruled by organizational discipline, which was my first lesson.

Furthermore, the Appointments Committee had both male and female members, primarily teachers who came up through the system, became inspectors, and then were recruited into head office. So they knew the system, as they had been in it for thirty years.

The other important aspect in getting it accepted was the role of the NSW Teacher's Federation. Whereas the Federation opposed the 'comparative assessment' model because it was such a departure from seniority, it did not oppose the 40 per cent approach because it was a form of seniority — a kind of skewed form of seniority if you like. Because the 40 per cent in effect is a subset of the full list, it is the list of women by seniority order, so we were just sort of taking them out and putting them up there and going 1, 2, 3, 4, and so on.

Now why was 40 per cent chosen? Originally, as I said, this was very scientifically calculated by developing a statistical projection based on the percentage of women in promotion positions, and taking into account the projections about retirement, plus the percentage of promotion positions as opposed to the system as a whole. I found out later that the original proposal, as calculated from the above data, was *70 per cent*, and it was bargained down. We had to argue the case for the reform to the NSW Government's Cabinet Subcommittee, because it had to go through as an amendment to the Education Commission Act. So we were summoned (that is, my boss as the Director of Industrial Relations and myself and my colleague, Kerry Hyland, who did the statistical analysis and had prepared the original Equal Employment Opportunity management plan, and whose original proposal it was) by the Cabinet Subcommittee and they said, 'Why 40 per cent?' Kerry provided her analysis of the statistics, showing how that figure had been derived, and then one of the members of the committee said, 'But surely it would seem fairer to people if you just established a list of women, and a list of men, and you just took one off the top in alternation.' A few seconds went by and he said, 'Hang on, that's 50 per cent.' Even though the 40 per cent had been very scientifically derived as a figure that would begin to adequately redress the dearth of women in promotion positions below the level of principal by establishing a 'feeder' mechanism for the comparative assessment of principals, none the less, it also became clear that the 40 per cent was the maximum acceptable figure. This is part of a phenomenon that I call 'male arithmetic', which means, 'How much do you women really want?'

Some random anecdotes illustrate the complexities of this process of change, and the relationship between theory, research and practice. In our research we had projected that the 40 per cent would never be reached for a variety of reasons: first, because of women's reluctance to be mobile in the system in the past; second, because of the chance factor involved in the vacancies coming through. The odds were against actually having selected schools that were going to become vacant. A number of things led us to project that we would only achieve 20 per cent or 30 per cent. Indeed, that is one of the factors by which the package was sold to the politicians. Even the dreaded 40 per cent was considered an upper figure. Ironically, every single deputy principalship offered to the women has been taken up except one. Part of the predictable backlash came from the men who said, 'But we did not think the women would accept the positions.' They did not, therefore, fight the proposal when it went through Cabinet as a political decision, on a bet that it would not actually come into full effect. Furthermore, with a stroke of a pen, it proved possible to change people's behaviour and expectations, because when the jobs were offered the women said, 'Yes, thank you very much.' Not only that, they had in fact put in applications broadly enough in terms of the schools that they would accept, that they could then be offered a position. The research was thus an inadequate guide: people reacted very differently once new opportunities became a reality!

The next issue which arose was the leadership issue. In the comparative assessment selection process, we had a criterion called 'leadership in the school'. What became clear was that, when people were being asked questions about leadership, there was an enormous overlay of gender related expectations. I started to understand that, particularly in primary schools, there was an implicit model of leadership which I now call the 'rugby league model': you know, the front row forward. Leadership was equated with a certain kind of masculine powerfulness, initiative, and 'take-chargism'. It was very hard for the women who were applicants to document an alternative model of leadership because that had not been spelled out. So in our criteria we were gender blind because we did not take account of the cultural weight of a certain kind of implicit notion that leaders have to be of a certain kind. An 'athletic' view of leadership is just one way I can characterize it. There was no room for an exploration of more subtle notions of how to establish authority. Because authority is what it is about. What makes a principal effective in a school is establishing authority, so when a principal says, 'This is the timetable,' people do not say, 'Who's she?' It is a subtle thing about arriving as a new appointment and getting people to accept your authority.

Additionally, many women accepted deputy principal positions under the affirmative action measure. This was not made public, so that ordinarily one ought not to know who got a promotion under affirmative action and who got it on straight seniority. But in our system, people read the seniority books like the Bible! They know in detail who was on what number relative to themselves. So the notion that it would all be subtle and private was completely naive.

Moreover, when some of the women, excited about their appointment under the affirmative action method, visited their new school to meet the staff, many were told, 'There is no point in you coming in because nobody here is going to work with you.' So under this system of appointment to a deputy principal's position, a *female* appointee's authority was undermined, *a priori*, by the attitude of the staff of the school. Both the 'comparative assessment' model and the '40 per cent affirmative action' model took people out of seniority order. Yet the former group only experienced complaints, but no harassment or victimization, whereas the affirmative action group experienced outright opposition and discrimination because they were women. That was a very serious problem.

The final anecdote refers to the process by which we achieved this reform. It involved the most extraordinary teamwork between a range of people, some of whom were carrying out very traditional male roles politically, and some, particularly the women in the bureaucracy, who were attempting to initiate change. The result was directly feminist-influenced political work. The most extraordinary kind of conspiratorial framework was established between (i) my male Director of Industrial Relations, who was very committed to this reform, partly out of conviction and partly out of wanting to have, as he says, 'runs on the board'; (ii) a Director-General who was very committed to making a change for women in the department because he came to power with a view that probably he had five years in office and he wanted to 'make a mark'; (iii) the female EO personnel within the department who were obviously very committed to getting the reform in; (iv) the Director of Equal Opportunity in the state, who was wanting to get the department to meet its obligations under the equal opportunity legislation; and (v) the Minister of Education, who was the most curious player in this whole process.

The Minister was distinguished by his having coined the term 'gender fascists' for the women who sought affirmative action within the Labor Party some years previously, a move he opposed bitterly. So he was a particularly interesting example of political flexibility when he supported this affirmative action measure, because he had been so overtly opposed to affirmative action within the Labor Party. He was convinced, and I give credit here to Alison Ziller, the Director of Equal Opportunity in Public Employment in NSW, of the virtues of this affirmative action proposal. What converted him were the arguments about educational leadership and excellence. He needed at that time to 'sell' public education. Yet it was a widely held view that the seniority system was promoting principals to their last school for the five years prior to retirement. In general they were uncaring and unresponsive to the community, and therefore failing in terms of the new demands upon principals. The Minister was very concerned to change that; left to his own devices, he would have brought in a complete merit system, but he had to be reined in because of the administrative impossibility if all applicants for the number of promotion positions per year were interviewed. It was also politically unacceptable to the teaching force in the Federation. Further-more, the Director-General of Education spoke out publicly against people being chosen after a twenty-minute interview supposedly on 'merit', as occurred in public service departments, on the grounds that it did not provide a full under-standing of someone's worth, whereas he supported the inspection system of the Department of Education, which he considered a very rigorous form of merit selection.

The argument then became, since everybody on the list had already been selected on merit, one of how to select from that pool. The Minister, having been converted to this two-part scheme, supported it quite unequivocally and stayed committed to the affirmative action. He got it through the legislature, he got it through Cabinet, he got it through the Labor Council, and he defended it. When there emerged a breakaway group of male teachers on the attack to get the proposal reversed, he said: 'Any teacher who harasses one of the women appointed under the affirmative action measure should be sacked.' On this issue it is nice to hear, because he was saying that such action was unacceptable and indeed unprofessional.

The irony was that, when the measure was introduced and the women accepted the positions, reverberations went through the system against the Minis-ter. The Minister went to his female advisors, and said, 'Where are your gender fascists now, why are you not supporting me, and why are there not thousands of feminists out there to support me for my courageous feminist act? So please write in support to the Premier!' It was so ironical. He felt he had taken an enormous political risk, and with an election coming up, yet somehow the vocal minority was silent. The women were not saying, 'Good on ya, Rodney!' When I said this many women got very angry and they said, 'Why should we be concerned about his ego?' But we need to contextualize his action within the framework of the gender politics of the time, that, having taken this enormous risk personally and politically, he felt 'miffed' that nobody said, 'He's done well.'

This also illustrates how the link between the Minister's female advisors and the EO Unit was critical. Every time it looked as though the reform was going off the rails, phone calls and midnight consultations were initiated just to make sure that a deadline was not missed, or the Cabinet minute did get up, or it did not get dropped from the agenda. Numerous crises were averted in this way. But we also had a very strong male/female alliance. It was remarkable that not only were there women who were very committed to the reform but there were men fighting for it as well. In some cases, certainly, for an entirely different reason, but there was enough common ground, so that whenever the reform came under threat, we were able to work together and get it through. It could not have happened without that combination of Director-General, Minister, Director of Industrial Relations, EO people in the Department of Education, EO people in the EO Agency, and sympathetic feminist advisors within the Minister's office, plus the female leadership of the Teachers' Federation, Jenny George. A very complicated alliance system was at work.

One final anecdote deals with the 'breakaways' or the 'tearaways'. These were the men attacking affirmative action and threatening to leave the union because the union would not support them. They claimed: 'Affirmative action is unfair, because it applies to 40 per cent of women without differentiating out '*x*' number of women who have genuinely been discriminated against.' They would have been agreeable to affirmative action, they argued, if we had selected out *individual* women who could actually document that they had lost places on the seniority ladder, because of 'time out' for child bearing and rearing, instead of giving it to *all* women. They feared that, for example, a young female teacher who had never had children and who in fact was not even married could profit from this affirmative action, and how *unfair* that is. If you unpack that argument, it means that the issue of discrimination was defined in a very crude manner, but still they were halfway to saying that some women have been hard done by.

By way of conclusion, let me direct this to those who are writing and theorizing about gender, particularly, but not only, in the educational context. Indeed, I see this as a broad women's studies/feminist issue. It seems to me that the question is how to theorize gender in a way that reflects the 'lived' reality of this experience, rather than using concepts that seem to me somehow quite archaic; that is, sex role socialization theory; the romanticized élitist/nurturant 'other' concept, which I think brings together Gilligan and the women's studies phenomenon; or the assimilationist model of Rosabeth Kanter which suggests that if we get enough women into high positions, the difference would vanish. None of these make sense of what we are experiencing, which is the genuine power of women as a political force. What I wish to suggest is that the experience of difference gives us, however minimal, significant political leverage in any particular context.

References

BLACKBURN, J. (1986) Productive and Excellent Women: equity, productions, excellence and women in tertiary education; *Australian Feminist Studies*, **2**, Summer, pp. 15–26.

EISENSTEIN, H. (1984) *Contemporary Feminist Thought*; Sydney: George Allen Unwin.

EISENSTEIN, H. (1991) *Gender Shock: Practising Feminism on Two Continents*; North Sydney: Allen & Unwin.

GILLIGAN, C. (1982) *In a Different Voice: Psychological Theory and Women's Development*; Cambridge, Mass. Harvard Uni. Press.

HARTSOCK, N. (1983) *Money, Sex and Power: Towards a Feminist Historical Materialism*: New York, Longman.

KANTER, R.M. (1977) *Men and Women of the Corporation*; New York, Basic Books.

Introductory Comments

Jill Blackmore and Jane Kenway

What is one to make of Hester Eisenstein's tale of the formulation and implementation of equal opportunity policies in the New South Wales Education Department in Australia? What is one to make of her claim that current and dominant feminist theoretical frameworks lack explanatory power when confronted with both the complexities of the gender politics of organizations and the dilemmas associated with feminist work within organizations? Why have we chosen this narrative to introduce a collection of papers under the title *Gender Matters in Educational Administration and Policy: A Feminist Introduction?* Let us answer all these questions together. Hester's story of the struggle to achieve some sort of 'gender balance' among school principals in the large education system of New South Wales indicates, in a powerful and rather poignant manner, how and why gender matters. It also points to certain themes which run through this collection. Her narrative demonstrates some of the ways in which histories of discrimination against women have become naturalized and institutionalized; how the gendered beliefs and practices of the past are represented in the present. These themes underpin many of the following chapters, which stem from the common recognition that the educational apparatuses of the state and the state itself have, over time, developed certain knowledges, policies and practices, rules and regulations, and ultimately certain patterns of power which have systematically structured unequal relationships between women and men, girls and boys. Feminist scholars in education have produced a wealth of evidence documenting the complex and often subtle ways in which this has occurred over time and continues to occur and, as the collection indicates, while there are many debates about how best to interpret this evidence, it is none the less conclusive. Of course, this is not to say that all educational administrators and policy-makers accept the evidence. As Hester's story shows, many not only refuse to do so, they actively oppose any policies designed to effect even the most meagre levels of redistributive gender justice. To such people, the gender order, unequal as it is, is the natural order not to be questioned or challenged. There is a form of wilful blindness in this view, a gender blindness which not only informs the resistant behavior of many conservative educators, it is also reflected in much of the educational administration and policy literature which in turn informs fields of practice and vice versa. Thus a circuit of mutually reinforcing conservatism and resistance is constructed. However, as Hester's tale also shows, feminist work in education is designed to break the circuits of exchange which largely benefit males at females' expense, which indicates another theme in the collection.

Many of the chapters which follow point both to women's struggles for change and to the never unproblematic outcomes of such struggles. Effecting change in complex organizations is never easy, as all policy-makers and administrators know, and changing the policies and the people who make and remake such organizations is no less difficult. A great deal of feminist energy has been spent in the development of theories which will inform the change process, in the conversion of such theories into policies and administrative practices and in rethinking theory in the light of practical experience. The range of ideas and experience is now considerable and a number of these come under review in the following chapters, though they reflect only some of the differences, debates and tensions among feminists and feminisms on this topic.[1] Further, as Hester and other writers in this collection indicate, the relationship between feminist theory and practice is somewhat fraught with tension and contradiction. This is because it is the subject of struggle between different sets of ideas and interests within and beyond the feminist movement. The politics within feminism, the politics between the sexes, and the relationship between them are, like all politics, complicated and because of this their outcomes are difficult to predict. Often the outcomes of struggles between the sexes are a matter of judicious and other sorts of settlements which arise as the result of disparities of power. Hester clearly demonstrates that this is the case. Sometimes such settlements have the effect of producing the sorts of changes feminists seek, and sometimes they simply readjust the *status quo* or change it in favour of certain women or girls over others. A number of chapters point to the ways in which this occurs. The politics within feminism are partly about praxis. Hester's discussion suggests that feminists need to engage more seriously in the continuing process of developing a praxis in and for education policy and administration. It is clear that all the writers in this collection share a belief that reflection, debate, critique and revision are an essential part of such feminist praxis. Let us now offer some brief introductions to the chapters to follow.

The first section, called '*Rereading' Educational History*, includes three accounts of the ways in which gender has been treated historically in various educational contexts. Kerreen Reiger teases out the historical relationship between the emergence of modern organizational structures and the family. She shows that these structures emerged in such a way as to equate the masculine with the public sphere and technical rationality and the feminine with the private sphere, affectivity and emotionality. She traces the shift in managerial/organizational style from the hierarchical, patriarchal bureaucrat to the flexible, multi-skilled corporate manager, but sees the latter as no less 'masculine' than the former. She argues that there is a need to rethink and reconstruct the public/private relationship and not just to focus on transforming the public domain. Jill Blackmore picks up on similar themes within education. She argues that educational administration has been constructed, since the mid-nineteenth century, as a 'masculinist enterprise', in which a particular type of 'hegemonic masculinity' has become associated with bureaucratic rationality. In contrast, she observes that teaching has been constructed as a feminine activity, an extension of the nurturant mother. She explores the manner in which this dichotomy has occurred and identifies a dynamic process which links the gendered division of labour and organizational cultures to particular ideological constructions of masculinity and femininity in specific historical contexts. In the final chapter, Deborah Tyler provides an example of the ways in which the relationship between the public and the private was historically reconstructed during a time in the 1930s when professional experts in the name of science began to intrude on all aspects of social life. Deborah links the dominant discourses of child psychoanalysis and developmental psychology which informed pedagogy, to the 'production of the perfect child' and the construction of the 'good teacher' in the child-centred pedagogy of the kindergarten. A central theme of these three papers is the ways in which the particular dominant versions of rationality in various public spheres had highly gendered implications.

In the second section, under the title *Contemporary Issues*, a number of topical and controversial issues associated with gender and other reforms are addressed. Joanna Wyn and Bruce Wilson's chapter develops a critique of current policies for reforming girls' schooling and offers an alternative approach. They argue that any adequate analysis of the policy objective of 'common outcomes' between the sexes must be informed by a material and cultural, as well as a gender, perspective. They suggest that the *National Policy for the Education of Girls in Australian Schools* produced by the Schools Commission of the Commonwealth of Australia contains contradictory imperatives; that although gender differences and cultural diversity are recognized, they are cast as a deficit not an asset for girls and women. Joanna and Bruce specify strategies and policies which they believe would produce more equitable material and cultural outcomes for and among girls. Jane Kenway's chapter looks at the ways in which certain aspects of gender reform policies have been translated into practice in schools, and points to a number of difficulties and dilemmas which have arisen as a result. More specifically, she focuses on the enormously popular movement to enhance girls' post-school options by encouraging them into 'non-traditional' fields of study (maths, science and technology) and employment. She examines the theoretical, pedagogical and political implications of this movement and suggests that those feminists who are promoting it must refine their thinking more carefully if this particular discourse is to work in girls' and women's best interests.

Helen Bannister's chapter examines the work of those who argue for and support the development of assessment strategies which recognize and value gender differences. Helen notes that most such work draws from developmental psychology and object relations theory, and makes the case that such theories and their associated assessment strategies fail to adequately explain and attend to differences in the performance and response of girls and boys to science and mathematics. In developing this argument, Helen argues against the naturalizing and essentializing categories of male and female which are evident in these theoretical frameworks. She suggests that such theories of learning have had the effect of actually producing gender differences in achievement and that a more powerful way to understand such apparent differences is to attend to the manner in which teachers themselves generate them. In the following chapter, Gaby Weiner explores the question, 'What would constitute a feminist evaluation?' She argues that evaluation is a field which has been dominated by the 'boys club' and makes the case that while more recent democratic approaches to evaluation might appear to include women, such an appearance is deceptive. Such approaches, she believes, sadly lack a feminist perspective, and thus cannot lay claim to being democratic. Drawing from critical and feminist theory, she suggests some elements of a critical, feminist evaluative practice which would take into account the complexity of the process of evaluation and attend to matters of gender. Attention to complexity is similarly evident in the following chapter by Terry Evans. Terry offers a case study which brings vividly to our attention the gender politics which are part of school life and the ways in which government policies on the issues of school governance and 'pupil mix' are worked through 'on the ground'. This chapter shows, in stark relief, some of the tensions which arise when institutions attempt to address one set of social differences and injustices, and fail to recognize and attend to others. In this case, gender struggles occur over the education of children with disabilities.

The chapters in the third section, entitled *Political and Administrative Theory: Some Feminist Challenges*, focus particularly on the state and on administrative practices. In different ways they all offer a feminist critique of the particular field under scrutiny and suggest modes of thinking and acting which are more amenable to the women's diverse and wide-ranging concerns. Anna Yeatman places feminist struggles in the broad context of the politics of the state, noting many of the complexities and contradictions that this involves as members of the 'new class' (certain women included) struggle to keep social justice issues on the policy agenda. She particularly emphasizes the importance of the state for feminist projects and highlights the dangers to this which are posed by the current privatizing and marketizing political agendas of both the Liberal and Labor parties in Australia. Barbara Preston's chapter on the social wage, and universal versus residual social services, vividly demonstrates, through example, some of the points made by Anna. Barbara's chapter points to the positive and negative ways in which the state may participate in the structuring of wages and in the provision of social services. Her discussion of universal social services is an important contribution to the public/private education debate and offers a set of principles which affirm and enhance the case for public education at both the school and tertiary level. However, the implications of her chapter go beyond the matter of education, for if Anna's argument about the importance of the role of the state for women is correct then clearly the development of a strong case for universal social services is crucial. Barbara's paper alerts us to the importance for feminism of an engagement with policy issues which may, at first glance, not directly appear to be 'women's issues'.

In her chapter, Clare Burton offers a critical introduction to the notion of corporate planning, identifies some of its more powerful metaphors, and suggests ways in which workers for Equal Employment Opportunity may temper some of the ideological power of the corporate plan in the interests of gender equity. In the current era, with corporate management strategies on the ascendency in educational administration around Australia and elsewhere, Clare's line of thinking is timely and helpful. Shirley Grundy's chapter, which concludes this section, addresses the matter of educational leadership. Shirley classifies different modes of educational leadership as technical, practical and emancipatory, identifies the key features of each, and asks to what extent 'emancipatory praxis' is possible in the current climate.

Feminist Praxis is the title we have given to the final section which includes only one chapter and which in certain senses draws the themes of the collection together. In this chapter, Lyn Yates focuses upon some theory/practice dilemmas, and a number of other issues which are of significance to feminist teachers, administrators, policy-makers and academics alike. Lyn also uses certain policy initiatives to point to the important intersections between gender and other forms of social division and shows how class and gender, particularly, are implicated in knowledge production. Finally, she identifies many of the contortions, contradictions and conundrums which are inherent in many policy formulations which are intended to produce equality.

The purposes of this collection are, as we said at the outset, to make problematic many of the truth claims and dominant tendencies in the field of educational administration and policy, and to introduce feminist perspectives into the mainstream/male-stream. Above and beyond this, our purpose is to alert readers to the depth and scope of feminist scholarship and to raise a number of issues for feminists who work in the area. Clearly there is a myriad of other issues which deserve attention and our selection has in some senses been rather random. However, we do not claim that this collection should set the agenda or that its status is definitive. Rather, our hope is that it will provoke many new ideas and stimulate many new directions in a field of theory and practice which, for far too long, has been the province of white, middle-class men.

Note

1 For an extended discussion of the range of feminisms in education see KENWAY, J. (1992) *Revisions: Feminist Theories in Education*, Geelong, Deakin University Press.

Section 1

'Rereading' Educational History

Chapter 1

The Gender Dynamics of Organizations: A Historical Account

Kerreen Reiger

Although the study of organizations has been a form of academic big business for many years, relatively few writers take adequate account of the historical context of the emergence of modern forms of administration. Rather, much organizational sociology, like sociology in general, tends to operate with its own form of what American writer Russell Jacoby (1975) has called 'social amnesia', the inability to think critically about the past. Yet the founding father of the study of modern organization, Max Weber, made it quite clear that the reason for studying bureaucracy was to delineate the nature and direction of society itself. Our concern with organizations, and with their gender dynamics particularly, should be not just with organizational structure and operation, but point us towards consideration of the nature and direction of society itself. Many commentators have noted the pessimistic conclusions Weber reached in studying modern forms of organization, writing very powerfully and passionately about humans becoming little cogs in the machine, and despairing that the world might know 'no other men but these'. Unfortunately, in many ways, we now take for granted and live our daily life in the world that Weber foresaw — but not entirely. Many feminists, and indeed women who would not claim to be feminist, have resisted this world in practice and more recently have been trying to formulate an alternative theoretical rationale for other ways of doing things.

This paper contributes to debates about desirable organizational forms for the future. It does so by discussing the ways in which modern organizations arose out of a formulation of public life predicated on the exclusion of women, but have none the less, come to rely significantly on women's labour. With contemporary, less autocratic, management styles, they even seem to be more attuned to traditional feminine human relations skills, but they continue to make little allowance for the demands of 'private life' on personnel, for family needs are still to be merely 'personal'. In view of the different responsibilities of women and men, their experience of managing the 'private/public' split, and of the processes of the workplace, remains dissimilar. The gender patterning of modern organizational forms is a more complex matter, therefore, than simply the proportions of each sex in particular positions. I argue that feminist debates over how we should assess and respond to the dilemmas presented by modern organizations need to recognize the ambiguity or unevenness and contradictions in the historical processes through which they emerged.

17

Feminist writers have developed substantial critiques of the position of women in modern organizations (Kanter, 1975; Wolff, 1977) and of the very form of legal-rational bureaucracy itself (Ferguson, 1984; Gould, 1979). It is not my purpose here to try to explore these in detail, but rather to draw out the salient issues for taking a historical perspective.

Several defining features of modern organizations are central to their structure and operation. We are familiar with most of these for we live with them daily: their hierarchical, specialized division of labour; the centralized authority; the impersonal social relations in which behaviour is guided by formally established rules. In spite of the pretence of organizational theory that bureaucracy, and indeed its own theory of management, is value-neutral, there are a variety of ways in which such an organizational model actually reproduces gender inequality in society (Kanter, 1975; Ferguson, 1984; Wolff, 1977). It does so, for example, by confining women to lower positions in the hierarchy and by sex-typing of tasks. There is substantial evidence that women, by and large, carry on the maintenance activity of an organization, thereby achieving lower status and rewards, for greater prestige and material benefits are associated with higher-echelon management roles.

To some extent this has been seen as just an unfortunate by-product of assumptions about women's social role and outdated male attitudes. These are thought to lead to forms of discrimination, such as towards women seeking promotion. Liberal feminist advocacy of legislative remedies for these problems has presupposed that eventually women will be able to enter organizations, in both the state and the private sector, basically on the same terms as men. Radical feminists, however, have claimed that this is too naive an expectation and, even if true, would be a sell-out of women's interests. By contrast, they have argued, (for example, Ferguson, 1984) that modern organizational forms represent a conjunction of patriarchal social relations and those characteristic of industrial capitalist corporations. They reproduce the sexual division of labour and reinforce the dominance of the instrumental values more associated with men.

Describing bureaucracy as both structure and process, Ferguson, for example, argues that 'bureaucracy, as the "scientific organization of inequality", serves as a filter for other forms of domination — those of class and race, as well as sex, projecting them into an institutional arena that both rationalizes and maintains them' (Ferguson, 1984, p. 8). In particular, bureaucratic discourse institutionalizes technical rationality, the concern with means rather than ends, and the compartmentalization of social life and segmentation of social relationships, or, to put it bluntly, chopping things up and cutting out personal relationships. It is in women's experience of community, of caretaking, of mingling of self and other that Ferguson, like other radical feminists such as Adrienne Rich (1976), finds both the basis of critique of current social arrangements, and the source for an alternative social vision. Sometimes the resulting critique relies on an implicit essentialism, suggesting that women would somehow 'naturally' organize social life better than men, but there is another possible argument underpinning the claim, one which stresses women's existing practice, rather than something to do with their intrinsic nature.

In order to assess this argument and its implications, we need an understanding of the past. The historical picture, however, is a quite complex one. If we explore the relationship between the emergence of the public sphere in which organizations are primarily located, and the structuring of the private sphere, we can be clearer about links between masculinity, public life, and technical rationality and those connecting femininity, private life, and affective or emotional relationships. Furthermore, we can critically examine historical processes cutting across both. During the twentieth century not only has technique, as Ellul (1964) calls it, spread to the domestic sphere but there has also been, in the public sphere, renewed interest in human relations, in what would seem to be 'feminine' types of skills. After discussing the processes associated with the nineteenth-century separation of public and private spheres, and then twentieth-century developments, I shall go on to take up a feminist analysis from what women actually do by exploring very briefly some examples from my own research.

We start, therefore, with understanding the emergence of the public and private and the gender dynamics that are essential to both. First, then, bourgeois society and the separation of public and private spheres. A great deal has been written about the ways in which industrial capitalism has polarized aspects of life which previously had an everyday lived unity (such as Zaretsky, 1976; Shorter, 1975). As the labour market drew men and, for a time, most working-class women and children out of the household, the bourgeois society promoted the ideology of separate spheres for women and men. This was linked very closely with a particular notion of the family and of domestic life. The form of the family developed by the emerging bourgeois class — the traders, the merchants, the early industrialists, the urban folk, particularly of Protestant religious background, in Western Europe — had several main features (Poster, 1979). I do not think we can understand the gender dynamics within modern organizations without an understanding of this historical process of the formation of masculinity and femininity in the eighteenth century in Western Europe. Some of the main features of the bourgeois model of the family became institutionalized in modern organizations. Its notion of masculinity was a particular one; it was an emphasis on men as rational, unemotional, logical, authoritive figures, but it also entailed a certain notion of men's sexuality. I am particularly intrigued by, and always delight in quoting, American writer and historian Barker-Benfield's (1976) discussion of the nineteenth-century debates about sexual energy, having seen plenty of examples of similar themes in medical sources in the Australian context. This bourgeois notion of masculinity strongly emphasized a concept of the rational man, but beneath that was said to be the irrational sexual man, who had to be kept under control. There was a great deal of discussion about energy within the body, how it had to be diverted into work, and, therefore, how sexuality had to be repressed. Much of this nineteenth-century notion of sexuality continues to underpin understandings of men's sexuality. The crucial point, of course, is that ideas of masculinity were clearly counterposed to notions of femininity. Many historians (for example, Shorter, 1975) have described the Victorian bourgeois image of womanhood in terms of images of true womanhood, the angel in the house, the nurturing figure who was the centre of home and family. Woman was pure emotion in some cases, but certainly not pure sexuality; she was asexual if she was anything. She was irrational, she was nurturing, but primarily wife and mother. She thus provided the ideal complement to the breadwinner, father figure. Other aspects of the bourgeois notion of the family were also significant, including the growing emphasis on the importance of the private sphere as an idealized, even sanctified, realm. The house and home became increasingly portrayed as a refuge from the outside world. With that went a growing emphasis on the importance of children and hence the genesis of scientific preoccupation with childhood development.

The dichotomization of relationships into those appropriate to the public and private spheres became a central feature of nineteenth-century thinking. For example, the Melbourne Methodist paper, *The Spectator*, described the home and family as 'the haven of rest and peace, a sphere of privacy from which the world with its storms and rude alarms is shut out, a place in which all inmates are known and loved and where we can never feel the chill of a stranger' (8 May 1882). The chilly world, then, of business and politics was also that of science and technology, of reason rather than emotion. Quite clearly it was to be the sphere of men rather than women. In effect, women were needed at home to provide the nurturing and sexual relationships which were by definition excluded from the rational bureaucratic world. Accordingly, women's entry into that world implicitly threaten such dichotomization. Indeed, they would threaten its very order. I think some feminist theorists such as Dorothy Dinnerstein (1976) have paid some attention to the sexual aspects and the psycho-dynamics of women's entry into the public sphere and the way that threatens the 'rugby league' model of leadership (see Eisenstein in this collection). Women threaten many of the basic preconceptions of the rational bureaucratic world, and Dinnerstein and others argue that women's presence there, in contradicting many of the assumptions upon which the world of modern organizations was based, is central to understanding the social processes now going on within the public sphere, sexual harassment being merely the most obvious example.

However, the separation of spheres was never as real in practice, of course, as it was in theory. Moreover, as I have discussed in some detail elsewhere (Reiger, 1985), it was the target of attack from those wanting to rationalize even the private sphere. The new professional-managerial class, from doctors and administrators to psychologists and kindergarten teachers, wanted to extend the mode of operation typical of the business and professional world to home and family life as well. This professional-managerial class which grew rapidly in the early twentieth century was the major proponent of instrumental rationality with its commitment to modern scientific and efficiency techniques. Along with Taylorism in industry and the perfecting of bureaucratic structures of administration, the new class, as they are often now being called, also tried to reshape the home and intimate family relationships. In my earlier book (Reiger, 1985), I outlined the preoccupation of infant welfare professionals with weighing and measuring of food stuff and babies, and that of psychologists with rationalizing sexual behaviour and child bearing. However, there are many more examples of the practices of the 'experts', of the influence of their general mentality and outlook. They were especially concerned about the 'irrationality' of mother love and how it needed to be kept under control, diverted and reshaped. In the process of establishing institutions to do just this, they attempted to take child bearing and rearing increasingly under their own control.

Pressures mounted on women as housewives and mothers, pressures to be more orderly and scientific in running the house and mothering. Domestic science, of course, and other aspects to do with the schooling of girls were to play a major role in this project. In the American context too, as Ehrenreich and English (1979) have argued, women have been the target of a massive onslaught of professional intervention. Much of it, of course, has been designed to adjust them to the demands of modern society. Others have talked about it in terms of the pressures to turn them into consumers — Anne Game and Rosemary Pringle's discussion of the 1950s, for instance (Game and Pringle, 1984).

None the less, the movement has not been as one way, all from the public sphere into the private sphere, as that makes it seem. Although the formal structure of bureaucratic organizations embody, as Rosabeth Kanter has pointed out, a 'masculine ethic of rationality', and this has been supported by management science, since the 1930s the human relations school has challenged that ideology. There has been growing recognition of the significance of informal processes in organizations, that is, that it is not just the formal structure, but also the personal and informal dynamics that count in explaining the overall pattern of organizational operation. And there has also been at least limited acknowledgment of the importance of fostering interpersonal skills within organizations.

The development of a somewhat different bureaucratic style, then, has been accompanied by a modification of influences from the public to the private sphere of home and family. Child-rearing advice, for instance, has shifted away from the strong emphasis before the Second World War on science and reason. Since the 1950s the same professionals, the psychologists and so on, have followed a different tack. What other writers have called, and what I would also refer to as, the emergence of a psychotherapeutic ideology has replaced that pre-war stress on efficiency and calculation. The development of marriage guidance, for instance, and the post-Spock era of child-rearing advice has privileged emotional rather than behavioural goals and psychological dynamics have come even more into the forefront of concern.

Such a development has been part of a wider cultural shift which has been described by Christopher Lasch (1979) in the North American context as the culture of narcissism or, as others would call it, the culture of the therapeutic; a search for, indeed a preoccupation with, meaningful selfhood. Lasch and others argue that the growing preoccupation with seeking a 'self' and with pursuing meaningful relations with others, has been occurring at the same time as the social conditions increasingly militate against personal autonomy and community interaction. Lasch claims that, in advanced western cultures, society is taking hold in the individual through a new style of personality structure, one that is profoundly shaped by the administrative apparatus of modern society.

The relationship between social structure and personality is not a new theme and is one directly related to debates on organizations. Other commentators since the 1940s have long since described the rise of 'organization man', in some people's term, or in Reisman's (1961) term, 'other-directed man', rather than 'inner-directed man'. Of course the gender here is not an accident. Many have traditionally seen the rise of organizational man as a progressive development, simply 'the emergence of a more organized and differentiated set of mechanisms for developing and regulating personality' (Parsons and White, 1964, p. 235). Now by contrast, Lasch, for instance, complains that the new bureaucratic rationality is paternalistic. He points to the rise of a new ruling class of administrators, bureaucrats, technicians and experts, who differ in style as well as in role from the old entrepreneurial élite. Corporate capitalism's system of social control, says Lasch, is internalized by the individual who becomes dependent on experts and the state and prey to the manipulation of consumerism. Unfortunately neither the established liberal account of organizational man, nor the conservative Left account of Lasch, explores the gender dynamics that this shift of cultural and organizational style has involved.

Feminists have, however, suggested that the change in organizational style from the earlier strict hierarchicalism and centralization of authority to new-style corporate management does not represent any genuine advance for women at all. Indeed, of course, it can be pointed out, as Kanter does, that the new-style shift to human relations never goes right through the whole organizational structure anyway. The management message is still very much the old nineteenth-century model of masculinity, the bourgeois notion of the unemotional man. Concern with relationships often does not extend that far up the bureaucratic ladder and, to the extent that it does, it represents an instrumental attitude to others. Ferguson pursues the theme of the 'feminization' of bureaucracy (1984, p. 99); she is not, however, referring merely to the traditional role of women as maintenance workers in organizations, the way in which women smooth over ruffled feelings, make the tea, keep the whole show running, as well as doing the typing and shuffling the paper. Rather, she argues that the skills traditionally developed by women as a result of their subordinate social status are those increasingly necessary for men, too, in order to survive the extension of the bureaucratic mode. These include skills of successful impression management — putting on a good face to others, knowing how to get around them, the ability to work in groups and to conform to the normative consensus of a group, and reliance upon the informal message systems as avenues of change. These features of traditional 'femininity' seem to be increasingly adopted by men within bureaucracies too, says Ferguson. 'As society becomes more bureaucratized', she says, 'we are seeing the feminization of the polity through increased administration' (Ferguson, 1984, p. 99). In other words, rather than the development of an environment really conducive to women gaining equality, fundamentally patriarchal relations remain, simply having taken on another 'face' in advanced western societies with this change in organization style. This is perhaps clearest in the case of Japanese industry in which *gemeinschaft* or personal, even clan-type, relationships actually characterize the public sphere. As we know, Japanese companies are organized around close personal involvement — staff go on holiday together, and have a high level of commitment. All employees, but primarily men, have this degree of involvement with the company which is lifelong. So *gemeinschaft*, or close-knit-type relationships, actually characterize the public sphere in the case of Japan (Deutschman, 1987). Of course, women's subordination is still more firmly entrenched than in western societies.

So it seems that it is not necessarily just the impersonal technical rationality of bureaucratic discourse which is the major barrier to gender equality. In order to discover what else might be going on in modern organizations, we need to ground our theorizing in a comparison of women's and men's lives. It is a fundamental norm of feminist discourse to start with women's actual experience, and for many people this means starting with the practical, day-to-day activities in which women engage (Ruddick, 1982; Rich, 1976; Smith, 1987). The feminist model of organization which has emerged from this argument is one most activists in the women's movement are now very familiar with, and it provides the basis of many services delivered by and to women, such as several in the health field. It has been well summarized by Joyce Rothschild-Whitt (1979) as a 'collectivist democratic model'; it interprets authority as residing in the whole rather than in a hierarchical structure of the people at the top. It minimizes formal rules, is characterized by holistic rather than segmented personal relationships, tends to be egalitarian with minimal division of labour, and emphasizes community or solidarity considerations rather than material rewards or task achievements. Ferguson goes so far as to claim that an alternative vision of collective life to the bureaucratic one is based on the concrete life experience of women, especially that as caretakers. Another writer, Kari Waerness (1987), talks about the 'rationality of caring'.

Most feminist case studies based on the line of argument just outlined tend to use as examples explicitly feminist organizations, women's health collectives, alternative schools, women's refuges and so on. Even if we look at women who have played a significant role in the past within the structures of traditional organizations, however, we can get some clues which we can build on for developing a feminist framework, and an example from my own research can suggest some pointers (see also Blackmore in this collection). What we can see is that the public/private aspect of women's lives are never as readily distinguishable as men's tend to be. Thinking about this, I reread the notes of one of the leading people supporting the establishment of kindergartens in Victoria in the early 1930s, Vera Scantlebury-Brown, who was the first director of Maternal and Child Welfare in Victoria. Dr Vera, as she was widely known, became a very important figure within the public service in Victoria in the 1920s and 1930s, until her death in the mid-1940s. Although she had a housekeeper and a nanny to care for her child, her professional and family roles intersected in all sorts of ways. One can see from reading her diaries that her struggles within the bureaucracy for funds, for adequate staff to establish a state-supported infant welfare system that would end the petty bickering of voluntary groups, were intensely felt at the emotional level. Likewise, her worries when her baby was unwell, or the household disorganized, flowed over into her professional life. After a Government House dinner party in 1929, she wrote, for example:

> I was kept waiting! Both with a policeman marking my car and an angry husband and a hungry babe waiting for me, and then a rush to get home in time. Alas, the theories! The afternoon wet, windy and cold, I had to take two doctors to the Tweddle baby hospital and was kept late — result — a worried mother and a poor wee babe. Damn! Tuesday was better (Scantlebury-Brown, 1929).

Her concern with social relationships at work as well as home was very significant throughout her diaries. On another occasion she commented:

> A vile day at the office, Miss Wigg in tears, which is upsetting and detrimental to progress. The posters and leaflets had to be sent out and so it was all very trying and headachey and on top of it the babe was a little upset. I'm ashamed to say how my stomach turns upside down when he's not perfect (Scantlebury-Brown, 1929).

Clearly, she believed all the right mothering ideology. 'It's difficult to be reasonable,' concluded Vera, but I do not think that Vera's definition of reasonable involved the bureaucratic notion of rationality. It did not involve the exclusion of emotion; rather, I think, what she meant was the balanced response to circumstances, some effective meshing of the demands of public and private life.

In my current research on several women's organizations I am exploring the emergence of parenting organizations as part of my interest in the interaction between professionals and women in the period after the Second World War. I am especially interested in groups such as childbirth reform groups and the Nursing Mothers' Association. This has meant investigating the ways in which women have even used highly bureaucratic structures and yet maintained a distinctly 'womanly' combination of orientation towards both task and process. The Nursing Mothers' Association is a highly complex organization and I am a long way from reaching a full understanding or assessment of it. But in one joint interview with several women who played major administrative roles, I was struck by their enjoyment of administration and sense of achievement of goals and their awareness of the ways in which their organization, in spite of its corporate management model, has remained distinctive. They were actually talking about the ways in which this was a women's organization as distinct from a men's. One said, 'Well, men don't spend so much time sitting and talking about how they feel in the first place.' The next said, 'Are you talking about hiring and firing, or just the administration in general?' I asked, did they mean in terms of organizational strategies? One said, 'They wouldn't worry about hurting people's feelings so much, we are much more, I think, aware of hurting or upsetting someone.' And another said, 'We don't expect people to belong to themselves as much, they belong to their husband and their children as well, whereas, I think as a man, they have families too but they expect their time to be more free.' 'Yes, if you belong to a men's organization,' said another, 'you just turn up because it says so.' None the less, these women also admitted that their organization, and they themselves, were not very good at handling conflict, and that for all its talk and often practice of caring and sharing (which is a favourite phrase), at times they had often been bitterly hurt by their treatment within the organization. But what certainly seems to come out from some work we have been doing on archival records as well as interviews, is the ways in which public and private life continually intermix, and on a daily basis (for an extended analysis of relationship between the economy and the family, see Reiger, 1991). There is never a real separation, even taking into account the highly bureaucratic formal structures of the organization, because their actual experience as women means that it simply never works the same way that it would for men. Where all this leads me, then, is to argue that not all aspects of bureaucratic organizations are necessarily problematic for women, but they indeed can and do benefit from some aspects of modern forms of organization as against traditional hierarchies. It may well be that women can actually use these bureaucratic strategies to get some effective change taking place.

The drift of much feminist analysis has been to want to collapse the distinction between public and private life entirely. That seems to have been the way some people read the 'personal is political' slogan. However, the above examples suggest that we need to reconstruct both public and private spheres, and that means also reconstruct the relationship between them. We can only understand that relationship by understanding the historical processes which I described earlier. Although hierarchicalism and seniority patterns in bureaucracies and the impersonal, rule-oriented, calculative model of behaviour have disadvantaged women in many ways, I think the core of the problem lies not in the public sphere alone. Rather, it is the relationship between public and private to a large extent, and in particular the historical emergence of, in effect, an institutionalized devaluing of private life. That is now a major issue for feminists in and out of organizations to face up to, and recent work, such as that of Marilyn Waring on reconceptualizing the value of labour (Waring, 1989), makes important advances in doing so. A historical perspective does help us understand the gender dynamics, the emotional complexities of this rational, masculine public sector and the significance of an established gender ideology which sees women as most properly belonging in the emotional sphere of the home.

All modern forms of organization, in spite of the style differences, in spite of the shift to a newer 'human relations' style, all of them presuppose that the work of daily life, the reproduction of the population, the production of food, of clothing, all that production of daily life, can make no legitimate claims on people's performance in the public world. It should just be out there and, of course, the unspoken and often spoken assumption is that women should take care of it, and for free, and that it should not impinge on the public world.

The assimilationist model of women entering the public world, the idea that they should enter it on men's terms, I would argue, is clearly not the answer. As critiques of affirmative action and equal opportunity point out (Game, 1984; Poiner and Wills, 1991; Burton, 1991), the assumption that women can and should simply become like men is not necessarily the direction that we want to go in. This means, of course, facing up to very real differences, not only between the responsibilities of women as a group and of men as a group, but also between different women's and different men's obligations, such as the care of children. It often tends to be couched only in terms of children, but also responsibilities for the ill or the elderly or for non-public sphere activities, just the many other things in life. Clearly, people do have different conditions of existence and ranges of responsibilities. This is emerging as a source of tension now between women themselves in the public sphere, in terms of people's availability for meetings, expectations of work demands, and so on. There are still many people accepting the institutionalization in our society of a masculine notion of the public sphere which does not recognize the legitimacy of claims of the private sphere. As I have argued above, this is not a world view in accord with many women's needs and experience. In conclusion, then, an historically informed understanding of the gender dynamics affecting organizations can assist us to critically analyse the present with a view to reshaping the future. Those in educational frameworks are hopefully better placed than those in industry to start the attempt to reconceptualize the relationship between public and private, and to correct the devaluing of the world of children and of everyday life.

References

BARKER-BENFIELD, G.J. (1976) *The Horrors of the Half-Known Life,* New York, Harper and Row.

BURTON, C. (1991) *The Promise and the Price: The Struggle for Equal Opportunity in Women's Employment,* Sydney, Allen and Unwin.

DEUTSCHMANN, C. (1987) 'The Japanese type of organization as a challenge to the sociological theory of modernization', *Thesis Eleven*, 17.

DINNERSTEIN, D. (1976) *The Mermaid and the Minotaur: Sexual arrangements and human malaise,* New York, McGraw-Hill.

EHRENREICH, B. and ENGLISH, D. (1979) *For Her Own Good: 150 years of experts' advice to women,* London, Pluto Press.

ELLUL, J. (1964) *The Technological Society,* New York, Alfred Knopf.

FERGUSON, K. (1984) *The Feminist Case Against Bureaucracy,* Philadelphia, Temple University Press.

GAME, A. (1984) 'Affirmative action: liberal rationality or challenge to patriarchy?', *Legal Service Bulletin,* 9, 6, pp. 253–7.

GAME, A. and PRINGLE, R. (1984) 'Production and consumption: Public versus private', in BROOM, D. (Ed.) *Unfinished Business,* Sydney, Allen and Unwin.

GOULD, M. (1979) 'When women create an organization: The ideological imperatives of feminism', in DUNKERLEY, D. and SALAMAN, G. (Eds) *International Yearbook of Organizations,* London, Routledge and Kegan Paul.

KANTER, R.M. (1975) 'Women and the structure of organizations: Explorations in theory and behaviour', in MILLMAN, M. and KANTER, R.M. (Eds) *Another Voice,* New York, Anchor Books.

JACOBY, R. (1975) *Social Amnesia: a critique of conformist psychology from Adler and Laing,* Boston, Beacon Press.

LASCH, C. (1979) *The Culture of Narcissism,* New York, Abacus.

PARSONS, T. and WHITE, W. (1964) 'The link between character and society', in PARSONS, T. (Ed.) *Social Structure and Personality,* London, The Free Press.

POINER, G. and WILLS, S. (1991) *The Gift Horse: A critical look at equal opportunity in Australia,* Sydney, Allen and Unwin.

POSTER, M. (1979) *Critical Theory of the Family,* London, Pluto Press.

REIGER, K.M. (1985) *The Disenchantment of the Home: Modernizing the Australian family,* Melbourne, Oxford University Press.

REIGER, K. (1991) *Family Economy,* Ringwood, Penguin.

RICH, A. (1976) *Of Woman Born: Motherhood as institution and experience,* New York, Norton.

REISMAN, D. (1961) *The Lonely Crowd,* New Haven, Yale University Press.

ROTHSCHILD-WHITT, J. (1979) 'The collectivist organization: An alternative to rational–bureaucratic models', *American Sociological Review,* 44.

RUDDICK, S. (1982) 'Maternal thinking', in THORNE, B. and YALOM, M. (Eds) *Rethinking the Family: Some feminist questions,* New York, Longmans.

SCANTLEBURY-BROWN, V. (1929) *Manuscript Diaries,* Archives, University of Melbourne.

SHORTER, E. (1975) *The Making of the Modern Family,* New York, Basic Books.

SMITH, D. (1987) *The Everyday World as Problematic: A feminist sociology,* Milton Keynes, Open University Press.

WARING, M. (1989) *Counting for Nothing: What men value and what women are worth,* Sydney, Allen and Unwin.

WAERNESS, K. (1987) 'The rationality of caring', in SHOWSTACK SASSOON, A. (Ed.) *Women and the State,* London, Hutchinson.

WOLFF, J. (1977) 'Women in organizations', in *Critical Issues in Organizations,* London, Routledge and Kegan Paul.

ZARETSKY, E. (1976) *Capitalism, the Family and Personal Life,* London, Pluto Press.

Chapter 2

'In the Shadow of Men': The Historical Construction of Educational Administration as a 'Masculinist' Enterprise

Jill Blackmore

Administration and policy-making in education have been, and still are, the province of men, although women make up a large proportion of educational workers. Educational theory and administrative practice have been dominated by men, who have acted as 'gatekeepers' in setting the standards, producing the social knowledge and decreeing what is significant, relevant and important in the light of their own experience. Historically, the consolidation of male hegemony in administration is also connected to the coincidence of the expansion of bureaucratic organization in education, the feminization of the occupation, and the emergence of teaching as a 'semi-profession'. Gender, therefore, cannot be separated from the ways in which children are taught, schools have been organized, and curricula have been shaped.

Yet the 'taken-for-grantedness' of the division of labour in education in which men administer and women teach is still evident in educational research. Apple commented that although the history of teaching is the history of a gendered work force, gender is still an 'absent presence' (Apple, 1983; Lather, 1987). In reasserting the feminine presence in education, historians have tended to reconsider the gendered definition of what constitutes teachers' work (Clifford, 1987; Apple, 1985; Lawn and Grace, 1987). As Clifford suggests, the focus has been on the differing career paths and life cycles of women through life history (Middleton, 1986; Acker, 1989); on the activity of women in teacher unions (Purvis, 1987; Ozga and Lawn, 1981; Oram, 1987; Hughey; 1989); and on the feminization of teaching (Williamson, 1983; Prentice, 1975; Grumet, 1981). In emphasizing the construction of teaching as women's work in ways which do not cast women as deficient, this body of research had neglected the historically significant and interrelated feature that men have increasingly come to 'administer' education as it has been taken over by the state and become more closely connected to the economy during the twentieth century (one exception being Hansot and Tyack, 1981).

My concern in this chapter is about how administration has been historically constructed as a masculine enterprise and different from teaching as a feminine enterprise. I draw from feminist critiques of labour process and market theory (such as O'Donnell, 1984) and critical culturalist perspectives of administrative and organizational theory (for example, Bates, 1986; Yeatman, 1990; Marshall and Mitchell, 1989) to facilitate my analysis of this gendered division of labour in education. A conceptual apparatus useful for my argument is that presented by Bob Connell in *Gender and Power* (1987). Connell links the macro-social ordering to the micro-organizational dynamics through the use of the concepts of 'gender order' and 'gender regime'. Gender order, as conceptualized by Jill Matthews, deals largely at the systemic and social level. As Matthews comments:

> Despite the extreme relativity of all the meanings of woman (and equivalently, man) all individuals and all societies tend to treat what they have created as women and men as essential, and as necessary to their sense of rightness and order. Indeed, they build up the specific and relevant differences and relationships between men and women into an order in its own right. This ordering according to gender is one of the main ideological and material grids within which social meaning is created, an ordering which encompasses the entire society, sub- or super-imposed on all other orderings. This gender order is a systematic process of power relations that, for the individual, begins at birth and turns barely differentiated babies into either women or men of the approved types, thereafter keeping them to the mark as the definitions change. It is a systematic process of power relations that, for the society, establishes a basic division of labour, an initial social differentiation that permeates and underpins all other distinctions (Matthews, 1984, p. 13).

Connell sees the gender division of labour as being a consequence of the interlocking of the gender order with the 'gender regime' at the institutional level. The concept of gender regime developed out of research which needed to 'describe the state of play in sexual politics within a school. . . . Among both students and staff there are practices that construct various kinds of femininity and masculinity: sport, dancing, choice of subject, classroom discipline, admin-istration and others' (Connell, 1987, pp. 99, 120). Connell comments that while the principle underlying the division of labour between paid and unpaid, 'men's jobs' and 'women' jobs', is to *separate*, the principle underlying the structures of authority, control and coercion, the hierarchies of the state, the family and the school, is that of *'unequal integration'* (Connell, 1987, p. 97). That is, there are two processes occurring simultaneously. It is the latter process, that of the 'unequal integration' of women, that deserves closer analysis.

A culturalist perspective takes into account the subtle and contradictory ways that the gender regime of schools and bureaucracies works against women, about how ideologies of femininity and masculinity inform and are informed by the 'gender order', and in so doing become hegemonic in that they gain common consent by the masses regarding the 'general direction imposed on social life by the dominant group' (Gramsci, 1971, p. 12). Furthermore, a culturalist perspec-tive recognizes the significance of myth, ritual, common-sense beliefs, shared valuings and meanings in the production and reproduction of gender relations at the level of the organization, the school, and also in the bureaucracy (Marshall and Mitchell, 1989; Hearn and Parkin, 1983). A cultural perspective suggests that embedded in organizations are subtle innuendos, images, valuings and languages which *exclude* many women, such as dominant 'masculinist' images of leadership and administration. At the same time, I would also assert that the cultural perspective recognizes that, while many images, myths and skill definitions may not be conducive to women, they can be transformed, undermined and replaced by more empowering visions of administration (see Blackmore, 1989; and also Grundy in this collection).

I take up from Connell's point that administration has become identified with particular 'masculinist' cultures which are hegemonic in particular administrative contexts. By this I mean that the values, ideologies and structures associated with dominant theories of administration and associated cultural practices favour certain images of masculinity at any one time. His analysis of the ways in which the state 'institutionalizes hegemonic masculinity' through a 'very active gender process' which has been historically constructed provides valuable insight into this. First, he points to the ways in which a hegemonic masculinity is 'always constructed in relation to various subordinated masculinities as well as in relation to women' (Connell, 1987, p. 183). Connell argues from a Gramscian perspective that, whereas certain masculinities become hegemonic, either by consent or coercion, there is 'no femininity that is hegemonic in the sense that the dominant form of masculinity is hegemonic among men', although at a level of mass social relations 'forms of femininity are defined clearly enough' (Connell, 1987, p. 183). One form is defined around compliance with women's subordination, what Connell calls 'emphasized femininity'; others are defined as resistance or non-compliance; and even others by 'strategic combinations of compliance, resistance and co-operation' (Connell, 1987, p. 184). This hegemonic masculinity does not obliterate all other forms of masculinity or maintain a total cultural dominance over women. Rather it has to work constantly in everyday social relationships which are sites of contestation, to adapt and change in order to remain dominant.

Second, he suggests that some women may feel 'comfortable' with this hegemonic masculinity, partly because of the constructed complementarity or 'fit' between dominant hegemonic masculinities and 'emphasized femininities'. But, he warns, hegemonic masculinity 'can contain at the same time, quite consistently, openings towards domesticity and openings towards violence, towards misogyny and towards heterosexual attraction' (Connell, 1987, p. 184). Third, he argues that this hegemonic masculinity is

> very different from the notion of a general 'male sex role' . . . [because] the cultural ideal (or ideals) of masculinity do not need to correspond at all closely to the actual personalities of the majority of men. Indeed, the winning of hegemony often involves the creation of models of masculinity which are quite specifically fantasy figures (Connell, 1987, p. 184).

Finally, Connell argues that hegemonic masculinities become institutionalized through the social categories employed by the state which define women as dependent, as well as the process of bureaucratization which is 'a tight fusion of the structure of power and the gender division of labour' (Connell, 1987, pp. 128–9). He takes up Carole Pateman's point that the state relies upon the changing patterns of gender relations and that a 'key part of this is a change in patterns of masculinity'.

From this cultural perspective, therefore, administration has become associated with a particular type of masculinity — that of the heterosexual, white, rational and technically capable male. A cultural perspective also suggests that bureaucracies and organizations such as schools are sites of contestation not only between different groups but also between different views of masculinity and femininity, 'as there is not one unitary hegemonic masculinity to which all males have access and all females are excluded. Embedded in our social structures are a number of 'masculinities'. Although one particular view of masculinity may be hegemonic at a particular time, this is countered by changing sets of relations which require its reassertion, transformation or demise' (Connell, 1987, p. 86). Working with this conceptual framework and that of labour process and market theory I now trace the history (or histories) of teaching and administration in Australia, to indicate various historical shifts in the images of administration which have dominated educational work.

Images of the Educational Administrator: 'The Benevolent Patriarch'

Teaching has long been an activity of women in the home (as mothers and governesses) and in the workplace. The pupil-teacher system upon which the denominational and common schools were dependent in colonial times in Australia relied on a ready pool of literate labour among the daughters of the *petite bourgeoisie* and working class, many of whom had been monitors while older students. Ironically, working-class women taught prior to the more publicized entrance of their middle-class sisters into the workforce in the late nineteenth century. Only when teaching came to be considered a more respectable occupation did the genteel daughters of the middle class (some with degrees after 1885), establish private dame schools. By the 1880s, 'teaching was unrivalled in combining respectability and short-term independence before marriage, or long-term security for those who preferred a career in teaching . . . a career which generally meant not marrying' (Dow and Scholes, 1984, p. 172; see Tyack and Strober 1981, for similar conclusions for America). In order to facilitate the entrance of the bourgeois daughter into teaching, the very definition of masculinity and femininity was reconstructed in the mid-nineteenth century. In both England and Australia, when women of the bourgeoisie in England gained access to male education in the late nineteenth century as a consequence of the women's movements, in order to remove the threat of being considered 'deviant' or 'unsexed', a redefinition of bourgeois femininity as the 'new woman' was required. It was a feasible ideal in the late nineteenth century, given that industrialization had created new occupational niches for 'well-educated women' which fitted with contemporary liberal beliefs in the 'political democratization' of the 'abstract' individual' (Purvis, 1987, p. 257).

Malcolm Vick in his South Australian study perceives that the same contradiction of the presence of women in paid work, although their prescribed sphere of activity was the domestic, was resolved by the elaboration of a view of a 'good teacher' which was premised upon a strict division of labour in which masculinity in the school, as in the family, was associated with discipline, authority and rationality (Vick, 1988). Thus the characteristics of the father were readily transported into the public roles of principal, administrator and professional. Femininity, meanwhile, was associated with caring and nurturing, irrationality and emotion, and what has been called 'the cult of domesticity'. Women followed their traditional familial caring functions into the public domain in schools, hospitals and welfare institutions, still under the patriarchal eye. Women carried these nurturing aspects (moral, spiritual, interpersonal) into their work as teachers, nurses and service workers.

At the critical time in the 1870s when the education acts in each colony established universal elementary education and invested the state with full responsibility for the child (as distinct from to the Church or the parent), the 'naturalness' of the categories of 'man' and 'woman' and their conventional attributes went unquestioned. Women teachers were to morally uplift both their pupils and their male colleagues; to bring with them domestic virtues and to carry out surveillance for the middle class upon the working class. Women stood on high moral ground, as complementary to the propensity of men's moral weakness. In fact, the moral capacity of women was perceived to be more critical than their skills or training. An inspector in the Victorian system in 1869 stated that female teachers' 'qualities which render them valuable at the same time render them sensitive and timid' (Victoria, 1869, p. 54; Bacchi, 1990).

At the same time, women's association with nature as that of men's with culture meant women were the 'biological inferior', requiring protection by the transcendant spirit of males who dominated the material world. Hence women's perceived incapacity to 'manage the material'. The nineteenth century bourgeois distinction of women as moral and men as material thus 'served to support the removal of moral, spiritual and interpersonal values from the public world of industry and commerce. Safely located with women in the domestic sphere, they were devalued and marginalized but kept alive in a haven for the work-worn alienated male' (Reiger, 1985, p. 21). Administration, as with all public life, was reliant upon a natural and paternal authority, the innate capacity to control the material world. Women, accordingly, were allocated the nurturant and emotive tasks in schools.

The state, therefore, was active in constructing educational administration as 'masculine'. Middle-class male politicians and educators sought to regulate and define teachers' work. Studies of schooling in the nineteenth century have clearly indicated that teaching offered an independent and relatively autonomous occupational niche for women prior to state intervention in the 1870s. Pavla Miller describes how in South Australia teachers were seen as independent contractors, who decided upon the 'subjects they taught, set the level of fees, employed, paid and trained their own pupil-teachers and assistants and sometimes built and owned their own school houses'. Although the supervising Board of Education 'seemed more ready to recognize and reward the qualifications and efficiency of male teachers, the basic rate of pay was the same for men and women' (Miller, 1986, p. 25). In Victoria, it has clearly been illustrated that until the 1906 Victorian Registration Act which required all teachers and schools to be registered, teaching was an independent career path for many educated women (Zainnu'din, 1984). Women managed and taught both boys and girls the liberal arts and 'accomplishments' curricula in numerous 'dame schools' and private academies. In 1867 there were 959 private schools employing 590 men and 1277 women in Victoria alone. These academies were unregulated by the state, but of increasing concern to the authorities. In Victoria, the Higinbotham Report in

1867 cited such academies as being a 'risk to the community' because they were not under public supervision (Theobald, 1984).

While state intervention in education in the nineteenth century was initially intended to

> mitigate class and religious differences; to promote a well-ordered society, a society of "respectable citizens", teachers as well as students and parents were expected to conform to the "correct values" of the mercantile bourgeoisie. This was to be achieved through uniformity of provision, inspection, payment by results and a direct line of control between Minister and the schools (Bessant, 1986, p. 38).

From the start, teachers were classified and promoted, as in the public service, by seniority and 'good conduct', the latter determined by the inspectors' reading of community values. Thus the characteristics of bureaucratic life — uniformity and hierarchy — surfaced early in public education.

In Victoria, male bureaucratic surveillance intensified and spread with the expansion of the state system of elementary education. Ironically, this expansion (as in the USA) was dependent upon the proliferation of rural one-room primary schools *managed* by young female teachers who had generally arrived at this position through the pupil-teacher system. By 1888, over 85 per cent of all pupil-teachers were females. Patriarchal control was largely maintained through the visitation of the male school inspector to the one-room school. Such surveillance was of both a sexual and a professional nature, the inspector checking for female moral impropriety as well as poor work (Theobald, 1984; Kyle, 1990). As education became increasingly important as regards national advancement and efficiency at the turn of the century, with Federation looming, state intervention and regulation over education and teachers' work increased. This had the effect of constraining the career opportunities for educated middle-class women, as Marjorie Theobald (1984) and Ailsa Zainnu'din (1984) have shown, with the demise of most private academies after the 1906 Registration Act. Furthermore, wage differentiation based on sex legitimated the sexual division of labour. Thus patriarchal authority in educational administration was institutionalized and normalized by the state legislation, regulation and bureaucratization well before 1910.

In the USA, Myra Strober, David Tyack and Elisabeth Hansot have likewise connected the bureaucratization of teaching in larger urban schools after the 1830s as exacerbating the division of labour. Male managers of schools were accorded greater public status and therefore 'natural managers', whereas female teachers were not only cheaper and supposedly more nurturing with children, but also more compliant. That men took on the public role of administrator and instruction of senior classes and supervised many junior female teachers caring for the younger children in a highly controlled institution was not only highly economical, given the 'cheapness' of female teachers, but also construed as 'natural'. For as Carolyn Steedman argues, from the start childhood education conflated the 'mothering' of young children into 'educating' them so that teachers of young children became what Carolyn Steedman calls 'mothers-made-conscious' (Steedman, 1985). Nursery and early primary school were the context 'in which good mothering and good pedagogy were part of the same process of aiding child development' (Walkerdine, 1987, p. 173). Women came to primarily teach younger children up to the stage prior to induction into public life, which was then undertaken by the objective, rational and authoritarian male as senior teacher and administrator.

'The Rational Man'

The development of the educational bureaucracy was therefore dependent upon the ideology of 'separate spheres' of the domestic or 'private' world of women and the 'public' world of men. At the same time, the bureaucratization of education coincided in the decades preceding and following Federation in 1901 with a period in which 'radical knowledges' flourished — nationalism, Darwinism and socialism (Allen, 1988, pp. 159–60). But such 'radical' knowledges did not refute the public/private division. Instead, they were informed by Enlightenment ideas of the capacity of *man* to control *his* environment, and nature through science became entrenched in administration (Lloyd, 1984; Sydie, 1987). It has been well documented how women were excluded from this equation of control and science. Marjorie Theobald comments on how particular subjects (such as mathematics and psychology), derived from the double birth or 'rationality' and 'modern man' in the twentieth century, assumed a specifically historical character which has been submerged in the logic of the discourse of rational man from the nineteenth century. Conversely, she argued that, while science was constructed as masculine, the humanities were associated with the female mind. A major consequence, in the early decades of the twentieth century, was the 'translation into mass educational practice of the mutually impoverishing split between masculine "rationality" and feminine "intuition"' (Theobald, 1987, p. 162). The nexus between the female mind and the humanities was historically constructed at a time when the patriarchal ordering of society had to be renegotiated as the new industrial order emerged from the older aristocratic world. Ironically, those negotiations were informed by an intuition that somebody within the unfamiliar and disturbing society which was emerging must retain those qualities of nurturance and selflessness which are necessary in a just society.

It was science and reason, however, which were to inform the new managers and the state in its progressive programme of social engineering after 1901. Claiming the status of science for their field provided legitimacy for an emerging class of professional managers, experts in the field of health, welfare, psychology and education, among them educated middle-class women. In so doing, these experts denied most women the possibilities of controlling even their own domestic environment (Reiger, 1985). The development of science through education was also seen as promoting national economic efficiency and international trade competitiveness. The social efficiency movement of the early twentieth century informed the field of educational administration through the adoption of principles of 'scientific management' (Bates, 1986). These new managers in education also sought to claim that reason was their virtue and that education could be made more efficient through control mechanisms of science such as mental testing (McCallum, 1990; Bacchi, 1990).

Kerreen Reiger elaborates upon a particular ideological formation of the above conditions whereby masculinity was equated with the public and with technical rationality while femininity was equated with private and affective relationships, largely as a consequence of the nineteenth-century bourgeois capitalist separation of the public and the private. This promoted an ideology which portrayed the family as an emotional and moral haven from the world. As Reiger argued in the previous chapter, some of the main features of the bourgeois model of the family became institutionalized in modern organizations at this time. The hegemonic image of masculinity associated with administration was one which stressed the rational, unemotional, logical and authoritative aspects of human behaviour. On the other hand, 'the woman as container soaks up and contains the irrationality which she best understands', as the moral arbiter and emotional manager in the private sphere (Walkerdine, 1987, p. 59).

Conversely, women's entrance into the public sphere in the early twentieth century, particularly at the top as administrators, implicitly threatened this simple dichotomization of life into the public and private, male and female spheres. Any association of women with the material was also 'threatening to masculine-defined cultural reality'. For example, Noelyne Williamson describes the irrational fear of male bureaucrats regarding the feminization of teaching, as indicated in their overt attempts to exclude women from the teaching service in the early 1900s in NSW in favour of lesser qualified and experienced males. Williamson attributes this to the 'teacher as mother' stereotype which allowed women to teach young children and girls art, music and health, but which denied women's capacity to teach upper classes because it would 'disadvantage male students' because females 'lacked the economic and political punch characteristic of the public authority of men' (Williamson, 1988, pp. 26, 32–3). It is a view which was still present in 1973 and espoused by an inspector. Women are, he stated,

> naturally designed for the office of teaching the young; they have more sympathy than men, they know almost intuitively where a child's heart lies. For young children, therefore, female instruction would be most efficient, and if for teaching older children a female is not on the whole as well adapted as a male the loss would be sustained only by the boys over 12 years of age (quoted in Williamson, 1988, p. 31).

In Canada, while regional differences existed on patterns of feminization and there was no overt attempt to rectify a perceived 'imbalance' of the sexes, it was common that the character of a teacher's work underwent subtle changes as more women entered the classroom. New subjects were included in the curriculum, and daily classroom teaching was increasingly structured by outside authority (competitive examinations). At the same time, the monitoring roles of teachers increased during lunch and recess hours as well as over the health of children, thus extending the mothering aspect (Danylewycz and Prentice, 1986).

In the USA, Geraldine Clifford maps out how fears of feminization proliferated in the period 1885–1915 when female teachers became a majority in both elementary and secondary teaching, when the majority of high school graduates were female. A campaign was run to stop school administration becoming 'feminized' after the First World War by favouring males in the recruitment of teachers and administrators on the grounds that boys, especially black youth, needed male role models (Clifford, 1987, p. 7). In the USA in 1909, Ella Flagg Young, the only female superintendent of schools in Chicago, acclaimed the fact that in 1905 the females comprised 17.9 per cent of elementary school teachers and 61.7 per cent of elementary school principals (Tyack and Hansot, 1982, p. 183). Young was part of a wider women's movement both in the teachers unions and connected to broader social reform movements concerneed about democracy and equality which emerged in the early decades of the twentieth century. These female teachers sought to claim the top administrative positions in education, equal pay, and condemned the way in which 'scientific management was turning teachers into operatives who had to do the bidding of their superiors' (Tyack and Hansot, 1982, p. 181). But Young's optimism was not fulfilled. The change in the form of governance in the major teacher union (the National Educational Association) led only to symbolic gains for women teachers in terms of holding office. Their male colleagues within the union effectively utilized the ideology of professionalism to blur the cleavages between men and women, administrators and teachers, by calling upon unity on the grounds of professional integrity. Top male administrators and male-dominated school boards continued to make certain that women administrators were concentrated in the lower administrative echelons and that the male old-boys network was protected. A state superintendent, for example, informed his subordinates not to worry as 'I'm not going to send a person in petticoats to supervise your work' (Tyack and Hansot, 1982, p. 189). By 1972–3 female elementary teachers were 84 per cent, whereas females held only 19.6 per cent of the elementary principalships; females constituted 46 per cent of high school teachers but a mere 1.4 per cent of high school principalships (Tyack and Hansot, 1982, p. 183) Men in power, therefore, had to actively work to exclude women.

That the feminization of teaching or the intrusion of women in administration could cause such alarm suggests that it was perhaps more fear of competition of women with men in the public domain which created a 'crisis in masculinity'. Control over boys in the classroom was not the issue. More likely it was control by women over men in public life. The latter view is becoming increasingly recognized as issues of sexuality are seen to be more central to the gender dynamics of organizations and cultures (Rose, 1988; Oram 1987; Hearn and Parkin, 1983).

State intervention in education from the late nineteenth century, therefore, both institutionalized and legitimized the public/private dichotomy implicit in liberal political thought of the time, and in so doing particular hegemonic ideologies of masculinity and femininity. This dichotomization between the public and the private has, according to Pateman and other feminist theorists, denied women equal access to public positions (such as administration) while maintaining a liberal rhetoric of individual choice and equality (in education more than employment) (Eisenstein, 1985; Pateman, 1989). The public/private dichotomy has defined that that which occurs in the public sphere is rational, instrumental, productive and effective — and activities in the private sphere of the family and home have been defined as irrational, expressive, consuming and ineffective. In addition, the public sphere has historically been defined as being a masculinist sphere of economic as well as political activity in that the masculine identity has been closely bound to the notion of the breadwinner. The Harvester judgment of 1907 in Australia, for example, established a family wage in which the male was the breadwinner of a family unit, and women and children were legally defined as dependants. Just as the liberal view of the social contract between individual and the state was premised upon the male as representative of the family, that is, the fraternal social contract, so it was embedded in this notion of the family as an economic unit (Pateman, 1989). In this way women, even when at work in the public sphere, came to be categorized in particular ways and perceived differently than men: as feminized (and sexualized) service workers; as members of the helping professions in furthering their mothering skills; as targets of sexual harassment; as cheap and low-paid unskilled workers; as casual workers without commitment due to a preoccupation with domestic work; as supplemental workers; as working wives or working mothers. This is the masculine subtext of the division of labour and these different perceptions of the quality of women's presence in the paid workforce testify to the cognitive and ideological dissonance between femininity and the worker role in classical capitalism (Chambers, 1986, p. 5).

Administration, therefore, came to be associated with the image of the rational, logical and objective male early in the twentieth century, in a period of social and economic dislocation, although there was significant evidence to suggest that administration in reality was not exclusive to men. While the early educational bureaucracies took on the patriarchal model of authority and discipline, embedded in the Weberian 'ideal type' bureaucratic model which informed state education systems, by the Second World War there was a new model of administration which was propagated as a neutral free science. Connell comments:

At the same time, the tradition-centred patriarchal authority of the nineteenth century that was criticized at the level of public politics by liberal rationalists such as Locke represented the hegemony of a particular type of masculinity. Over the period in which both the modern state and the industrial economy were produced, the hegemony of this form of masculinity was challenged and displaced by masculinities organized around technical rationality and calculation. The system of industrial capitalism was constructed by this shift as well as by class dynamics; and so was the characteristic form of state bureaucracy sketched above (Connell, 1987, p. 131).

Various 'sciences' have informed administrative theory and practice. While biological explanations of sex difference (social Darwinism) were increasingly challenged in the early twentieth century, other explanations arose to take their place, for instance, that of psychological difference during the 1920s and 1930s (Bacchi, 1990; McCallum, 1990). With the popularization of eugenics and notions of fixed intelligence after the First World War, theories of psychological difference were well propagated within educational circles. McCallum argues that 'the theory of natural differences between individuals was made to perform the specific task of explaining differences in achievement amongst social groups, such as between State and private school pupils, and occupational groups', and, I would add, between men and women (McCallum, 1990, p. 88; Bacchi, 1990). Educational notions were likewise informed by such individualistic and psychologistic models which meant gender, race and class difference were unproblematic. Equality of opportunity, for example, had by the 1940s come to be interpreted to mean different treatment according to individual difference. It was translated in education into the notion of merit, defined as innate ability (as indicated by IQ) plus effort.

Likewise, merit was a central feature of the Weberian notion of bureaucratic rationality which distinguished between fact and value, means and ends. The Weberian ideal mythologized the view that bureaucracies were neutral organizations necessarily dependent upon hierarchy, specialization and a strict division of labour. In turn, the discourse of bureaucratic rationality and its associated emphasis on procedural justice was called upon when embedded masculine biases were challenged. The following case history illustrates how what Hester Eisenstein calls the 'gender of bureaucracy' is embedded in the so-called neutrality and objectivity of particular liberal concepts of merit and bureaucratic practice; of how women's presence creates a 'crisis in masculinity' and a redefinition of administration (Eisenstein, 1985).

The Case of Julia Flynn

Julia Flynn was appointed as the first female assistant Inspector of Secondary Schools in Victoria in 1914. As such, she wrote sections of the *Annual Report* of the Victorian Education Department and took a fairly high profile in matters of curriculum and examination reform. When, in 1928, the position of Assistant Chief Inspector of Secondary Schools was advertised, Flynn, as one of the most senior officers, objected on the grounds that the only salary rate mentioned was for males. After appealing to the Minister of Education, all senior women were personally notified of their eligibility. When Flynn's appointment (at four-fifths the advertised rate) was announced and duly passed by the Public Service Commissioner, it was widely and publicly commended. But with the retirement of the Director-General of Education the following year, the position of Chief Inspector, temporarily occupied by Flynn, was duly advertised. The advertisement stated that 'a male was required', although this infringed the Women's Qualification Act of 1928 which disallowed discrimination on the grounds of sex. Martin Hansen, the new Director of Education and former Chief Inspector, argued that 'a woman could not do the work . . . required as Chief Inspector'. In defending his position against widespread and public protest from parliamentarians, women's organizations, *The Age*, his Minister and a less than enthusiastic male-dominated union, Hansen stated that secondary education was 'pre-eminently boys' education', and thus required 'male supervision'. In administrative terms, he argued, a female appointment was inappropriate as

> the Chief Inspector has to interview parents and councils, discuss all manner of details, even those dealing with sanitary arrangements, holding inquiries into complaints often involving sex matters, and these duties, I am satisfied, a woman should not be called upon to undertake (quoted in Hannan, 1975, p. 5).

Hansen not only defined administrative work as necessarily masculine, but argued that work which women typically did in the family and in other 'nurturing' occupations was not deemed suitable for females in an administrative context. That is, the same task carried out in the private sphere by women was redefined in the public as a male attribute and enterprise. Once again, Flynn won her appeal against the male appointment on the grounds of seniority and merit.

And again, Hansen actively utilized so-called 'neutral' procedural and administrative means to subvert her position. He extended the probationary period specified by the public service regulations from three to six months, during which time he actively criticized her work.

What emerged was that Hansen had the tacit support of a new conservative Minister of Education during this time. Meanwhile, Hansen's justification for this unusual treatment shifted from the general argument that it was not that *women* were incapable of the administrative tasks required of the position but that the personal fitness for the job of this particular woman, Julia Flynn, was not proven. That is, he shifted the issue back to 'personal inadequacy' and lack of competence in a way which blamed the victim. At the same time, Hansen confidently wrote to Flynn in a private letter, recognizing her 'self-confidence' and 'legitimate ambition', but insisted that she lacked 'a necessary broad vision and clear imagination' and had been unnecessarily 'slow and academic' in her planning of postprimary reorganization. He again suggested that she accept the more appropriate position of Assistant Chief Inspector which would enable her to concentrate on girls' education as she had previously, a focus she had been directed by him to take (Hannan, 1975, p. 9). Flynn was sensitive to what she considered was Hansen's antagonism to women in general, and so stated in her letter to the public service commissioner:

> His [Hansen's] actions and his correspondence suggest that he has endeavoured to create a state of mind which would render me unfit for the duties of the position. His confidential letter appears to have been written with the intention of intimidating me from appealing to you . . . no man appointed to a corresponding position has been subjected to such unusual tests in his probationary period (quoted in Hannan, 1975, pp. 10–11).

This letter was then used by Hansen as signifying her 'psychological' unsuitability. Finally, at the end of the six months the Commissioner upheld the decision that her appointment be terminated. Despite the public outcry by teacher unions and women's organizations of all political persuasion regarding this injustice against women, no inquiry eventuated. The Premier argued that the case did not relate to governmental policy or the Woman's Disqualification Act, but 'related entirely to the *administration* of the Education Department', for which the Director was responsible (Hannan, 1975, p. 13). This instance, although clouded by issues such as the changing power relationships between the Minister and Director, and union (male-dominated) concern over administrative appeal procedures, is evidence of what one historian conceded as late as the 1970s as the 'public personnel practice in Australia based on the concept that all responsible positions should be a male enclave' (quoted in Hannan, 1975, p. 15).

This case study indicates, first, how supposedly neutral bureaucratic procedures are open to interpretation, and how 'merit', as are all judgments of competence and worth, is culturally and, in this instance, male defined. Merit is seen not to be a neutral measure of ability but is based on the perceived achievements or 'success' of those who have historically dominated (generally white middle-class heterosexual males) and therefore based on criteria which are often gender, race or class biased. Merit is not a value-free or objective measure but is used by those who have succeeded because a particular interpretation of merit maintains their advantage (Burton, 1987). Second, in this historical instance, it indicates how male collegiality, both overt and covert, served to maintain power structures beneficial to male dominance in administration rather than good education and how particular organizational arrangements favoured 'masculine' values (Burton, 1987; Martin, 1987). It was, in effect, what Clare Burton refers to as the 'mobilization of masculine bias'. The fact that the activity by the males in authority to maintain their hegemonic practices as the norm is often 'inefficient' and 'contradicts' their 'rationality rhetoric' is ignored.

Third, it indicates how the public domain as the province of men was characterized as rational, ordered, instrumental and productive as distinct from the activities of the private domain of woman in the family — woman as nurturant, expressive, irrational and economically unproductive. Ironically, Hansen usurped what was traditionally 'female' labour in the family (dealing with social and sexual relationships) and placed it into the realm of masculine activity since it was in the public domain. Fourth, it illustrated that the claims of bureaucratic or technical rationality are more what Cathy Ferguson calls the 'scientific organization of inequality' in that it serves as a filter for those other forms of domination, projecting them into an institutional arena that both rationalizes and maintains them (Ferguson, 1984, p. 8).

The myth of bureaucratic rationality which dominated the expanding state educational bureaucracies after 1945 presumed the Weberian 'ideal type' which characterized the bureaucrat as being impartial and rational and the bureaucratic structures and processes as necessarily being hierarchical and neutral. 'The Weberian model of rational administration, therefore, is itself a powerful rhetorical and ideological resource for maintaining commitment to the organization' and particular gendered relationships (Martin, 1987, p. 444).

Recent critiques of the post-war period have indicated how organizational theorists have relied heavily upon a false detachment of organizations from the personal and the political since the public/private dichotomy was deeply embedded in theories of administration (Hearn and Parkin, 1983). On the one hand, individuals were defined in organizations by their gender. Those individuals who did not conform to particular norms of organizational behaviour were seen to be deviant or inadequate (homosexuals, for example). Given that the image of a good administrator was a white, heterosexual, middle-class man, this meant all women and some men were by default deviant (both from other women and men), inadequate (in that they did not fit the image), and even unsexed (in attempting to do male work). In particular, Talcott Parsons' broad distinction between 'the masculine and feminine personality', the instrumental and the expressive, which became influential in sociology during the 1950s and 1960s, was interpreted as meaning 'other things being equal, men would assume more technical, executive and "judicial roles"', women more supportive, integrative and "tension managing roles"' (Carrigan *et al.*, 1987, p. 39). On the other hand, the personal/private lives of workers was ignored in organizational theory. Thus there was what Hearn and Parkin call a 'desexualization of organizational life' at the same time that there was a 'resexualization of everyday public life' (Hearn and Parkin, 1983).

The instrumental–expressive dichotomy became deeply entrenched along gender lines at the same time that organizational theorists ignored difference and fell back on male versions of organizational life as the universal. The model of administrative leadership was that of the autonomous competitive individual (male) who was motivated solely by material rewards. It was (and still is) premised upon a view of the unitary, rational subject which emerged in western culture during the seventeenth century and which features in the social scientific discourses and in the apparatuses of administration as the abstract legal subject of individual rights, of responsibilities and obligations: that is, the individual citizen (Lloyd, 1984; Pateman, 1989). Social theory during the 1950s and 1960s was built around the instrumental–expressive dichotomy as a given. And so the growth of large educational bureaucracies and the development of teaching as a profession during the following decades intensified gender differentiation (Connell, 1987). Indeed, the intensification of hierarchical authority, the trend towards fragmention of work into specialist tasks, the reliance upon role orientation and the reduction of worker autonomy characteristic of modern bureaucracies has even been justified as a *consequence* of the increasing presence of women. Sociologists in 1969 argued:

> Women's stronger competing attachments to their family roles and . . . to their clients make them less likely than men to develop colleague reference group orientations. For these reasons, and because they often share the general cultural norm that women should defer to men, women are more willing than men to accept the bureaucratic controls imposed upon them in semi-professional organizations, and less likely to seek a genuinely professional status (Simpson and Simpson, 1969, pp. 199–200).

So far, I have focused upon one factor which has interacted and contributed to particular constructions of sexuality which have dominated organizational life, to produce what Connell calls the 'gender regime' within organizations. That is, the historical dichotomy between the public and the private which was institutionalized and legitimized at the turn of the century concurrent with the early formation of state education systems, the professionlization of teaching and the bureaucratization of education in general (Connell, 1987; Ferguson, 1984).

A second important factor was the way in which male educational administrators seeking 'collective mobility' and public legitimacy for their profession during the twentieth century, particularly after the Second World War, claimed for educational administration the status of a science (Blackmore, 1989). They did so not only because science was seen to be a more 'objective' form of knowledge production during the post-war period, but also because scientific knowledge promised those who practised administration and policy development predictability, comparability as well as objectivity, thus imparting greater authority to administrative experts. The epistemological foundation of the view of administration as a neutral, rational and value-free enterprise in the period after the Second World War was positivism. Underpinning emergent organizational and management theory since the 1950s, positivism made privileged claims to objectivity, predictability and universality, claims which separated means from ends, facts from values. Decisions were attributed to the position and not the individual, thus absolving individuals from moral and ethical responsibility (Bates, 1986). The dominant model of 'scientific' educational administration which came to be accepted in the USA as well as Australia until the mid 1970s, was built, therefore, upon particular conceptions of human behaviour and knowledge which were exclusionary of female knowledge and experiences. In so doing, the theory movement in educational administration maintained the *status quo* in justifying administration as men's work by assuming some men's experience was universal.

Other aspects informed administrative theory after the 1950s. For example, while the early human relations movement of the 1950s produced a new concern about the 'human' and 'informal' aspects of organizations, it was still framed by the view of the individual as being the 'universal male' capable of being 'integrated' into and in agreement with organizational objectives. Given that during the 1950s there were fewer women in senior administrative positions than any other decade of the twentieth century, it is not surprising that organizational theories were modelled upon male work and life experiences (Blackmore, 1989). Educational administrative literature which draws from these theories still proliferates with notions of the 'rational bureaucrat', 'organizational man', 'corporate man', the 'Man in the Principal's Office' (Hearn and Parkin, 1983; Shakeshaft, 1987).

At the same time, the proliferation of testing and classifying (both gender biased) in personnel management and education since the early twentieth century has given 'scientific' weight to arguments about women's unsuitability for administration, although women have become increasingly 'acceptable' in the workplace. Wendy Hollway talks about psychological assessment in organiza-, tions as being the 'technology of the social' which derives from what Foucault sees as the mutuality of a power-knowledge relation which has been produced in other historical contexts. Hollway illustrates how the 'fair science' of occupational psychology shifted from the 1950s as 'fitting the right man to the right job' in order to maximize profitability, to 'humanizing work' during the 1970s by organizing corporate 'well-being' and improving the 'quality of working life' through management techniques such as performance appraisal by colleagues, peer assessment and professional development (Hollway, 1984). But, as Venn points out, psychological explanation accounts for the deviations and does not question the normality of the norm (Venn, 1984, p. 131). And in each of the above instances, the control of labour required new techniques of management to accommodate shifts in the labour market, the crisis in capital accumulation and the contradictions and dissonance between the daily experiences of women and various ideological contructions of femininity.

As in the previous century, when various contradictions emerge new ideologies of femininity mediate these contradictions. During the 1960s there was a high demand for female labour in teaching since males had access to more lucrative forms of employment. So state and non-state ideologies about women in that period stressed the dual roles of work *and* family, encouraged women into higher education and training, while social and welfare services were extended to allow women to participate in particular segments of the labour market. At the same time, women's entrance into the labour market did not mean access to the power implied by paid work, as indicated by the few women who entered the upper employment echelons of educational administration as either principals or bureaucrats. The exclusion of women from these positions was justified on the grounds of women failing to 'fit' the 'masculine' model of educational leadership.

Leadership, as a masculine activity, as I have argued, has been traditionally associated in liberal capitalist democracies with 'so-called' male traits of aggression, individualism, and competition. Any display of the 'feminine' qualities of emotionality, caring or sharing are perceived, therefore, as weaknesses in managers in a technocratic and hierarchically organized workplace, and strengths in teachers of young children (Blackmore, 1989). Hence during the 1970s the significance of socio-psychological theories of women's incapacity to lead, their 'fear of success' and 'lack of aspiration'. These notions of female inadequacies, such as lack of self-esteem and career motivation, have to some extent become used unproblematically to 'explain' the underrepresentation of women in educational administration.

'The Multiskilled Manager'

Whereas the period from 1900 to 1945 saw the demise of a patriarchal model of administration in education and a shift towards a bureaucratic model premised on bureaucratic rationality of the 1950s and 1960s, there has been a significant shift in organizational theory since the 1970s towards cultural approaches, with an emphasis upon new forms of organizational behaviour — teamwork, and interactive and communicative skills. Organizational culture emerged as a central conceptual framework in 1980s business literature and in educational administration during the 1980s, often linked to increased productivity. A highly popularized business version of corporate culture emerged, derived from both the post-war human relations movement and notions of technical rationality (see, for example, Deal and Kennedy, 1982). Its objective is still the 'unequal integration of the individual' into the organization although its language is that of community not self.

In Australia, the desire to promote a 'productive culture' has seen education more closely oriented towards short-term, instrumental economic ends, and a move from the liberal humanism of public administration to the economic rationalism of corporate management. Informed by economic models of human behaviour, the emphasis in corporate management is on outcomes not inputs. The assumption is that public and private organizations do not have different logics, that both are producing goods for public consumption (Considine, 1988). It reworks the notion of worker to that of producer, of citizen to that of consumer, regardless that the product being sold is education. This logically leads to a view of organizational structures as being necessarily instrumental, requiring high levels of accountability between relatively autonomous units of work. Accountability must be to the client and to national economic objectives. This accountability is not via rules and job specifications as in the old, legally bound bureaucratic mode or organizations, but rather through negotiable contracts with senior management or clients. Corporate management therefore claims to provide increased flexibility for workers and organizational units which in turn facilitate flexible arrangements through these individualized, competitive contracts (Yeatman, 1990). In education, this is evident with the push towards school-based decision-making and devolution as the means to produce both a more efficient but also more equitable and responsive system of education. At the same time accountability is to be ensured by standardization of measures to facilitate comparability between programmes and individuals (such as programme budgeting, performance appraisal and performance indicators).

In turn this has led to a new form of hegemonic masculinity associated with the notion of the multiskilled manager. Yeatman talks about how the new discourse of corporate management in public administration based upon private sector models encourages the recruitment of a 'new technically-oriented élite recruited on merit as defined in terms of higher education credentials' (Yeatman, 1990). These new managers have replaced the liberally educated upper-class male intelligentsia who generally had a high degree of substantive experience in the field and some commitment to reducing social inequity of post-war public administration. The multiskilled manager is expected to possess a package of generic skills and competencies which allows him or her effectively and efficiently to 'manage' *any* field of administrative activity. The best attribute of such a manager is a *lack* of personal commitment to or experience in the field of activity (such as health, education, welfare) as such involvement or even substantive knowledge of the field is seen to represent particularistic not universal interests. This managerial élite works within a corporate culture which espouses notions of process and people, but always operates within a framework of scientific management which encourages a view of management as a matter of specific technical tasks rather than raising substantive ethical questions. Yeatman comments: 'Equal opportunity in this context comes to be reframed in terms of what it can do for management improvement, not in terms of what it can do to develop the conditions of social justice and democratic citizenship' (Yeatman, 1987, p. 341). In this view, equity and democratic work practices must be seen to contribute to productivity and cannot be justified in their own right.

As with scientific management, corporate management assumes a stance of neutral judgment according to objective criteria. But embedded in the notion of corporate management is a culture, a particular view of social life and organizational activity which upholds particular values and is exclusive of others (see Burton in this collection). The hegemonic potential of corporate culture lies in its ability to readily subsume and appropriate social justice and affirmative action strategies into its corporate planning, under the guise of representation and participation. Corporate culture co-opts and subsumes more radical discourses of industrial democracy, using participative rhetoric for managerial ends. In so doing, it effectively incorporates equal opportunity language into its managerial discourse through an ideology of consultancy (not democracy) and consensus. In a time of scarce resources, the dominant corporate goal of efficiency is a strong one which legitimizes certain activities and decisions which are not conducive to equity or worker's interests in general.

At the level of the individual, merit and success are judged against 'objective' (although sometimes negotiated) criteria, such as performance appraisal. The corporate management view assumes consensus about organizational goals; and a monolithic and homogenous version of culture (Hearn and Parkin, 1983). It focuses upon the individual rather than institutional factors when explaining success or failure. This is contrary to research which indicates that merit, skill and success are value-laden and context-bound terms (Burton, 1987; Martin, 1987). Women are judged differently in the organizational culture in which male models of 'success' dominate.

Yeatman points out that the irony of the corporate culture (as elaborated by the private business world) is that it appropriates those very characteristics seen to be 'feminine' in terms of interpersonal skills, empathy and displaying behaviours which are more affective and personal, and utilizes them for the benefit of the company or organization (Yeatman, 1990). Good managers are those which display and utilize such 'generic skills'. This is most evident in the ways the nature of the school principalship has been reconceptualized — principals are now expected to be facilitators, communicators, team leaders, instructional leaders, and so on. So while women may gain access to middle levels of administration which focus upon the interpersonal, they continue to be excluded from upper levels of educational administration in any great numbers. Even then, they are unequally integrated into this new administrative mode because of the culturally exclusive practices and images arising from a new, particularly persuasive and co-optive form of hegemonic masculinity.

Conclusion

What I have attempted to show is that there have been shifts over time in the ways in which ideological constructions of masculinity and femininity and their various cultural manifestations have interplayed with the sexual division of labour within educational organizations and the wider labour market. For example, in the eighteenth and nineteenth centuries, the sexual division of labour (both in terms of who taught which children and what knowledge and who held adminis- trative power) was justified as being 'natural' and morally justified due to the nature of women (as the physically weaker sex, lacking in rational capacities). Women, because of their different attributes, first entered the 'public domain' of teaching as an extension of their nurturing role, to complement and support male activities. From the start, women teachers were paid less because they were assumed to be dependants of men and because of their ready availability. The science of eugenics and evolutionary theory of the nineteenth century considered women to be psychologically, physically and cognitively different from men, thus reinforcing gender stereotypes and rationalizing the complementarity of women's dominance in the home sphere to men's dominance in the public sphere. As women have participated more overtly in waged labour, and with the introduction of mechanization and then more sophisticated technology, arguments about women's socio-psychological 'unsuitability' for leadership have displaced biological and then moral judgments in determining what is appropriate women's work (Bacchi, 1990). At the same time, the dominant ideology of instrumental rationality inscribed in positivism and the type of 'masculine' science of administration it informs continues largely unchallenged, even in the 1990s. Furthermore, this rationality is compatible with the strategies of administration and the maintenance of particularly gendered images of administrators and administrative work and, implicitly, of teachers and teachers' work.

In turn, the emphasis of the 1980s on generic managerial skills and competencies, forces us to think anew the complex ways in which skills and images have been historically constructed and redefined in specific administrative and educational contexts in gendered ways. Indeed, women and women's skills of emotional management have been co-opted by a different, but no less dis- empowering, discourse of corporate culture. The dilemma lies in the ideological power of such notions of merit and neutrality and in their capacity to facilitate systemic forms of control, as well as to require individuals and organizations to address issues of equity. While an individual woman can appeal to notions of neutral procedure and merit and thus succeed 'in a man's world' according to her ability, this leaves unchallenged the hegemonic masculinity embodied in these principles and structures of administration. Alternatively, recognition of the non-neutrality of the merit principle and bureaucratic procedure is strategically problematic for feminism, given that these have been the touchstone of equal opportunity legislation.

Finally, it is necessary to think about the role of the state in defining and redefining what constitutes teaching and administrative work, for the state has been active in 'both institutionalizing hegemonic masculinity' (for example, family wage) and 'expending great energy in controlling' (such as equal opportunity legislation) (Connell, 1987, p. 128). In that sense, the state should be seen, not as a monolithic, unitary, nor even a necessarily masculine, entity acting for or against women, but more as 'a political process whose outcome is open' (Franzway *et al.*, 1990; Deacon, 1989; see also Yeatman in this collection). While this view of the state allows for change in ways which can benefit women, the problem is to develop strategies of change which can work effectively in specific contexts. Critical attention must be made of how, in a period of economic rationalism, the nature of teaching and administrative work is being theorized and redefined, a process in which the state and the unions are active through award restructuring, in ways which exacerbate the sexual division of labour and facilitate exclusionary cultural practices. Such machinations have the potential to either promote new forms of hegemonic masculinity in education or facilitate women stepping out of the shadows.

References

ACKER, S. (Ed.) (1989) *Teachers, Gender and Careers*, Lewes, Falmer Press.

ALLEN, J. (1988) 'Rose Scott's vision; Feminism and masculinity, 1880–1925', in CAINE, B., GROSZ, W. and DE LEVERPANCHE, M. *Crossing Boundaries: Feminism and Critique of Knowledges*, Sydney, Allen and Unwin.

APPLE, M. (1983) 'Work, gender and teaching', *Teachers College Record*, 84, 3, pp. 611–27.

APPLE, M. (1985) 'Teaching and "women's work": A comparative historical and ideological analysis', *Teachers College Record*, 86, 3, pp. 455–73.

BACCHI, C. (1980) 'Evolution, eugenics and women: The impact of scientific theories on the attitudes to women 1870–1920', in WINDSHUTTLE, E. (Ed.) *Women, Class and History: Feminist Perspectives on Australia 1788–1978*, Melbourne, Fontana Collins.

BACCHI, C. (1990) *Same Difference: Feminism and Sexual Difference*, Sydney, Allen and Unwin.

BATES, R. (1986) *Management of Culture and Knowledge*, Geelong, Deakin University Press.

BESSANT, B. (1986) 'The school — the institution and its controlling bureaucracy', in ANGUS, L. (Ed.) *Schooling for the Social Order*, Geelong, Deakin University Press.

BLACKMORE, J. (1989) 'Educational leadership: A feminist critique and reconstruction', in SMYTH, J. (Ed.) *Critical Perspectives on Educational Leadership*, Lewes, Falmer Press.

BURTON, C. (1987) 'Merit and gender: Organizations and the mobilization of masculine bias', *Australian Journal of Social Issues*, 22, 2, pp. 424–35.

CARRIGAN, T., CONNELL, B. and LEE, J. (1987) 'The sex role framework and the sociology of masculinity', in WEINER, G. and ARNOT, M. (Eds) *Gender under Scrutiny: New Inquiries in Education*, London, Hutchinson.

CHAMBERS, C. (1986) *Lessons for Ladies: A social history of girls' education in Australia 1870–1900*, Hale and Ironmonger Marrackville.

CLIFFORD, G. (1987) ' "Lady teacher" and politics in the United States, 1850–1930', in LAWN, M. and GRACE, G. (Eds) Teachers: *The Culture and Politics of Work*, Lewes, Falmer Press.

CONNELL, R.W. (1987) *Gender and Power*, Sydney, Allen and Unwin.

CONSIDINE, M. (1988) 'The corporate management framework as administrative science: A critique', *Australian Journal of Administration*, 47, 1, pp. 4–18.

DANYLEWYCZ, M. and PRENTICE, A. (1986) 'Revising the history of teachers: A Canadian perspective', *Interchange*, 17, 2, pp. 135–46.

DEACON, D. (1989) *Managing Gender: The State, the New Middle Class and Women Workers 1830–1930*, Melbourne, Oxford University Press.

DEAL, T. and KENNEDY, A. (1982) *Corporate Cultures: The Rites and Rituals of Corporate Life*, Reading, Addison-Wesley.

DOW, G. and SCHOLES, G. (1984) 'Christina Montgomery', in SELLECK, R. and SULLIVAN, M. (Eds) *Not So Eminent Victorians*, Melbourne, Oxford University Press.

EISENSTEIN, H. (1985) 'The gender of bureaucracy: reflections on feminism and the state', in GOODNOW, S. and PATEMAN, C. (Eds) *Women, Social Science and Public Policy*, Sydney, Allen and Unwin.

FERGUSON, K. (1984) *A Feminist Case Against Bureaucracy*, Philadelphia, Temple University Press.

FRANZWAY, S., COURT, D. and CONNELL, R. (1989) *Staking a Claim: Feminism, Bureaucracy and the State*, Sydney, Allen and Unwin.

GRAMSCI, A. (1971) *Translations of Selections from Prison Notebooks*, trans. by HOARE, Q. and HOWELL-SMITH, J., London, Lawrence and Wishart.

GRUMET, M. (1981) 'Pedagogy for patriarchy: the feminization of teaching', *Interchange*, 12, 2/3, pp. 165–83.

HANNAN, T. (1975) 'Julia Flynn and the Inspectorship of Victorian Secondary Schools 1928–9', *ANZ History of Education Society Journal*, XLIV, 1, pp. 1–19.

HANSOT, E.W. and TYACK, D. (1981) *The Dream Deferred: A Golden Age for Women School Administrators*, Stanford, Institute for Research on Educational Finance and Governance, Stanford University.

HEARN, J. and PARKIN, W. (1983) 'Gender and organizations: A review of the literature', *Organisation Studies*, 4, 3, pp. 219–42.

HOLLWAY, W. (1984) 'Fitting Work: Psychological assessment in organizations', in HENRIQUES, J., HOLLWAY, W., URWIN, C., VENN, C. and WALKERDINE, V. (Eds) *Changing the Subject: Psychology, Social Regulation and Subjectivity*, London, Methuen.

HUGHEY, J. (1989) 'Equal pay campaign in the Queensland Teachers Union', in HENRY, M. and TAYLOR, S. (Eds) *Battlers and Bluestockings*, Canberra, Australian College of Education.

KYLE, N. (1990) 'Policy, politics, parsimony and pragmatism: The state and the rural school in colonial New South Wales', *History of Education*, 19, 1, pp. 41–54.

LATHER, P. (1987) 'The absent presence: Patriarchy, capitalism, and the nature of teachers' work', *Teacher Education Quarterly*, 14, 2, pp. 25–38.

LAWN, M. and GRACE, G. (1987) *Teachers: The Culture and Politics of Work*, Lewes, Falmer Press.

LLOYD, G. (1984) *The Man of Reason: 'Male' and 'Female' in Western Philosophy*, London, Methuen.

McCALLUM, D. (1990) *The Social Production of Merit: Education, Psychology and Politics 1900–50*, Lewes, Falmer Press.

MARSHALL, C. and MITCHELL, D. (1989) 'Women's careers as a critique of the administrative culture', Paper presented to AERA, San Francisco, March.

MARTIN, B. (1987) 'Merit and Gender', *Australian Journal of Social Issues*, 22, 2, pp. 436–51.

MATTHEWS, J. (1984) *Good and Mad Women: The Historical Construction of Femininity in Twentieth-century Australia*, Sydney, Allen and Unwin.

MIDDLETON, S. (1986) Feminism and education in post-war New Zealand: an oral history perspective in OPENSHAW, T. *et al.* (Eds) *Reinterpreting the Educational Past*, New Zealand Council for Educational Research, Wellington.

MIDDLETON, S. (1987) 'Educating Feminists: A life history approach', in ACKER, S. *Teachers, Gender and Careers*, Lewes, Falmer Press.

MILLER, P. (1986) *Long Division: State Schooling in South Australian Society*, South Australia Netley, Wakefield Press.

O'DONNELL, C. (1984) 'Market theories of the labour market and women's place in it', *Journal of Industrial Relations*, 26, June, pp. 147–65.

ORAM, A (1987) 'Sex antagonism in the teaching profession: Equal pay and the marriage bar 1910–1939', in ARNOT, M. and WEINER, G. (Eds) *Gender and the Politics of Schooling*, Milton Keynes, Open University Press.

OZGA, J. and LAWN, M. (1981) *Teachers, Professionalism and Class*, Lewes, Falmer Press.

PATEMAN, C. (1989) 'The fraternal social contract: Some observations on patriarchal civil society', in *The Disorder of Women*, Cambridge, Polity Press.

PRENTICE, A. (1975) 'The feminization of teaching', *Histoire Sociale*, 8, pp. 5–20.

PURVIS, J. (1987) 'Social class, education and the ideals of femininity in the nineteenth century', in ARNOT, M. and WEINER, G. (Eds), *Gender and the Politics of Schooling*, London, Hutchinson.

REIGER, K. (1985) *The Disenchantment of the Home: Modernising the Australian Family 1880–1940*, Melbourne, Oxford University Press.

ROSE, S. (1988), 'Gender antagonism and class conflict: Exclusionary strategies of male trade unionists in nineteenth-century Britain', *Social History*, 13, 2, pp. 191–208.

SHAKESHAFT, C. (1987) 'Training school administrators: The making of the man in the principal's office', *Teacher Education Quarterly*, 14, 2, pp. 59–67.

SIMPSON, R.L. and SIMPSON, I.H. (1969) 'Women and bureaucracy in the semi-professions', in ETZIONI, A. (Ed.) *The Semi-professions and their Organization*, New York, The Free Press.

STEEDMAN, C. (1985) '"The mother made conscious": The historical development of a primary school pedagogy', *History Workshop*, 20, Autumn, pp. 135–49.

SYDIE, R.A. (1987) *Natural Men/Cultured Women: A Feminist Perspective on Sociological Theory*, Milton, Keynes, Open University Press.

THEOBALD, M. (1987) 'Humanities, science and the female mind: An historical perspective', *Unicorn*, 13, 3, pp. 162–5.

THEOBALD, M. (1984) '"Mere accomplishments"? Melbourne's early ladies schools reconsidered', *History of Education Review*, 13, 2, pp. 15–28.

TYACK, D. and HANSOT, E. (1982) *Managers of virtue: Public school leadership in America 1820–1980*, New York Basic Books.

TYACK, D. and STROBER, M. (1981) 'Jobs and gender: A history of the structuring of educational employment by sex', in SCHMUCK, P. and CHARTERS, W. (Eds) *Educational Policy and Management: Sex Differentials*, New York, Academic Press.

VENN, C. (1984) 'The subject of psychology', in HENRIQUES, J., HOLLWAY, W., URWIN, C., VENN, C. and WALKERDINE, V. (Eds) *Changing the Subject: Psychology, Social Regulation and Subjectivity*, London, Methuen.

VICK, M. (1988) 'Trained or incompetent? Historical perspectives on the training of teachers', Paper presented to the ANZ History of Education Conference, Canberra.

VICTORIA, (1869) *Parliamentary Papers*, Seventh Report of the Board of Education, Melbourne, Victorian Government Printer.

WALKERDINE, V. (1987) 'Sex, power and pedagogy', in ARNOT, M. and WEINER, G. (Eds) *Gender and the Politics of Schooling*, Milton Keynes, Open University Press.

WILLIAMSON, N. (1983) 'The feminization of teaching in New South Wales: A historical perspective', *Australian Journal of Education*, 27, 1, pp. 22–44.

YEATMAN, A. (1987) 'The concept of public management and the Australian state in the 1980s', *Australian Journal of Public Administration*, 46, 4, pp. 13–15.

YEATMAN, A. (1990) *Bureaucrats, Technocrats and Femocrats: Essays on the contemporary Australian State*, Sydney, Allen and Unwin.

ZAINNU'DIN, A. (1984) '"The poor widow, the ignoramus and the humbug": An examination of the rhetoric and reality in Victoria's 1904 Act for the Registration of Teachers and Schools', *History of Education Review*, 13, 2, pp. 29–42.

Chapter 3

'Setting the Child Free': Teachers, Mothers and Child-centred Pedagogy in the 1930s Kindergarten

Deborah Tyler

'At the age of six', announced Christine Heinig in 1939, principal of the Kindergarten Training College, 'it is difficult indeed, on any economic level, to find a perfect child' (Heinig, 1939a, p. 222). Children, born perfect, were 'damaged' between birth and school, in such a way that their maximum capabilities and potential for happiness would never be realized. Heinig based her statement on the evidence of an extensive body of scientific studies of the child, including the work of Piaget and Gesell on development and attainment. She cited a 1933 publication to demonstrate the solid base in scientific fact which underpinned her comments. Her source, Murchinson's *A Handbook of Child Psychology*, spanning one thousand pages, was able to cite the findings of, for example, 250 studies of sex differences, 80 studies on the development of the emotions, 90 studies of mental growth, and 256 studies of language development (Heinig, 1939a, pp. 218–223). The child, as an object of scientific study, had definitely arrived.

Nor was the question of responsibility for this damage, those producing imperfect children, left hanging. Heinig, and hundreds of other child development experts, solidly implicated parents, and in particular mothers, in the production of the imperfect child. Mothers, through their mode of child rearing, stood between their child and healthy development. In Heinig's view, these thousands of studies had done no more than 'prove the obvious' but she concluded that 'these obvious facts give practical workers a strong platform from which to work and have served to impress on us the importance of really getting done some of the obvious things' (Heinig, 1939a, p. 222). For Christine Heinig and many others acquainted with the child through science, the nursery school and kindergarten provided the ideal site for doing these 'obvious things' and for producing the perfect child.

The value of an educational intervention which covered the child from two to six years was seen by psychologists and educationalists to be self-evident. Studies of children defined as problems or as delinquents routinely asserted the importance of a child's earliest years in determining what kind of adult a child would become. It was those years, between the baby health centre and the beginning of formal schooling, when the child was left to the uncertain care of mother or other untrained adults that the 'damage' was done. By the time compulsory schooling began it was simply too late to undo this damage: habits were formed, characters blighted, intellects dulled. At the very best, valuable time would be wasted trying to untangle the sticky mess that unsuitable child rearing had made of the child's mind, and expenditure of time that made, in the words of another training college principal, the 'foundation of victorious childhood' impossible to lay (Gutteridge, 1931, p. 108). According to Christine Heinig, these scientific studies had established the necessity for 'someone to pick up the child' between the baby health centre and the school (Heinig, 1938, p. 159). That someone was not the child's mother, but the kindergarten or nursery school teacher.

The kindergarten teacher was equipped for this task because her teaching was based on 'growth facts instead of "isms"'. The programme she followed, said Heinig, was 'not based on a preconceived idea of what children ought to do but a truly scientific programme following the developmental needs of the child' (Heinig, 1939a, p. 219). It was her training in the science of child development, and the co-operation in proper management of the child that mothers would give through the effectivity of her techniques, that would assist in the production of the perfect child, the child that science had decreed that all children could become.

We need to ask what aspects of a mother's child-rearing practices, relationships with the child and ultimately of her nature were viewed as inhibiting the production of the perfect child, and the ways in which this knowledge of the failings of mothers informed the teacher's understanding of her own position and the relationship between home and school. We need to explore, too, the processes through which the activities of mothers have become central to a contemporary common sense concerning the educability of children, educational achievement, classroom behaviour and so on.

Following the work of Henriques and others in *Changing the Subject* (1984), and in particular that of Valerie Walkerdine, I explore in this paper the foundations of child-centred pedagogy in the discourses of developmental psychology and child psychoanalysis (Walkerdine, 1984). These two discourses, while distinct theoretically, acted in concert in pedagogic practice, informing teaching strategies intended to promote the child's intellectual and emotional development respectively. The paper moves through three stages, focusing first on the shape of the perfect child, the child produced through the knowledge of science, second on the ways in which the failure of mothers to produce this child was understood in child psychology, and third on the kindergarten teacher herself, the construction of the practices of the 'good teacher' within child-centred pedagogy.

The Perfect Child of Science

Rather than there being an essential child who had waited in the wings of time to be discovered by science, 'the child' of child psychology depended for its production on already existing conceptions of the nature of the child and of what is to count as scientific procedure (for an analysis of the production of 'the child' of child psychology see Riley, 1983, pp. 42ff). Psychology's claims to truth about the nature of the child, claims produced through psychology's status as science, have become central to educational practices and a contemporary common sense, giving those claims a centrality here. The child of child psychology is a child stripped of social relations, a child who is constituted in science simply as 'child', not as daughter, son, friend, brother, sister, black, white, female, male and so on. These matters were deemed relevant only in so far as they impinged on the development of the individual child — they did not signify different ways of being a child. This does not mean that the discourses and practices of developmental psychology have not contributed to the production and institutionalizing of differences. But these differences were constituted within child psychology, producing a typology of children — for example, the seclusive child or the anxious child — and were made meaningful through their deviation from that other child, the perfect child.

What then was the nature of the child 1930s science claimed to know, the 'growth facts' that Christine Heinig referred to? D.M. Embleton, a leading Melbourne psychiatrist, described the human baby in blunt, if characteristic, terms: 'The infant begins life as a completely dependent parasite and by parental example and application must be transformed into a socially useful, independent citizen' (Embleton, 1936, p. 749). Other writers softened this message through reference to biology and comparison with animals, claiming that in early dependence and an extended period of childhood lay the essence of humanity and the greater intelligence of the human being (see, for example, Isaacs, 1929, pp. 8–10). To take on the really complex tasks of human society could require a period of development spanning 25 years (see, for example, McRae, 1932, pp. 14–16). But, despite these provisos, the perfect child, the child science knew that every child had the capacity to be, would move steadily towards total independence by taking every opportunity to exercise greater control and autonomy. Independence was the key to the perfect child and the well-adjusted adult: 'Mental health calls for a gradual "weaning" from the dependence of babyhood to an independence that will stand the child in good stead all through life' (Gutteridge, 1931, p. 107). As will be discussed later, it was in the cultivation of independence that many mothers were found wanting.

The attainment of independence was not only socially desirable, but part of the nature of the child. A defining feature of the child's nature was the desire to take on this essential task of development and move towards independence and maturity. Rather than requiring transformation by the agency of parents and others, if possibilities for independence were provided, the child would fulfil its nature by transforming itself. Christine Heinig saw this principle as axiomatic to the pedagogy of the kindergarten:

> The second guidance technique is to allow the child to do for himself.
> The toddler is just beginning to feel his own power to do. He seems by
> nature full of the desire to acquire social virtues, such as independence,
> self-help, neatness, concentration on a self-initiated task. He is also full
> of the desire to work hard . . . to the point of tears and fatigue, and he
> takes pride in accomplishment (Heinig, 1938, p. 156).

Moreover, by facilitating the child's desire for independence, a second defining characteristic of the perfect child would be able to show itself. For the child to be moving towards independence also meant taking responsibility for one's self and one's actions, and discovering that the desire to do something was not sufficient reason in itself for doing it. Dr P.M. Bachelard, a Melbourne psychiatrist, regarded this discovery by the child as a crucial indicator of its progress towards 'full humanity' but warned that the child would naturally make this discovery as its intelligence 'opened'. The child who was forced into obedience would never discover 'inner discipline' and would come only to resent the rules, not regulate the self (Bachelard, 1939, p. 110). The child was capable of self-regulation, and to realize its full potential must become so.

Alongside independence and self-regulation came the child's progress towards rationality. The pre-verbal dependent baby had no option but to experience and express frustration directly and openly, no means of understanding or controlling its emotions and desires and consequently no character as such. Bachelard emphasized that the child was not born rational, but did have the potential to become so and thus fully human (Bachelard, 1939, p. 112). Language development appeared as the central means for the promotion of reasoning in the child, providing a naturally occurring vehicle for the expression of wishes and the resolution of conflicts. But for the child to develop into a rational being depended chiefly on the ways the irrational part of its nature was brought under control, and while language, 'unfolding intelligence' and the child's own desire to mature were useful assets, the achievement of rationality was the most difficult test confronting the child, and where the need for careful treatment from those around was most acute (see for example, Bachelard, 1939; Gutteridge, 1932, pp. 112, 115).

Mary Lush, one of the older group of kindergarten directors who had embraced the knowledge of science and altered her practices in the kindergarten and the training she offered to students accordingly, explained the child's struggle to achieve rationality as a struggle between the demands of growth and the ease of regression. 'In all children', she advised parents, 'there is the life urge to growth, to achieve manhood or womanhood, and not only physical, but mental and emotional maturity.' At the same time, she warned, in all of us there is a 'regressive tendency' which makes it attractive to wallow in the privileges and pleasures of babyhood. The child's developmental challenge lay in resisting the pull of such pleasures, leaving them behind, and moving steadily forward to the development of an independent personality and the mentally healthy satisfactions derived from maturity and from controlling the seductive lure of infantile desires (Lush, 1932, p. 7).

Susan Isaacs, a well known member of the Kleinian school who was immensely influential in the training of Melbourne kindergarten teachers and others through her many publications and her appearance at the New Education Fellowship Conference in Melbourne in 1938, offered an even more alarming and powerful picture of the perils in the path to rationality and the tempting pleasures that invited a child to remain irrational. Isaacs portrayed the baby as an intensely sensual being, exulting in the movements of the bowel and the sensations of sucking the mother's breast. At the same time the baby was prey to the immediate and overwhelming impact of anger and wants, simultaneously hating and loving the breast, occupying, in Isaac's phrase 'an unchartered ocean of immediate desires'. It was only gradually, and never in a fully guaranteed way, that the child was able to gain distance from desire and control immediate impulse (Isaacs, 1929, pp. 28–30).

As was common with this literature, Isaacs moved quickly from description to prescription, defining the activities of the mother and the teacher in relation to the nature of the child. This advice is worth noting briefly here, as it makes the meanings of rationality much clearer. Her advice was complex and depended on the mother keeping her own nature under control, her desires at arm's length:

> If we indulge *our* love for the child by excessive kissing and caressing, rather than by intelligent provision for his interest in things and events, we cannot be surprised when he fails to leave behind his own primitive modes of affection (Isaacs, 1929, p. 113).

And, while Isaacs's use of 'he' here is intended to include both sexes, she is even more explicit about the inappropriateness of physical affection between mothers and sons. With boys, Isaacs gave her advice as a command:

> There should be no demand for caresses or for open expressions of love. . . . They want to be manly, and to be treated as manly, and they can well appreciate the indirect expression of love in courtesy, consideration and in providing for their material and spiritual needs (Isaacs, 1938, p. 619).

It is worth noting here that Isaacs was regarded as one of the most *laisser-faire* and least prescriptive of scientists of the child, and indeed these particular prescriptions leap from her text, and are the more notable for that. She describes a number of features of the mother approved by scientific discourse (the exclusion of passion, the mother who services the needs of children by suppressing her own needs and desires) which will be returned to in this paper. Her words also point to the dual functioning of scientific knowledge of the child with, on the one hand, claims to truth concerning a discovery of the already existing nature of the child; and on the other, a productive effect in generating that nature, including sex differences, through the regulation of the everyday practices of mother and teacher.

The final defining characteristic of the child of science was that aspect of the child produced by developmental psychology as its object of study. Without the claim that the child was by nature an organism that passed through a series of ordered, measurable stages to maturity, a science of child development was an impossibility. The scientific meanings of the child cohered around the child as an 'integrated unit' who moved through an ordered sequence of development, a movement whose origins and direction lay in the child itself. Development was held to be an ordered process, determined by an inner logic, an inner clock.

The discovery of this developmental clock, which laid down a universalized developmental path through which each child passed in observable stages, was the most significant of the achievements of child psychology, covering intellectual, social and emotional development. The work of the American Gesell, who derived intellectual support from Piaget, was extremely influential in Melbourne and was described by one Kindergarten Training College principal as a bible in the training of kindergarten teachers during the 1930s and 1940s (Lyon, 1988) Gesell's theory of maturation was received in the same spirit of enthusiasm which greeted other major discoveries: science had discovered the logic of the child's mind. Christine Heinig conveyed something of the excitement that greeted such knowledge and the ways in which maturation became an organizing principle of child-centred pedagogy in a 1937 article for the *Australian Educational Review*:

> We have discovered *maturation*, that simple but heretofore elusive under-
> standing of growth, without which we have for so many years been
> wasting children's time and dulling their interest in learning. Since
> research has shown us that teaching certain interests and skills is fairly
> useless until both physical and mental growth have ripened to the point
> where the human machine is able to deal with them, we are broadening
> education instead of speeding it up and shortening it. If in accordance
> with findings, reading abilities do not mature until a child is about seven,
> reading does not need to be taught as such until the child's second year at
> school (Heinig, 1937, p. 15).

Theories of maturation and the ordered development of the child did not only
centre on intellectual abilities, but covered all aspects of the child. For example,
May Gutteridge, giving examples of behaviour that were natural to the 3-year-
old, explained:

> By three years . . . there also comes a definite feeling of responsibility for
> the younger children and a wish to help adults. If this is not forced or
> over-suggested, it comes from the child as a definite step in develop-
> ment. . . . It comes to boys and girls alike, built up step by step as the
> first experience of this kind is happy and successful (Gutteridge, 1932,
> p. 19).

Despite her confidence that caring and helpful behaviour came naturally to
both girls and boys, the examples given of this kind of behaviour and the ways in
which the kindergarten environment facilitated its emergence, are exclusively of
girls, a pattern repeated in the work of other writers on the kindergarten. What is
important here is the ways in which the discourse of developmental psychology
which defined the child as the point of origin of behaviour was in the universalized nature of the child, timed by an inner clock. Moreover, the developmental clock provided the means of measuring the child's progress, and was
productive of normalizing expectations of what to count as development, and
when different capacities should emerge from the child.

Clearly the implications of this were, and are, considerable and the meanings
of order within the discourses of child psychology are complex. However, I want
to turn to another way in which the notion of 'order' became an essentialized
aspect of the nature of the child.

While the logic of ordered development held the key to the child's mind, the
notion of the child's inner order was extended to include the child's necessary
relationship with the external world. But of the nature of the child, the child of
development psychology and Kleinian psychoanalysis, was the desire for and
appreciation of an ordered existence. A desire for order, stability and predictability in everyday life, producing the importance of routines and certainties,
arose naturally from the inner truths of the child's own development. While the
extension of a science of mind to a science of social relations in this way was
possible only through a slippage or fluidity in the meanings of order, such fluidity
was crucial in providing a scientific rationale for preferring some modes of child
rearing to others. For, as with those other universalized features of the child, if the
child's inner nature, expressed through a desire for order, was not replicated in

the social arrangements of the child's upbringing, a 'lack of fit' between child and environment would result, displaying itself in unhappiness, a failure to maximize individual capacities and a failure to adjust socially. Mary Lush portrayed the necessity for this match between the inner child and the external environment through reference to the knowledge domain of the physical sciences. For this match not to exist, she said, 'is like living in a world where natural laws are apt to be temporarily suspended, where the law of gravitation sometimes functions and sometimes does not, where fire sometimes burns and sometimes does not' (Lush, 1932, p. 2). She provided the example of a child who, aware that his mother was depressed and upset, was reluctant to engage in play that would dirty his clothes. This child, in Lush's terms dealing with an unstable mother, was confronted with a lack of match between his inner nature and the social world. Such a child was unable to develop (Lush, 1932, p. 2).

Paradoxically, then, the child's inner order, which combined with innate intelligence determined everything of importance about the child and provided the path along which the child would move, was capable of disruption. The potential for this disruption was ever present, and to a degree normal. For example, the child on first entering the kindergarten could be expected to display behaviour regarded as characteristic of a younger child, until the mentally healthy child adjusted his or her inner mental world to the new external world and ordered development resumed. The child's capacity for making such an adjustment depended on the external world corresponding with the 'fact' of development, a correspondence found in the kindergarten but not in all environments. Severe disruption of this inner order was the terrain of abnormal psychology, but the 'facts' of child development produced through the knowledge domain of child psychology meant that explanations and solutions should be sought in the social world, to discern where the lack of match occurred. For the perfect child, the child of science, to be produced, necessitated a freeing of the child from aspects of the social world which would otherwise impinge upon development. Mary Lush quoted a mother who had been helped to this realization by participation in a child study class, saying, 'I now spend less energy in managing the child and *more on preventing upsets in myself*' (Lush, 1932, p. 3. My emphasis). Within this discourse, all those matters which took a child's attention from the primary task of development by placing the child as a social actor inhibited the possibility of producing the perfect child.

The child's needs emerged smoothly from the 'facts' of child development, produced through the nature of the child. Like the facts of developments, these needs were universal, regardless of the social, material or cultural location of child and parents. The list of the child's needs within the discourses of child psychology appears endless, and can perhaps most usefully be considered as cohering around the facilitation of those aspects of the child's nature produced and universalized through the sciences of the child. For example, Susan Isaacs identified the child's need for 'stable attitudes of feelings in those around him' as essential to the facilitation of self-regulation, a need for firm control as essential to the growth of rationality, a need for security as essential to independence and so on (Isaacs, 1938, p. 613).

Isaacs, and other writers on child development, focused extensively on the child's need to play, understood to be the natural business of childhood, essential to all aspects of development and the means by which the child self-directed the pace of development. Given the centrality of play to development, the child needed the provision of appropriate play materials, suitable for each stage and to encourage the move ever onwards to maturity. Moreover, the child needed to be free of adult interference in play, achieved through the mother's respect for its importance and the provision of a safe and stimulating environment. Mary Lush gives a sense of the proliferation of needs produced through the discovery of the importance of play to child development:

> *Another* practical consideration is the need for looking ahead. . . . In this respect many homes have a crying need for more space. A playroom can be regarded a necessity. . . . But space for vigorous outdoor play is also needed. . . . For the older child a workshop is almost a necessity. . . (Lush, 1932, p. 10).

Along with the need for play in the production of normal development came its therapeutic importance and the view of play as providing a window on the child's mind, or, in Susan Isaacs words 'the shortest and surest way of gaining knowledge of his feelings and attitudes, his questions, his interests, his wishes (Isaacs, 1937).

Related to play was the child's need for companions of the same age or same developmental stage. Like play, the provision of suitable companions was essential for all aspects of development, particularly for co-operative behaviour and social adjustment more generally. Through the companionship of either children, in Christine Heinig's view, the child learnt to: 'become a responsible member of the group . . . to respect others' rights, to maintain his own, to use language as a means of communication, and to have a direct quality in his dealings with adults and children' (Heinig, 1938, p. 57). It was in relation particularly to the child's need for the provision of appropriate conditions for play in an environment where supervision and monitoring were both constant and unobtrusive, and for the provision of suitable companions, that attendance at a kindergarten became in itself an essential need of the child, necessary for normal development.

Smaller families, that new type of child the 'only' child, homes without adequate arrangements for play, all produced a near universal need for children to have access to nursery schools and kindergartens. While this need was particularly acute for inner-city children, where many kindergartens were located, the developmental benefits had application to all children. By placing her child in a kindergarten, a mother was able to ensure that these two key needs — play and companionship — were met. And placing the child in a kindergarten would bring the mother into contact with professional knowledge that would assist her to meet the child's other needs.

Psychology's claims to know the nature of the child, and the rate and path of development, produced the need for this knowledge to be known by the mother. Scientifically equipped, the effective mother would regulate her everyday life around meeting and anticipating the needs of her child. Like the child's other needs, the need for the mother's knowledge of the 'facts' of development originated in the nature of the child. Psychology, it was claimed, had done no more than facilitate the meeting of this need. Susan Isaacs makes this clearer, prefacing her comments by the introduction of another need, that of the child's need to be able to sense that parents had confidence in his or her future:

we can only gain confidence in the child's future . . . by learning something of what normal development is, of the ages at which the various
skills and social qualities we wish to foster typically appear in the course
of normal growth . . . the parent needs to know when the child can . . .
run and throw and play with other children, and what is suitable play
material for different ages (Isaacs, 1938, p. 613).

By knowing when the child was ready for different activities, Isaacs explained,
the mother would convey her faith in the child's potential to become fully
human, mature, through the ways her provision could replicate the child's own
ordered progress. By facilitating development in this way, the mother would
provide the emotional support that would relieve the child's anxieties about leaving the safety of infancy behind. The child's desires to develop fully and the
mother's desire for this to happen would thus coincide, and this match would be
known to the child. Moreover, her knowledge of normal development would
enable the mother to avoid causing 'emotional irritation' in her child, or the feeling of inferiority and other problems which a 'lack of fit' between the child's
developing capacities and environmental demands could produce.

For most mothers, social agencies like the baby health centres and kindergartens provided the most appropriate means for coming into contact with such
knowledge, and for professional guidance on the organization of daily life around
meeting the child's needs. A major portion of the kindergarten teacher's work
was around the education of mothers in appropriate child rearing. The mother's
willingness to co-operate with the kindergarten was, then, in itself a reliable indicator of her ability to mother through provision for the child's needs.

How Mothers Failed

Yet K.S. Cunningham, author of a 1932 ACER study on problem children,
found that kindergarten teachers reported that between 20 and 25 per cent of the
children they taught displayed problem behaviour of such magnitude that they
required special guidance from experts. The problems kindergarten teachers
reported included the failure of children to reach the norms for their age, poor
bladder control, and nightmares. They found children in kindergartens to be
neurotic, hyperactive, seclusive, emotional, egocentric and just plain inadequate.
They found children who lied, disobeyed, bullied, deceived, sulked and were
obstinate (Cunningham, 1937). Moreover, they classified 80 per cent of the home
environments of these problem cases as poor, and overwhelmingly attributed the
cause of problems displayed to the home. Just as Christine Heinig had, kindergarten teachers solidly implicated mothers as the cause of problem behaviour in the
kindergarten and the failure of children to develop in the way science decreed
they should.

How was the kindergarten mother failing to produce the perfect child? The
scientific mother, or the intelligent mother as she was most often described, was
able to meet her child's needs because she organized her childrearing around the
knowledge of child psychology, and expressed her love for the child through
meeting those needs that science had discovered. Importantly, she displayed her
intelligence and earned the appellation of intelligent because of her intellectual

recognition of the truth of psychology's claims. The kindergarten literature is full of references to mothers who, when confronted with the temporary manifestation of a behaviour difficulty like lying, responded according to the prescriptions of psychologists rather than the advice of other mothers or friends. Dr Anita Muhl, a psychoanalyst who lectured at the Kindergarten Training College, for example, reserved the title of 'intelligent' for those mothers who recognized that their child needed guidance beyond what they could offer. In such situations, their intelligence was rewarded by discoveries that the child's behaviour resulted from the 'unintelligent' act of someone else, often a servant or grandparent (Muhl, 1939, pp. 61–2). The 'intelligent' mother, like the kindergarten teacher, understood that the sheer range of knowledge about the child meant she could not be competent in all areas, recognized that she would require advice, and was willing to take and act upon it. Her relationship with this body of knowledge enabled her to keep her nature under control and to understand that facilitating the child's development, rather than expecting or requiring the child to answer her own needs, was the way to find satisfaction as a mother. The unintelligent mother represented, in the terms of child psychology, a triumph of knowledge over nature.

Yet the possibility that a mother would behave as an intelligent mother should depended upon the channelling of her desires for her children, stemming from the irrational love she felt for them as dependent babies, into a conviction that holding back herself was the way to do the best for them. To make her love meaningful and not destructive, she had to contain her love, love which was produced, it was held, through the child's early dependency, and express it through the facilitation of the child's independence. It was then, paradoxically, on this irrational love that the motivation to be an intelligent mother rested. As Christine Heinig explained, 'We know . . . that while children are very young parents are more easily influenced to make efforts and sacrifices that will benefit their babies than they are when children are older and more independent' (Heinig, 1939a, p. 219). And it was the irrationality in a mother's love that most often brought about her downfall, her classification into a 'type' of mother. The ways that mothers failed, as did their success, depended upon their relationships with the theories of developmental psychology and their ability to control their natures and the irrational origin of their feelings towards their children.

Just as the kindergarten teacher's training provided her with the categories and criteria through which she could recognize and classify problem behaviour in children, so it provided her with the categories through which she could classify mothers. The productivity of psychological knowledge in producing a typology for children and mothers is important to grasp here, as is the ever-increasing specificity of the categories. The category of 'seclusive' by which to recognize, classify and 'treat' a 'type' of child is impossible without the existence of a body of knowledge which produces the normal child as one who by nature requires companionship for optimum development. It is only by reference to such knowledge that a child can be 'seclusive'. Philanthropic institutions of the late nineteenth century classified mothers as decent or immoral and based the nature of their intervention on that division. The transformation of mothering from a moral question to a scientific one produced new ways in which mothers could be classified, and new 'types' of mothers. I explore some of these types before returning to questions of the mothers' nature.

Case studies of children displaying problems invariably referred to what 'type' of mother the child had, and this typology held significant clues to the child's treatment, or, as in most cases, the mother's treatment. The intelligent mother has already been discussed, and I want to discuss two other 'types' of mothers whose relationship to expert knowledge was the basis of their typing. Like the intelligent mother, the over-anxious mother was well acquainted with the theories of child psychology, but had the wrong relationship with them. For the over-anxious mother, an especial degree of contempt was reserved. A Newcastle doctor writing in the *Medical Journal of Australia* echoed the voices of many others, saying, 'one is cynical enough to be amused when he sees the modern young mother, bursting with psychological axioms, exhausted mentally and physically for months on end by the strain of bringing up her one and only child' (Minogue, 1936, p. 449). A second contributor claimed that working-class families were not able to cope with psychological child rearing. He quoted an example of a home in chaos because parents were afraid to punish a child physically, but did not understand how else she could be managed. He concluded, 'This, of course, was an extreme case, but it illustrates the effect of a smattering of modern psychological training upon an average working-class family' (Croll, 1936, p. 449).

Those closer to the kindergartens shared this sense of alarm about the inability of many mothers to develop the right relationship with the facts of child development. Many mothers appeared to find the balance between understanding their child as an individual and their knowledge of norms of development impossible to negotiate. Mothers became anxious that their child was 'falling behind' and tried to intervene to speed things up, not recognizing that by doing so they were interfering with development. Mothers, in their desire to meet the child's needs and to express their love in approved ways, mishandled the knowledge they possessed, and created problems that would otherwise not exist. Jean Wyndham offered a common example to the Australian Association for Pre-School Child Development in 1939:

> General in difference or resistance to food is another problem which the over-anxious mother often creates for herself. Height–weight tables and some knowledge on her part of calories and vitamins are often responsible for her anxiety to have the child eat a certain amount and certain kinds of foods. Her own anxiety is responsible for her tension, and this takes away her child's appetite (Wyndham, 1939, p. 102).

The mother of an 'only' child was held most likely to display over-anxiety, and to seek the help of child guidance clinics when there was no need to do so. Over-anxious mothers were advised to seek interests other than their child, or to have more children, to help facilitate the child's development.

Unlike the intelligent mother who constituted a 'type' of mother through the appropriateness of her relationship with the knowledge of developmental psychology, the over-anxious mother constituted a 'type' because of the over-*literalness* of her relationship with this knowledge. The 'ignorant mother' was also understood as a 'type' through her relationship with expert knowledge. The most numerous of all types, her ignorance resided in her lack of knowledge of child development. Without such knowledge, she was deemed unable to rear a child satisfactorily. Without such knowledge, her views or modes of child rearing worked only to produce the truth of her ignorance. Olive Dodd, the Free Kindergarten Union social worker, regarded ignorance of the 'facts' of child development to be the prime cause of difficult and problem children, saying of mothers,

> Too often they have married at a very early age, with the mother knowing little beyond the routine of the factory in which she has worked since leaving school. Consequently there is inconsistency — over-indulgence and over-severity — and no routine (Dodd, 1939, p. 142).

While conceding that housing was affected by economic constraints, Dodd told her audience that it was parental ignorance that led to the rearing of children in boarding houses and overcrowded dwellings. Only an ignorant mother would fail to see the consequences of this for child development, she claimed, and by reorganizing priorities arrange life differently (Dodd, 1939, p. 139). Many kindergarten teachers were themselves shocked by the conditions in which children lived, and did much to try and alleviate the edge of poverty by organizing food and clothing. But, in common with experts on child development, Dodd did not believe that material conditions held the key to the possibility of producing the perfect child. Rather, that possibility depended upon the 'type' of mother and the ways she managed the domestic environment and her relationships with the child to avoid the problems of poverty impinging to the child's development. An intelligent mother, though poor, would be able to produce the perfect child.

In many respects the kindergarten owed the conditions of its existence to the presence of ignorant mothers, in the obvious sense that it was the ignorance of child development that had, it was held, revealed the necessity for kindergartens. A large part of its function, and of the kindergarten teachers' work, was maternal education. Many mothers, then were not to be permanently locked into ignorance, but could gradually be brought to knowledge. Mothers who were 'willing to learn' were approved and affirmed by the teacher. Such mothers were regarded with sympathy rather than contempt, and were likely to be able to develop a good relationship with the teacher, a relationship that nevertheless was framed by the kindergarten teacher's recognition of the mothers' ignorance and need to know (see, for example, the discussion of 'Johnny's mother', Harrison, 1939, p. 144).

An indicator of more permanent and wilful ignorance was a 'refusal to cooperate' with the kindergarten's requests and advice. 'It is not every family that can be successfully helped,' Olive Dodd declared (Dodd, 1939, p. 141). The wilfully ignorant mother was not motivated, it appeared, by an irrational love for the dependent infant to try and do what psychology knew was best. Ultimately, much more than her classification as ignorant was at stake. If she failed to be convinced to regulate her mothering, then her capacity to love her child, to be a 'mother', was also in doubt. The mother who 'refused to co-operate' could well find that this constituted a relinquishing of her claims to her child.

The typology of mothers outlined above is certainly not exhaustive. The intelligent, the over-anxious, and the ignorant mother constituted particular types of mothers through their relationship to the knowledge base of child psychology, and it was through changing that relationship that a mother could become a different type. But other mothers were placed in 'type' according to their perceived ability to control their nature, for example the 'over-protective' mother. And, as I have pointed out, it was a mother's ability to control her nature by expressing the irrational love she had formed for the dependent baby through the child-rearing practices approved by child psychology, that underlay even the intelligent mother's relationship with this knowledge. A mother's love had to be harnessed, but at the same time the origins of that love were understood to be irrational. The mother's nature was regarded as the most untrustworthy factor in the battle to apply scientific facts to child development.

At bottom it was the mother's biological relationship with the child that inhibited her role in child development, the ties of blood and pain that bound her to the child. 'Objective guidance', said Christine Heinig, 'can often best be given by someone who is not a blood relative or emotionally involved' (Heinig, 1938, p. 156). Many other experts viewed the closeness of the connection between child and mother as preventing her from seeing the child clearly and dispassionately, preventing her, in effect, from sharing the relationship that science had with the child, where the child was an object to be observed, monitored and so, known. Although Susan Isaacs suggested that mothers could participate in the production of scientific knowledge by systematically recording their child's behaviour, this was not a task that many mothers were regarded as equipped for (Isaacs, 1939, p. 68). Mothers were related to their child through nature, not science, and could not take the necessary steps back for scientific observation.

The purpose of the science of child development was the production of the perfect child. Mothers, it appeared, frustrated that purpose by the belief that their child was already perfect, or at least by a belief that love and meeting the child's physical needs was sufficient to see their child through. Olive Dodd spoke of the 'infinite pains' that had to be taken to convince a mother that her child was in need of special guidance, only to find that at the last minute the mother would not consent and would draw the child back. Dodd noticed that although mothers were very keen to seek out assistance for the child's physical ailments, the same did not apply when the kindergarten teacher classified the child as mentally deficient or as having a behaviour problem (Dodd, 1939, pp. 141–2). John Williams, a psychiatrist who lectured at the Kindergarten Training College, advised students that 'fond parents' would try to 'explain away' what science knew was 'backwardness' and maintain that the child would catch up (Williams, 1938, p. 147). Lindsay Male, a Perth expert, oozed contempt for the blindness of parents who failed to recognize a child's defects, and allowed their irrational love to prevent proper action being taken:

> Parents will frequently tell you that the child is 'nervous' when it is really an imbecile . . . it is essential that such a child be . . . admitted to a suitable institution. It is wrong that a normal healthy child and potential good citizen should be sacrificed because of sentimental attachment to one who can never enter into the economic sphere (Male, 1938, p. 1057).

Even where the child displayed other problems, Male advised that if parents could afford it, the child should be sent to a boarding school where 'weekend holidays are not permitted and where the child returns home only at the end of term, even this is sometimes too often' (Male, 1938, p. 1058).

Kindergarten teachers were, of course, not dealing with children who could be packed off to boarding school for objective management, but they were dealing with mothers who by nature appeared to be poorly equipped to manage their children effectively. And they were dealing with very young children who were 'most closely' bound by their mothers' irrational love. It was this irrational love, formed for the dependent baby, a love that came naturally through its importance for the baby's survival, that had to be redirected toward the facilitation of independence.

Jean Wyndham asked her audience at the 1939 Australian Association for Pre-School Child Development the question: 'Do all mothers want their children to grow up and be independent of them? Do they give them the opportunity?' (Wyndham, 1939, p. 103).

The answer to this question shadowed much of the child development literature and informed many of the prescriptions on child rearing. The mother's nature, her desire to keep her child a baby, made her a poor partner for science. John Williams wrote of 'the fussy, over-anxious or emotionally starved mother who attempts to keep the child infantile by not allowing it to make attempts to feed or clothe itself, or mix with other children' (Williams, 1938, p. 146). The satisfaction that mothers derived from such activities, the desires they sought to fulfil, is not made clear, nor was there any attempt to probe what aspects of a mothers' everyday life might be productive of such desires. There are, of course, many other ways in which the actions of such mothers could be read. Even Susan Isaacs suggested that a busy mother might not feel she had the time to wait while a child endeavoured to feed itself when other work was calling. More widely, the origins of a mother's behaviour were assumed to be in her psychological make-up. The intelligent mother would understand the child's birth as the first act of separation from her. At the right time she would insert a cup between her nipple and the child's mouth, and orient her child rearing in its every detail to emphasize the child's separation from her. But most mothers continued to clasp their children to them, and never allowed psychological weaning to take place.

The Kindergarten Teacher and the Perfect Child

Equipped with this knowledge of what science understood to be a developmental path followed universally by all children, and the failings of mothers, the kindergarten teacher entered that peculiar space, the kindergarten, to facilitate the production of the perfect child. How was she to avoid the mistakes that mothers themselves made, and how was she to express that 'love for little children' that was claimed to be the prime prerequisite of the kindergarten teacher, in ways that were constructive? (Anon., 1927, p. 19). My exploration of these questions centres on the teacher's place in the kindergarten, her relationship with the children she taught and the ways practice was informed by the failings of mothers and regulated her distance from them.

Picture the kindergarten teacher in the environment of the kindergarten. Her task is to construct a space that was, in Heinig's words, 'scaled to the size of the child whose eye level is at about thirty inches from the floor' (Heinig, 1938, p. 156). The child's world at the kindergarten was to be based on a perfect illusion. The illusion was one of dominance and control over the environment, nothing was to speak to the child of their lack of power. Mothers, it should be remembered, spoke to their children of their lack of power continuously, by placing themselves as a social actor in the child's world, an actor who spoke of do's and don'ts and inserted themselves and their demands between the child and his or her play, between the child and development. But in the kindergarten all was different, child-centred not mother-centred. Furniture was child-sized and carefully graded so that the 2-year-old occupied tables and chairs that were different in size from those for the bigger or older child. Toilets and their partitions were child-size, stretchers for the afternoon sleep were of a size that the child could readily move, playthings were such that each child could seek for themselves those that were appropriate for development (for descriptions of the kindergarten environment see, for example, Heinig, 1938 and Gutteridge, 1932). In all, the child was to experience itself as powerful, autonomous and active, in an environment that did not produce conflict, or 'emotional irritation', an environment based around the child's 'natural rhythms' of play, rest, food and bowels, where rationality reigned supreme. As Christine Heinig explained, 'Problems on all age levels are avoided when life is conducted on a natural and ordered schedule' (Heinig, 1938, p. 156).

But where is the kindergarten teacher in this child-sized environment? Christine Heinig is again useful, presenting the vision that would greet a visitor to the kindergarten of a 'home-like colourful place where a small group of children are independently, definitely and happily busy with alert but inconspicuous supervision from the teachers' (Heinig, 1938, p. 156). The good teacher formed part of the background to the busy children, she did not present herself as a social actor in this child world. Although one expert advised parents to treat their children as part of the furniture, this description accords much more with the position of the teacher within child-centred pedagogy (Male, 1938, p. 1056). By effacing herself, she took up her proper location as part of the child's environment, scarcely more significant, it would seem, from the child's perspective than those other features of this child world. By merging with the background, she freed the child. As Heinig explained, 'children thus freed . . . are themselves active' (Heinig, 1937, p. 14).

Active children and the passive teacher discreetly facilitating that activity through the provision of an environment based on the 'growth facts' discovered by science are two central images that pervade kindergarten literature and its descriptions of child-centred pedagogy. The strength of these images in constituting what it is to be a good teacher in this set of pedagogic practices is well depicted in the writings of Mary Lush. Her writings in the 1920s and 1930s convey a picture of the teacher moving ever further into the background. In *Progressive Kindergarten Methods*, written in 1926, she advised a move away from the teacher-centred curricula of the early kindergartens and the abandonment of group activities, such as circle games led by the teacher. The teacher, she said, must not 'personally dominate the children' for 'where guidance checks activity the principle of growth is arrested' (Lush, 1926). By 1939 Lush was concerned that even with the complete elimination of teacher-directed group activities, some children were able to 'cling to the teacher mentally and emotionally as a sort of mother substitute, and so retard progress toward independence'. The teacher was clearly still too much 'there', too conspicuous on the child's horizon. Lush advised that teachers needed to take even more steps back, so that 'the child can show what he really is' (Lush, 1939, p. 173).

Lush's prescriptions gives the key to what the good teacher *was* supposed to do in the child-sized world, albeit a task that the child was not to be conscious of her performing. She was to observe what each child 'really was' and in addition to making discreetly sure that each child was having the 'right' experiences and that each child's kindergarten world matched the inner facts of development, she was to observe, record and regulate the child from the vantage point of her training. For while the child's attention was to be directed inwards and to the other children in their thirty-inch environment, her gaze was to be directed at the child.

Child-sized toilets, for example, not only enabled the child to become independent, but also enabled the teacher to observe the frequency with which children used them, to monitor their success or failure at maintaining the schedule the teacher had set, based on the ordered rhythms science knew were natural. The provision of a meal not only meant that the child was fed, but that the teacher could 'make records of daily food intake, behaviour expressed and techniques used' (Heinig, 1938, p. 158). The child engaged in play was not only having development facilitated, but was monitored for how she played, with what, for whether play was always solitary or always in a group. And the good teacher would ensure that the child was unaware of her surveillance. The perfect child would, in any case, be absorbed in the business of development. The teacher was trained to carry in her apron pocket 'a small pad on which to jot down information — but this should be as inconspicuous as possible, as it may lead to or cause distraction and self-consciousness' (Harrison, 1939, p. 147).

Continuous observation of the child was essential if the possibility of being a good teacher was to be fulfilled, and this surveillance, like the manner in which the child was to be 'set free', required the teacher to keep her distance from the children she taught. Although experts agreed that it was the child's psychological make-up that determined that the young child should have only one teacher, the evaluation by self and others as a good teacher depended on a set of practices that eliminated the mutual gaze that formed the relationship between the mother and child. It was from this mutual gaze that the child was to be 'set free' in the kindergarten. The perfect child would not feel the teacher's gaze, would not desire to return it. Nor would the good teacher want to capture the child in this way. And, like the intelligent mother, the good teacher recognized that she herself did not have the knowledge to help the problem child. Her skill lay in identifying the child with problems and consigning the child to a specialist (see, for example, Heinig, 1939b, p. 116). In this and many other ways, the good teacher performed the endless ritual of giving up the child, of 'setting the child free'. The good teacher, through her training, was able to perform the act which the mother, through her nature, was unable to perform.

Nor was the teacher's gaze directed solely towards the child. It was also directed toward that other woman, the child's mother. The mother's behaviour, her relationship with her child, were all to be recorded by the teacher. The teacher's training in the failings of mothers informed what was significant about this relationship, what she should be alert for, what she should observe. May Gutteridge trained her students to pay particular attention to the way the child dealt with being left at the kindergarten by the mother, for the way the child coped with separation 'affords a good index of this relationship'. She provided an example of a child identified as K, aged 19 months, attending nursery school who had arrived happily on his first day and continued this pattern, 'laughing and singing and meeting his mother with a smile' (Gutteridge, 1932, p. 120). Such behaviour demonstrated the effectivity of the mother's efforts to encourage independence and a smiling child at the end of the morning also indicated the teacher's success, the way she discouraged the clinging child who would make her a mother substitute. The good teacher was to express her love for the children she taught through her relationship to the knowledge domain of child psychology and through her adherence to a set of pedagogic practices that derived from it.

Unlike the mother who in the discourse of child psychology had by nature an investment in keeping the child dependent, the teacher, by training, was to construct her investment and evaluate success by the facilitation of independence. To make this claim is not to claim that kindergarten teachers fitted smoothly into the position that science had produced for them. Indeed, there is much evidence to suggest otherwise, that indicates that many kindergarten teachers found themselves seduced, in Carolyn Steedman's phrase, by 'the pressure of little fingers' (Steedman, 1987). Among such evidence is that the careers of many of these 1930s kindergarten teachers spanned a lifetime, a lifetime in which they remained childless. Often kindergarten teachers set up clubs that ran after school hours. Rather than the extension of their working day, they recorded their pleasure in having the children they knew as infants come to tell them stories of their day at school. These clubs were increasingly discouraged for taking the teachers' time and attention from their real work. The kindergarten teachers defended them (see for example, Lush, 1939, p. 175). But, in so far as kindergarten teachers gained their satisfaction from their work through forming emotional attachments to the children they taught, they had stepped outside the boundaries of what constituted a good teacher in the 1930s kindergarten.

Conclusion

The kindergarten teacher's place, too, was defined through her relationship with the knowledge of child psychology. She was to understand, as May Gutteridge explained, that her place was in the background, that she was never to raise her voice nor interrupt a child (Gutteridge, 1938, p. 117). She was not to see herself as a social actor in this child-centred space, she was not to be a source of prohibitions. She was to evaluate her success by the distance she maintained from the failures of mothers, from the ways she recreated in her everyday work a ritualized separation from the children she taught and from the way she used her knowledge to control what science produced as her nature.

Christine Heinig stated that follow-up studies of kindergarten children's school performance showed that:

> children who have had these advantages are 'better' children. Teachers of older children who welcome independence of thought and action are glad to have these six-year-olds enter their groups and look to them to supply ideas and leadership (Heinig, 1939, p. 221).

It was the regulation of the everyday practices of mothers and teachers that made possible the production of these 'better' children, children who were better at being the child that science had deemed part of the nature of all children. As indicated previously, children, mothers and teachers did not fit smoothly into the positions that science had produced for them. But, importantly, as Heinig suggests, the 'good' primary school teacher, like the kindergarten teacher, was one whose practices were defined through child-centred pedagogy, and this teacher, unlike other teachers, would welcome 'independence' and would look to particular children to supply group leadership, rather than sourcing leadership to herself. And this teacher would recognize and affirm the behaviour of those who were 'better' at being children. Their closer approximation to the perfect child of science would serve to differentiate them from those other children, children who were 'less good' at childhood, who did not follow the 'normal path', whose 'development' had been 'arrested' by unscientific mothering and whose class-room performance and behaviour could be expected to reflect those 'facts'. The teacher's training in the techniques of observation and monitoring, the recognition of significant behaviour and the categories for recording behaviour meant, in effect, that the good teacher 'only had to look' to enable her to differentiate the 'better' child from those others. Her training worked to produce a self-evident and seemingly natural connection between the activities of a mother and the child's classroom behaviour, including signs of educability and predictors of educational success.

It is implicit in this paper that the claims of child psychology are not the only ways to understand, care for or educate children. But it is also implicit that these claims have been real in their effects, that, for example, the ways in which the good teacher has been defined leaves many teachers feeling guilty, anxious and inadequate, fearing that they are not good enough. Confronted with the child who continues to display behaviour defined as a problem in an educational setting, the teacher has little alternative but to blame herself, or to source the cause of the child's failure back to that other woman, the child's mother. Either she is not a good teacher, or the mother is not a good mother. Unless the child happens to be the perfect child of science, neither teacher nor mother are free to affirm each other's practices within this set of knowledge.

References

ANONYMOUS (1927) 'Kindergarten teaching as a vocation for girls', *Australian Educational Review*, iii, 2, October.

BACHELARD, P.M. (1939) 'The psychological approach', Australian Association for Pre-School Child Development (AAPSCD), *First Biennial Conference*, 30 January–4 February.

CROLL, G. (1936) 'Difficult children', letter to the Editor, *Medical Journal of Australia*, 11 April.

CUNNINGHAM, K.S. (1937) 'Problem children in Melbourne schools', *Australian Educational Studies* (First Series), Melbourne, Australian Council of Educational Research.

DODD, O. (1939) 'The social worker in the kindergarten', AAPSCD, *First Biennial Conference*, 30 January–4 February.

EMBLETON, D.M. (1936) 'The problem of child guidance: Adaptability and delinquency', *Medical Journal of Australia*, 30 May.

GUTTERIDGE, M. (1931) 'The mental hygiene of childhood', *Medical Journal of Australia*, 24 January.

GUTTERIDGE, M. (1932) 'The story of an Australian nursery school', *Australian Educational Studies* (First Series), ACER, Melbourne, Melbourne University Press.

HARRISON, H. (1939) 'The keeping of school records', AAPSCD, *First Biennial Conference*, 30 January–4 February.

HEINIG, C. (1937) 'Current trends in education', *Australian Educational Review*, ix, 2, September.

HEINIG, C. (1938) 'The training of the pre-school child', *Medical Journal of Australia*, 30 July.

HEINIG, C. (1939a) 'Child development as promoted by the facilities for child and parent education in nursery schools and kindergartens', Australian and New Zealand Association for the Advancement of Science (ANZAAS), *Proceedings*.

HEINIG, C. (1939b) 'The use of a specialist', AAPSCD, *First Biennial Conference*, 30 January–4 February.

HENRIQUES, J., HOLLWAY, W., URWIN, C., VENN, C. and WALKERDINE, V. (Eds) (1984) *Changing the Subject: Psychology, Social Regulation and Subjectivity*, London, Methuen.

ISAACS, S. (1937) in the foreword to Marjorie Thorburn, *Child at Play: Observations*, Allen and Unwin, London; quoted by Anon, *Medical Journal of Australia*, 28 May 1938, p. 934.

ISAACS, S. (1938) 'The importance of the child's emotional life', in CUNNINGHAM, K.S. (Ed.) *Education for Complete Living*, Proceedings of the New Education Fellowship Conference, Melbourne, Australian Council for Educational Research.

ISAACS, S. (1929) *The Nursery Years*, London, Routledge and Kegan Paul.

LUSH, M. (1926) *Progressive Kindergarten Methods*, Lothian, London.

LUSH, M. (1932) 'The child in the home', in Victorian Council for Mental Hygiene, *The Growing Child*, Educational Research Series, No. 12, Melbourne, Melbourne University Press.

LUSH, M. (1939) 'Changing emphasis in kindergarten work', AAPSCD, *First Biennial Conference*, 30 January–4 February.

LYON, H. (1988) Interview, ex-Principal of the Kindergarten Training College, Melbourne.

MALE, L. (1938) 'The unsatisfactory child', *Medical Journal of Australia*, 18 June.

McRAE, J. (1932) 'The child and the school', in Victorian Council for Mental Hygiene, *The Growing Child*, Educational Research Series No. 12, Melbourne, Melbourne University Press.

MINOGUE, S. (1936) 'Difficult children', letter to the Editor, *Medical Journal of Australia*, 28 March.

MUHL, A. (1939) 'Inter-relationships between physical and mental health', AAPSCD, *First Biennial Conference*, 30 January–4 February

RILEY, D. (1983) *War in the Nursery, Theories of the Child and Mother*, London, Virago.

STEEDMAN, C. (1987) 'Prison houses', LAWN, M. and GRACE, G. (Eds) *Teachers: The Culture and Politics of Work*, Lewes, Falmer Press.

WALKERDINE, V. (1984) 'Developmental psychology and child-centred pedagogy: The insertion of Piaget into early education', in HENRIQUES, J. *et al.* (Eds) *Changing the Subject: Psychology, Social Regulation and Subjectivity*, London, Methuen.

WILLIAMS, J. (1938) 'Mental hygiene of the pre-school child', *Medical Journal of Australia*, 30 July.

WYNDHAM, J. (1939) 'Behaviour difficulties of nursery school and kindergarten children which require special guidance', AAPSCD, *First Biennial Conference*, 30 January–4 February.

Section 2

Contemporary Issues

Chapter 4

Improving Girls' Educational Outcomes

Joanna Wyn and Bruce Wilson

Introduction

What kind of policy approach is most likely to improve significantly the outcomes of all girls? This has been a fundamental concern of feminist educators for many years. An important priority has been to investigate the reasons for discrimination against and differential achievement by girls and women in educational settings, their experiences in those settings, and strategies likely to bring about change. Since the 1970s the complexities of the situation have become more apparent (see further, Kenway, 1990). Women have learned much about what they share and what can be gained through collaborating with each other in the struggle for social change. At the same time, early assumptions about objectives and strategies have been undermined by the persistence of occupational segregation and the apparent determination by many girls and women to place a continuing priority on relationships and domestic concerns (Wilson and Wyn, 1987). Furthermore, it is now recognized that the experience of particular groups of girls and women is deeply influenced by their differing material and cultural circumstances; that to look at gender alone is insufficient and inadequate. The significant influence of other forms of social division (class and racial conflict, for example) in shaping the educational and social outcomes achieved by girls and women has been widely researched and clearly demonstrated. Educational policy has been increasingly influenced by the efforts of feminist teachers, policy-makers and parents. The result of this influence and of policy is evident in the feminist practices of many schools. These included, among much else, the use of single-sex classes, counter-sexist resources and support groups, and the development of particular classroom methods. However, despite all this laudable effort, it is not at all clear that it is achieving its desired effects. One of the reasons for this, in our view, is that policy-makers and practitioners have failed to conceptualize their intentions adequately; more specifically, they have failed to clarify and identify the specific outcomes they are working towards. Rather, intentions are couched in very vague generalities.

A focus on outcomes is important because it helps to draw attention to the vision of society that is implicit in particular policies or programme strategies. Too often, government policies have been framed in terms of only one perspective on an issue or problem, obscuring important dimensions of the process of bringing about social change. A discussion of outcomes raises questions about the legitimacy and the kind of contribution expected from particular groups in a society. In educational terms, the attempt to specify desirable common outcomes is vital because it offers a framework for analysing the characteristics of personal and social life considered to be essential for all people to participate fully in their society. Even though the phrase 'full participation' has been widely used in statements of policy objectives, there have been very few efforts to indicate what is meant in practical terms. We suggest that it is worthwhile exploring the concept of 'common outcomes'; distinguishing the material from the cultural. This approach is explored in the latter stages of this paper, but first, we shall take a look at major government policy on the education of girls.

A National Policy

In 1987 the Commonwealth Schools Commission released its *National Policy for the Education of Girls in Australian Schools* (NPEG). As it is this document which has continued to inform subsequent policies on girls' education in the various states of Australia, it is worth returning to it in order to assess its underlying attitude on the matter of outcomes. This policy drew on the experiences and reflections of teachers and policy-makers in the decade after the publication of *Girls, Schools and Society*, Winnicot (1975) — the document which began the national policy imperative to improve the education of girls. While drawing attention to the gains that have been made during that time, the report also identified continuing shortcomings in the education system.

The National Policy was a comprehensive and in many senses far-sighted document directed towards guiding the direction of change and the co-ordination of effort across states and across the public and private sectors. This document suggested that the main issue at stake was the provision of more equitable education for girls, which would encourage girls and women to participate more fully in all aspects of public life. In this document the Commission has consolidated Commonwealth policies, referring to 'full participation in society' as the aim of equal outcomes from schooling. However, the argument continues to reflect considerable inconsistency in its understanding of the concept 'equality'. Johnston (1983) identified four basic, different and to some extent contradictory 'logics' of equality which have recurred in various ways in education policy documents subsequent to the Karmel Report (1973). All four logics of equality are represented in the NPEG's 'Shared Values and Principles' and 'Shared Objectives' to guide the development of programmes. They are:

(*a*)   a compensatory logic — defining the problem in terms of producing optimum mobility in a competitive, individualistic, market society.

In the NPEG, improving outcomes for girls is seen as necessary because of the continued relative inequities in girls' post-school opportunities, in terms of post-secondary education and access to employment, despite improving school retention rates;

(*b*)   an equality of respect logic — stressing a notion of valuing people equally, based on their common humanity.

One of the Shared Values and Principles of the NPEG is that girls and boys should be valued equally in all aspects of schooling. A Shared Objective is 'to provide a supportive and challenging school environment for learning in which girls and boys are equally valued and their needs equitably catered for' (p. 34);

(c) a mainstreaming logic — subcultures require the resources and skills to be able to compete effectively in mainstream schooling.

The NPEG Report makes one of its Shared Objectives 'to ensure that boys and girls have equal access to and participation in a school curriculum which contributes to full and equal participation in economic and social life' (p. 33). A further Objective is: 'to ensure that school resource allocation policies and practices operate in ways which are consistent with principles of equity and relative need' (p. 34); and

(d) power over circumstances — participating with others to change the circumstances that block the aspirations and hopes of identifiable social groups, whether the group identity be based on class, ethnicity or gender.

A Shared Value and Principle of the NPEG is that 'schooling should reflect the entitlement of all women, in their own right, to personal respect, to economic security and to participation in and influence over decisions which affect their lives' (p. 28).

The use of all four logics may not reflect confused thinking on the part of the Commission as much as an attempt to incorporate the approaches which have influenced policy to date. Each of the logics of equality has an important contribution to make to an understanding of these issues. However, the inherent confusion (and contradiction) among them makes it difficult to provide guidance for schools. The 'framework for action' provided by the NPEG Report is an attempt to translate the broad principles of social equity and of good educational practice into practical suggestions about what can be done in schools to implement the policy.

The range of strategies that are suggested as a means for achieving the objectives cover all aspects of schooling, from the resources used in classrooms to the administrative structure itself. The National Policy suggested that fundamental curriculum review would have to take place if its objectives were to be implemented. A number of specific reforms are suggested, including changes to gender-stereotyped areas of the curriculum, change in particular curriculum areas to enhance girls' participation and achievement, and the development of a new curriculum to include significant areas of knowledge of particular significance to girls which are presently omitted. The document also suggested specific ways in which the school environment could become more supportive for girls, in terms of teaching practice and classroom management, school organization and practice, and the social, cultural and physical environment. Changes such as these would make schools a more comfortable ('girl-friendly') environment for girls and young women. What is not evident, however, is how and if these changes would affect outcomes from schooling.

The suggestions for change derive from a critique of schooling, and the Commission is relatively clear about what is not desirable. However, a vision of the outcomes that would be wanted is missing. Some clues are provided through the use of the terms 'equity' and 'equality', and in the aim to encourage girls and women to participate fully in all aspects of society. These ideas do not provide a coherent framework for action, however, and in this policy document simply serve to provide an umbrella which obscures the tensions between the four logics of equality. Because of this there are a number of issues which are taken for granted throughout.

Issues

The Commission aims to provide a national policy that would benefit all girls and women. What is meant by 'all girls and women'? This question can be answered by exploring three dimensionns.

Are all Girls the Same?

In a number of places the NPEG acknowledges that girls and women bring with them a range of perspectives based not only gender but also on class, ethnicity and race, which affect their experience of schooling. There is a tendency for cultural and language differences to be seen as something to be valued, rather more than something that can also provide the basis for disadvantage, liability and racism. The specific 'needs' of particular groups of girls are largely seen to be catered for through affirmations of various sorts.

Although seen as a worthwhile goal, the aim of affirming cultural differences is barely supported. It is suggested that cultural differences may be affirmed through the teaching of community languages, by having regular and consistent contact between home and school, and by providing a framework for improving schooling that derives from 'a variety of cultural perspectives'. However, these ideas are contradicted in the Report's treatment of two further issues.

Individual or Group Goals?

The idea of affirming cultural differences supports the view that all girls and women are not the same. However, in some important respects the National Policy underestimates the existence of cultural and social groupings. Instead, the goal of improving girls' self-esteem, self-confidence and identity is given prominence, leaving the onus for change with individuals. This may be helpful to some girls and women under certain circumstances, and it is an attractive strategy for dealing with the day-to-day issues of the classroom. The weakness of this approach is that it sidesteps the question of why it is that particular groups are systematically marginalized and exist in a less powerful relation to other groups. Furthermore, the reference to raising girls' self esteem, self-confidence and identity has the effect of treating girls as a single category, all of whom it is assumed need the same 'treatment' (see further, Kenway and Willis, 1990).

Unless strategies for change consider the social and cultural context in which girls and women live they may undermine the position of those who the policies are intended to help. For example, it is often assumed that young women who live in non-English-speaking households are subject to particularly 'sexist' practices in the home. While this may be so in terms of feminist perspectives, there are strengths in the vision of womanhood to which these young women adhere and on which they rely. Such a strategy may also suggest a negative view of their cultures, to themselves and to others. It requires an especially sensitive approach to draw attention to the negative aspects of particular cultural practices while still maintaining their strengths. This means that rather than focusing on the individual student, it is necessary to help all students to develop an awareness of the ways in which social division in our society affects different groups.

A Deficit Approach

Recognizing diversity is also compromised if the problem to be solved is regarded as a deficiency in the experience, knowledge or skills of girls and women. This approach has been especially popular in discussions of the 'problem' of 'girls and maths,' as the articles in this collection by Kenway and by Bannister demonstrate. Only relatively recently have some begun to question the current outcomes of mathematics teaching and to argue that the process of mathematics teaching and the mathematics curriculum itself should be substantially revised.

The Commission believes that special measures are needed to ensure that those programmes especially designed to combat educational disadvantages relating to poverty, and to cultural differences or other factors such as geographical isolation and intellectual disabilities, serve the needs of girls as well as boys (1987, p. 16).

This approach locates the blame for lack of educational achievement with individuals or 'disadvantaged groups' rather than with schooling practices. While it is important that schools have the resources they need to develop worthwhile programmes, the receiving of funding on the basis of 'disadvantaged groups' should not result in a deficit view of these groups. This approach easily slides into a rationale for providing particular groups with 'special help', while leaving the mainstream curriculum untouched. This approach, too, avoids exploring the underlying power relationships between groups which create and maintain inequalities. It is in terms of this relationship that the question of outcomes should be framed.

Policy which consolidates the assumptions written into past documents does not go far enough in providing a sound basis for developing the future education of all girls and women. Because of their cultural perspectives, groups of girls and women continue to place a priority on concerns and relationships that are easily undermined and marginalized by schooling. Strategies are required which recognize the diversity of groups from which girls and women come while clearly delineating the future outcomes from schooling for all girls and women.

Outcomes

What is meant by 'educational and social outcomes' in this context? In the Australian debate the concept was drawn initially from the work of Halsey, who had attempted to clarify the concern with equality in the following terms:

the goal should not be the liberal one of equality of access but equality of outcome for the median member of each identifiable non-educationally defined group, i.e., the average woman or negro or proletarian or rural dweller should have the same level of educational attainment as the average male, white, white-collar suburbanite (Halsey, 1972, p. 8; quoted in Karmel, 1973).

After its decade of experience with various types of programmes, the Commonwealth Schools Commission reiterated its commitment to the concept of equality of outcomes in *In the National Interest* (1985). This was an important contribution, as the rhetoric of 'equity' in the PEP programme had served to muddy the waters considerably. Did 'equity' mean fairness in terms of individual treatment, fairness to groups, did it imply a focus on access to a range of opportunities, or did it retain the determination to achieve more equal outcomes? The Commission reasserted the view that the concept of equality of outcomes

. . . emphasized the idea of distributing success more equally in schools, and not just seeking to impose social equality through schooling . . . public authorities should not merely ensure a necessary minimum of provisions, or even equality of provision, but should, where necessary, allocate resources and effort to reduce inequalities in achievements and in the social distribution of outcomes. The idea of inclusiveness and co-operation thus came to the fore (Schools Commission, 1987, p. 30).

In other words, 'equality of outcomes' was an approach which emphasized the valuing of all students and their backgrounds and encouraged learning strategies in which all students could participate equally and from which the outcomes would be equally worthwhile. The Commission tackled the criticisms that this approach implied a 'levelling down' and that individual differences were being ignored. They argued that these criticisms reflected a very narrow perception of the purposes of education and suggested that all students were capable of excellent performance in their own terms. All children should be encouraged to have a vision of what is potentially achievable and should recognize that excellence can be displayed in many domains of life, not only through academic work.

What does this mean for girls? Girls' experience of schooling has shifted significantly in that their retention rates at least until the end of year 12 are now higher than for boys. The problem, to some significant extent, is that their representation in post-school course and training options and in specific fields of employment is significantly different from that of boys. Overcoming these patterns is not just a matter of educational reform; it requires a challenge to the nature of social division which affects society as a whole, specifically those structures and processes which render as marginal the experience and perspectives of girls and women, leaving them vulnerable both materially and culturally.

Common Outcomes

At the very least a statement of common outcomes should give priority to recognition of the social and cultural concerns valued by women. What follows is an attempt to signal a more comprehensive outline of the common outcomes that might be expected for all students, encompassing the priorities not only of girls but also other groups whose social and educational accomplishments are marginalized at present. It is assumed that the existence of significant material and cultural division in society would imply different curricula in order to ensure that the common outcomes were achieved.

Material Outcomes

This dimension of outcomes is concerned with the immediate and tangible evidence about what happens to young people when they leave school to enter adult life. The following categories reflect different kinds of interests and require further discussion to determine an appropriate order of priority. These are starting-points for such a discussion.

- *Retention rates, credentials, further education*

  At the present time there is a relatively clear and hierarchical kind of streaming built into the credentials with which young people leave school and the types of options which they subsequently have. It goes something like this:

  tertiary professional course
  tertiary course
  full-time, potentially stable employment
  trade training
  full-time employment
  Technical and Further Education (TAFE) course
  traineeship (or similar)
  part-time work
  short-term training (public or private)
  unemployment.

  Within each of these levels, there is a further hierarchy, part of which is determined by the predominance of males or females in that particular type of course, profession or trade. If this approach is generally applicable, a number of questions arise:

  (*a*) What is the 'cut off' point (in other words, which of these options are unacceptable)?

  (*b*) Are social characteristics such as gender, ethnicity or class significant in shaping the choices which young people themselves would make between these various options?

  (*c*) Would parents and students tend to agree/disagree with teachers on which were the preferred options?

  (*d*) What records do the schools have about which of these options are achieved by their students, at what point of time?

  (*e*) What kinds of specific assistance are provided by the schools in relation to each of these options?

- *Specific knowledge, skills (academic, legal, health, and so on)*

  These outcomes are perhaps best related to the content of school curricula. They concern the kinds of knowledge included in the curriculum and their accessibility to all students, together with any information collected about student performance in demonstrating their particular capacities.

(a) One strategy for examining this topic would be to look for records of performance in specific subjects such as 'women's studies', 'parenting', 'health and human relations', 'legal studies', 'work education', 'community studies', or similar subjects (where the intention is to address directly aspects of the students' present social circumstances and needs).

(b) It may be that particular learning strategies such as action-research projects, cross-age tutoring or media projects provide a context where students can develop and acquire knowledge which relates directly to their own experience yet also provide a basis for critical examination of broader social structures and the possibilities of change. Indications of student involvement in these kinds of activities and the products subsequently produced might provide an avenue for assessing progress in these areas.

(c) Another approach may emerge through 'home group' or 'pastoral care' sessions, where teachers can deal more informally with whatever matters seem to be important at the time, as well as providing a more systematic coverage of knowledge appropriate to adult practices. Teachers themselves would have to develop appropriate criteria for recording the kinds of learning undertaken by their students.

(d) In some schools, of course, there are also specific staff whose responsibility is to deal with the immediate problems or crises that students may have; in some cases these can be developed as learning situations and records kept of the strategies adopted by students to improve their approach to handling specific situations.

- *Occupational record*
  This kind of information is presumably available in few, if any, schools. It is difficult to collect, and to be of use needs to be based on data obtained at least 18 months after the students have left (because of 'natural' unemployment and the early job-changing that many students do). However, ultimately the kind of occupation that a young person obtains and their commitment to their work are two of the best indicators that are available in order to assess whether the schools have had some distinct effect in improving the outcomes which their students might otherwise have expected to obtain. It would be particularly important to seek sufficient detail on the kinds of domestic commitments which young women have and how it affects their entry to the labour market.

- *Adequate housing*
  This aspect of student outcomes raises similar difficulties to those encountered in compiling occupational records. Nevertheless, given the significance of youth homelessness, it may be another useful means of assessing the outcomes achieved by young people as they become adult members of their society. Having adequate housing is closely related

to income level but it also provides a tangible indicator of what young people have learned about their rights and their resourcefulness (and co-operativeness).

Cultural Outcomes

Cultural outcomes represent a much more difficult area when it comes to trying to develop appropriate criteria for assessing what has been achieved. These are the outcomes of schooling which reflect 'power over circumstances' (power over circumstances means participating with others to change the circumstances that block the aspirations and hopes of identifiable social groups, whether the group identity be based on class, ethnicity or gender (quoted earlier from Johnston, 1983, p. 26)).

- *Personal dignity*
  This reflects the priority of wanting young people to have a strong sense of themselves as individuals in a social context. It involves the twin components of self-esteem and confidence on the one hand, and arti- culateness and the capacity to express oneself in a thoughtful, honest, and 'unthreatened' way within a group. By the time that students reach high school much will already have happened to affect their sense of dignity; there is a great deal of evidence which demonstrates the particular relevance of these issues for girls. Opportunities for expressing their opinions and undertaking activities which examine the circumstances of girls can contribute to enabling them to establish a new perspective on themselves. Observation of their participation in various decision- making or small-group situations can provide feedback on their growth in this regard.

- *Social legitimacy (sense of belonging)*
  Effective participation in social activities depends not only on the pre- sence of personal dignity but also on the development of the sense of legitimacy that comes from feeling that one belongs to a group; that as a member of the group, or of society, a person has the right to exercise influence over its shape and over the important decisions which are to be made. While women and girls place a priority on relationships and co- operative activities, their identification with belonging to a group does not seem to extend to exercising the right to demand change. This kind of energy is channelled much more into coping than it is into changing the circumstances which oppress them.

- *Exercise personal and social power*
  The nature of the cultural outcomes achieved is most likely to be demonstrated in the action taken by young people to influence, as much as they can, the situations in which they find themselves and to provide constructive solutions to problems which they may encounter. Examples may be found well before they leave school:

— dealing with personal relationships
— choice about jobs or further education
— negotiation with family
— negotiation with employers
— negotiation with landlords
— join a political party or movement
— involved in community activities
— take action on own behalf with police, etc.
— critical assessment of media (etc.) messages.

This discussion of outcomes and how they might be specified in order to provide more concrete directions for policy and programme development is inevitably tentative. However, this task should be seen as a high priority if policy development is to provide clearer guidelines for school-based action. The rhetoric of 'full participation in society' simply does not help either to outline a vision of the kind of society that is desired or to suggest the scope of practical curriculum or organizational change.

If we are to develop and administer policy that improves the outcomes for all girls and women, it needs to be recognized that the common outcomes for which we aim affirm the strengths of girls and women from different class and cultural backgrounds. Given the existence of social division and the significance of people's own cultural perspectives, unless these differences are not only recognized but valued, particular categories of students will continue to be marginalized.

References

COMMONWEALTH SCHOOLS COMMISSION (1985) *In the National Interest*, Canberra, Australian Government Publishing Service.

COMMONWEALTH SCHOOLS COMMISSION (1987) *National Policy for the Education of Girls in Australian Schools*, Canberra, Australian Government Publishing Service.

HALSEY, A.H. (Ed.) (1972) *Educational Priority, Volume 1: EPA Problems and Policies*, London, HMSO.

JOHNSTON, K. (1983) 'A discourse for all seasons? An ideological analysis of the Schools Commission Reports, 1973–1981', *Australian Journal of Education*, 27, 1, pp. 17–32.

KARMEL, P.H. (Chairman) (1973) *Schools in Australia*, Canberra, Australian Government Publishing Service.

KENWAY, J. (1990) *Gender and Education Policy: A Call For New Directions*, Geelong, Deakin University Press.

KENWAY, J. and WILLIS, S. (Eds) (1990) *Hearts and Minds: Self-Esteem and the Schooling of Girls*, London, Falmer Press.

WILSON, B. and WYN, J. (1987) *Shaping Futures: Youth Action for Livelihood*, Sydney, Allen and Unwin.

Chapter 5

'Non-traditional' Pathways: Are they the Way to the Future?

Jane Kenway

Introduction

During the 1980s an educational discourse developed which sought to enhance girls' post-school options by altering their relationship to so-called 'non-traditional' school subjects (maths, science, technology and manual arts). When given a choice, girls are to be encouraged both to select such subjects and to make 'non-traditional' choices within such subject groupings, such as physical rather than biological sciences, higher-level rather than lower-level mathematics. Teachers and others are to develop educational means by which girls will achieve greater success in or a stronger identification with such subjects when they are part of the compulsory school curriculum. Further, girls are to become empowered through the reconstruction of the processes and contents of the curriculum.

In Australia, the various strands of thinking which constitute this discourse have been sponsored and developed by numerous and extensive government grants for the conduct of research, projects, conferences and workshops, and for the development of curriculum packages and kits, videos, journals, registers, newsletters, bibliographic guides, promotional materials (increasingly glossy), bridging courses, access strategies and the like. Certainly, the significance of this body of work is not to be denied. Increasingly sophisticated and practical at its source, its potential to enhance girls' futures is indeed considerable. No less considerable is its capacity to produce new knowledge in the field of education generally and in the disciplinary areas which it seeks to reconstruct. For these reasons it must be constantly subjected to critical scrutiny by its developers and advocates, as well as by informed others. My main purpose here, therefore, is to identify and discuss some of the difficulties and dilemmas which confront the field and which have yet to be addressed in any adequate way. Let it be clear, though, that I offer this critique from a position of broad sympathy and support. I shall begin the paper by outlining the major premises of this discourse.

Jane Kenway

The Discourse Designed to Encourage Girls into 'Non-traditional' Domains

An Overview

Girls can do anything. Get smart with Maths. An electrifying career. Engineering, the people profession. Girls into Maths do go. Multiplying options and subtracting bias. Don't get filtered out. Girls count. Engineer a future. Girls are calculating. Science can take you beyond the experimental stage. Women of steel. Broaden your horizons . . .

These are but some of the puns and slogans which educators and others have developed in recent times in order to capture, in a memorable way, the problems and issues associated with girls' school subject and vocational 'choices'. Such puns are a shorthand, representing a discourse which consists of a very substantial body of research, policy and curriculum development in the gender and education field. This discourse identifies a strong connection between girls' schooling and their post-school options. It highlights women's largely subordinate and vulnerable position in the paid labour market and looks to their schooling as both a primary cause and means of redress. More particularly, it shows how females are horizontally and vertically segregated in both the labour market and in certain fields and levels of school knowledge, and draws causal connections between the two. Women's concentration in para-professional, clerical, sales and personal service occupations (see Mumford, 1989) is attributed, in large measure, to their lack of marketable credentials for entry into the full spectrum of occupations in the paid labour market. Women's work in such areas is often characterized by low pay and by little or no training, or the training is in-house, informal, on the job and uncertified. Associated with this is a lack of promotional opportunities. In contrast, men's work tends to be more associated with recognizable training and career structures — and this is increasingly so, given the current restructuring of the labour market. The occupations *not* traditionally associated with women, and the pay and security and in many cases power and status attached to them, are seen to require 'non-traditional' subject choices — hence the slogans, '*Maths multiplies your choices, Switch on to Science, Girls are getting in on the trade secret*' and so forth.

Questions which are central to this discourse are as follows: 'Why, when given a choice, do girls tend either to avoid 'non-traditional' school subjects or to choose selectively within them?' and 'What can concerned educators do to encourage girls to make alternative subject and vocational choices?' Answers to these questions abound, and it is my intention now to outline their scope and direction. Let it be said before I proceed further, however, that what I am about to do is describe, in a very short space and in a rather systematic fashion, what is in fact a vast body of literature which includes at its extremes scholarly treatises and promotional material (stickers, brochures, posters), carefully developed curriculum packages and tips for teachers. Moveover, within each such area, there is no unified view; different values and understandings produce different perspectives. There is a danger, then, that in what follows the discourse may appear more integrated, consensual and coherent and less multi-faceted, multi-voiced and dynamic than it really is. My intention is certainly not to deny its complexity, its moving frontiers or, in many cases, its sophistication, but rather to outline what seem to me to be its central features. Almost representing a social movement in itself, this discourse is action-oriented. Its unifying inspiration, and underlying imperative, of course, is the feminist movement's desire for gender and social justice.

Girls' Patterns of Participation in 'Non-traditional' School Subjects: Some Explanations

Why, when given a choice, do girls not participate as fully and successfully as boys in maths, science, technology and manual arts? This is clearly the mega-question which plagues the field, and answers have varied across time and theoretical and geographic space, and are somewhat differently inflected for each area. None the less, beyond broad claims about the sex-typed dualities which characterize society, the answers tend to centre on *the girl, the curriculum and the learning environment.* (These views are well elaborated in Sjoberg and Imsen, 1988; Kahle, 1985a and Kelly, 1985.) When the focus is on *the girl,* it is said that she lacks the appropriate aptitudes, attitudes and knowledge and makes the wrong choices. She, and her parents, are believed to be ill-informed about women's current patterns of participation in the paid labour market[1] and about the changed nature of the family,[2] and therefore they fail to recognize fully the likely realities of her future. These include the probability that she will be in (and out) of paid work for most of her adult life in either a two-income family, or as head of single-income family; that she can therefore not expect to be dependent on a man, certainly not in the traditional family form and not for a lifetime. The girl is said to be further deficient because she does not bring to 'non-traditional' school subjects a history of experience which facilitates her interest and success. Neither does she possess the 'cognitive style' which such subjects demand. It is also said that she fears the threats to her feminine identity and the challenges to the schoolgirl culture which such subjects seem to pose, and that she opts to avoid the unwelcome visibility and 'stirring' associated with being 'the odd one out' in a male domain.

When the focus is on *the curriculum,* the argument is that maths, science, technology and manual arts project a masculine image which alienates girls. Males are their dominant developers, propagators and consumers and therefore such subjects become identified as (and indeed are) their terrain, reflecting and building on their values, interests and learning styles and negating or ignoring those of girls and women. Such a point of view brings into question the truth claims of the various fields of knowledge. Indeed, as Sjoberg and Imsen (1988, p. 219) note of science, it questions their 'basic epistemological assumptions'. It thus also leads to the positing of alternative 'truths', to the search for new epistemologies and, indeed, into some very complex philosophical issues centring on problems associated with dualism and relativism (for science, see Keller, 1986; Tuana, 1989). Given the scepticism that pronouncements about the *masculinity* of the curriculum may attract even from those who recognize that the disciplines are not academically, politically or culturally neutral, I shall elaborate a little on this point. Aside from whatever else they are, the disciplines are also what Eagleton calls 'moral technologies'. They 'consist of a particular set of techniques and practices for the instilling of specific kinds of values, disciplines, behaviour and response in human subjects'. For example, he says that studies of Literature seek to teach people to be 'sensitive, imaginative, responsive, sympathetic, creative, perceptive, reflective' (Eagleton, 1985). The additional point which feminist scholars make is that the disciplines are also gender-inflected moral technologies, and that the so-called 'soft' subjects often (although clearly not always) resonate best with dominant cultural definitions of femininity, while the so-called 'hard' subjects do so with hegemonic definitions of masculinity (see further, Weinreich-Haste, 1986). As MacDonald (1979, p. 149) notes, masculine and feminine sexual and social identities are *built* on a series of hierarchical dualities which include the following 'instrumental versus expressive skills, public versus private knowledge, discipline versus spontaneous creativity' and, I might add, reason versus emotion and objectivity versus subjectivity. The case can quite readily be made that perceptions of knowledge draw on similar dualities, with science, maths and technology occupying the first and 'superior' pole in each case. Within maths, science and technology subjects, students are expected to reject the 'softnesses' mentioned above in favour of intellectual independence, rationality, certainty, control, rigour and emotional neutrality. This point about gendered hierarchical dualities is central to many of the arguments to follow in this paper and cannot, therefore, be over-emphasized.

When explanations of girls' lack of enthusiasm for the 'non-traditional' subjects focus on *the learning environment*, the following sorts of claims are made. It is said that teachers and timetables are unsympathetic towards girls with 'non-traditional' inclinations. Or, that teachers cultivate dependent learning in girls by being 'too caring'. Boys are seen to dominate intellectual and linguistic and other space, time and equipment, and to use such subjects as a means of demonstrating both their masculinity and their disdain for girls' attempts to work on 'their' terrain. Ultimately, girls' opportunities to learn are thus seen to be marginalized and minimized. Broadly, then, the argument is that the whole field positions girls and women negatively. In addition, it would appear that many parents, subject and vocational councillors and careers teachers and courses encourage girls to make traditional feminine 'choices'.

Strategies to Change Girls' Choices and Enhance their Participation, Identification and Success

What is to be done? Clearly the answers to this question will depend very much on (i) the work location of the concerned party or parties; (ii) how they conceive the problem; and (iii) the resources (time, money, energy, peer support, and so on) available to address it. While generalizations are therefore difficult to make, they are none the less possible. Most informed people these days see the problem as multi-causal and recognize the need to address it in a holistic manner — taking into account the girls, the curriculum, the learning environment and associated support systems. However, while some education policies and practices, curriculum packages (such as Lewis and Davies, 1988) and projects encourage and adopt such an approach, many others, particularly those at the school level, are more piecemeal, predictably focusing on one particular aspect of the problem.

A number of strategies have developed which seek to alter the attitudes and aptitudes of girls. Some attempt to compensate girls for their lack of scientific and technical or just plain expansive physical experience, and the earlier the better — hence, for example, the emphasis in pre- and primary schools on 'tinkering' materials and toys and Lego technics (see *Gems*, 1989). Other approaches offer girls a window on to their futures via information about the changing nature of the family, the current shape of the labour market and women's location therein and the access to wider career options which the 'non-traditional' subjects facilitate. In order to broaden their perceptions of 'feminine' possibilities and as an alternative source of identification, girls are also offered role models — images which run counter to the conventional — such as women in trades, women in science, women in charge (for example, the *Tradeswomen on the Move* programme). Some policy-makers believe that girls should not be given a choice of subjects; that for as long as possible they be required to study the 'non-traditional' subjects.

Alongside such attempts to change girls are attempts to change the curriculum — although it should be said that such attempts seem to be less common. It is to become 'gender-inclusive' or 'girl friendly', as the jargon has it (see further, Whyte *et al.*, 1985). Masculine bias is removed from course materials. The history and contribution of women in 'non-traditional' fields is recovered and put on display in booklets and on posters. Girls' genuine, rather than stereotyped (see Kelly, 1985) interests and concerns are to become important in the selection of topics, problems and examples. In particular, their concern for the everyday context and the social implications of the subject is to be accommodated. Further, alternative pedagogies are to be developed which articulate best with the learning activities which girls reputedly enjoy and with their cognitive style (see, for example, the work of the McClintock Collective, 1987). In this regard a number of educators who are concerned about girls' schooling have accepted the notion that there are broad differences in 'cognitive style', moral reasoning and ways of learning and knowing between males and females. Drawing heavily and somewhat uncritically from Harding (1986) and Gilligan (1982), who in turn draw from such feminist object-relations theorists as Chodorow (1978), the argument is put that while males have a psychic preference for autonomy, separation, certainty, control and abstraction, females are differently connected to the world through their relational and contextual preferences and their superior capacity to offer empathy and tolerate ambiguity. Hence, interactive, co-operative, contextual, intuitive, holistic and practical learning, and methods which draw on girls' linguistic and imaginative strengths, are encouraged.

In order to overcome the problem of a hostile learning environment, schools are to experiment with girl-only classes or girls are to be provided with same-sex role-model teachers, or both. Teachers are encouraged to undertake research, particularly 'action research', into the gender dynamics of their schools and classrooms (see Barnes, Plaister and Thomas, 1984; Lewis and Davies, 1988). Guidance councillors, teachers and parents are urged to constantly draw to girls' attention the connections between 'non-traditional' subjects and expanded post-school options.

The Political Spectrum: From Conservative to Radical — and Back Again?

What I have offered so far is a descriptive account of the overall discourse. However, I have also implied that different people or groups, for different reasons, will draw selectively from it and thus create their own interpretations of its central premises and purposes. It is important to note, then, that the discourse facilitates readings across a spectrum from radical to conservative, depending on the scope of educational, epistemological and social change anticipated. The most conservative reading is highly individualistic. It seeks to encourage girls' access to and success in the 'non-traditional areas' by 'skilling' them, but without altering to any significant extent the curriculum, the learning or the work environment. The main concern here is that girls pass through the 'invisible filter' into a wider than hitherto set of vocations and thus gain greater vocational and economic security. There are signs which suggest that this view has almost become the feminist educational orthodoxy of the late 1980s. A number of significant, mainstream policy documents now largely interpret gender equity to mean equal numbers of males and females in areas which have not traditionally attracted significant numbers of females. (Notably, they do not also interpret it to mean equal numbers in the 'non-traditional' areas for males.) We thus find, for example, the Commonwealth Tertiary Education Commission (CTEC) *Report for the 1988–90 Triennium* saying (in bold print) 'in engineering, despite an increase of four percentage points, the proportion of students who are women only reached 6 per cent in 1986, still a severe imbalance'. Access to and balance in such fields of knowledge and work seem, in many cases, to have become ends in themselves, despite the broader agenda for girls' schooling and girls' futures which was evident in, say, *The National Policy for the Education of Girls in Australian Schools* (Schools Commission, 1987). This more narrow view of gender equity now dominates the educational agenda, threatening to marginalize a number of equally important issues.

The more 'radical' reading has a range of different intentions and does not see the disciplines in such a narrow, instrumental way. It includes within its parameters feminist explorations of the sociology and philosophy of maths, science and technology as modes of knowledge and as actual practices in the educational arena and beyond. As I implied earlier, such explorations invariably involve some sort of critique of the content, *modus operandi* and social and cultural 'uses' of the particular knowledge domain. Men's 'truths' are often shown to be either untruths or part truths and the practices and outcomes of the field are often shown to be deeply discriminatory towards females (see Harding, 1986; McNeil, 1987; Griffiths, 1988; Jansen, 1989). Invariably such critique is accompanied by attempts to reconstruct the field's knowledge and practice in gender-sensitive ways and it is at this point, in particular, that many divergent paths are taken (for science, see Bleier, 1986; Tuana 1989). Unfortunately, it is not possible for me to document these in any adequate way here. Suffice it to say that a dominant tendency in current proposals for change draw their inspiration from cultural feminism (see Alcoff, 1988) and in particular from the work of Carol Gilligan (1982) who claims that whereas males' moral reasoning is dominated by an 'ethic of rights', females' is dominated by an 'ethic of care'. According to this view, such knowledge domains will only attract and retain significant numbers of females if they take into account women's and girls' 'ways of knowing', and in particular if they develop a stronger social conscience (see Weinreich-Haste, 1986). More broadly, the 'radical' positions rest on the premise that, despite their instrumental, technicist, discriminatory and alienating connections with masculinity, such knowledge domains also provide powerful 'tools' for interpreting and shaping experience, as well as a potential source of considerable pleasure and satisfaction. Further, they have the capacity to enhance as well as undermine and even destroy the human condition. It is thus argued that women's interest in such areas is not simply about gaining access to better-paid and more secure vocations, but about claiming the right to pleasurable and rewarding knowledge and work which offers females a greater capacity to understand and positively influence their worlds. These positions are to be located at the more radical end of the spectrum because they are largely concerned to reshape the male knowledge domains in ways which will both empower females and contribute to the social good. Such ideas find their way into the girls and schooling literature via the views of those who insist that science, maths and technology curricula must encompass a cultural, social and philosophical dimension or those who call for a radical reconstruction of the pedagogy of such subjects, or both.

Having identified a conservative to radical political spectrum, I should also point out that the matter does not end there: further complexities exist. Particular individuals and groups within this discursive field may take up multiple and ambiguous positions along this spectrum. Although this point will become clearer as I proceed, let me offer a quick example. Some groups suggest radical changes to curriculum and pedagogy, but adopt a rather simplistic and uncritical view of the 'invisible filter' and the structure of the labour market. They may encourage and celebrate the extension of 'feminine' principles to the 'male' domains, but at the same time implicitly define what is 'traditional' for women and girls as 'the negative other'.

Some Difficulties and Dilemmas

In the remaining pages, I shall identify some of the philosophical and political difficulties and dilemmas which beset this discourse. These seem to arise, in large part, from the following matters. The discourse designed to encourage girls into 'non-traditional' areas is informed by a body of knowledge which is constantly developing. Reworking, adjusting, reframing and refining its central propositions is what people in the field must constantly do. Propositional knowledge must be tested in classrooms and schools, and a dialogue between the theoretical and the empirical must be encouraged. A second dialogue to be encouraged is with those fields of enquiry beyond the 'non-traditional', in particular, those which might offer a wider contextual account of the complexities of the changing educational and social condition. However, a difficulty too infrequently acknowledged is that, in many people's minds, the field's more propositional aspects have hardened into 'truth', or, alternatively, its slogans have come to represent its totality. As a result, complexity, subtlety, ambiguity and indeed quite vigorous debate on a number of topics have become obscured by dogma. Also, because a certain intellectual insularity characterizes the field, it has a tendency to operate with a rather simplistic understanding both of bodies of knowledge and, indeed, the *realpolitik* beyond it.

Some Problems Associated with Dualism, Essentialism and Dogma

If so many of the propositions of the field — with regard, say, to performance, curriculum and pedagogy — were not so debatable or in need of further refinement, or both, perhaps its element of dogmatism would not be such a problem. However, neither the role model nor the single-sex strategy is without dispute (see Kahle, 1985a, p. 261, and Byrne, 1989, respectively), and object-relations theory certainly has its critics (see Fee, 1986). Too often in the 'girl-friendly' pedagogy which arises from object-relations theory, definitions of girls' ways of learning and of girls' interests and motivations are developed which tap right back into the gendered dualisms from which escape is sought. Here we confront a paradox which is central to certain radical interpretations of the field. Its critique of, say, science is based on the claim that science necessarily occupies the 'masculine' and 'superior' pole of a set of gendered cultural dualisms. Yet at the same time, it wants to reassert these dualisms, with an emphasis now on the 'feminine' side in the reconstruction of science as a field of knowledge, as school curriculum and pedagogy. This underwrites rather than challenges the masculine, monopolistic claim on certain forms of intellectuality, such as the 'rational', 'objective', 'impersonal' and so on. Further, gendered dualisms are confirmed, not transcended, and ironically, women and girls remain locked into traditional rather than expansive versions of femaleness — hence female difference is both naturalized and (re)produced. On the other hand, though, as I shall argue shortly, there is merit to the suggestion that the positive values which are often associated with women's varied but similar history, culture and experience become more significant in the public sphere.

A further difficulty here is that the search for 'girl-friendly' pedagogy often boils down to trying to identify the essential nature of girlhood. Yet this sort of essentialism is being challenged in the more general feminist and education literature as matters of class, ethnicity and race become a more explicit concern of many feminist teachers and researchers who increasingly recognize that students' identities cannot be reduced to one particular structural factor (see Weiler, 1988; Ellsworth, 1989; Weedon, 1987). The cultural *differences* which exist among girls have a considerable impact upon the ways in which they relate to the codes of the dominant culture embodied in all school curricula. Some writers might argue that a curriculum which recognizes the commonalities and the differences among girls faces what Yates (1988) calls 'the essentialist/pluralist dilemma'. However, it seems to me that now we have recognized *difference*, we must theorize anew what females have in common. Certainly there is no longer any place for either/or thinking. What we need instead, as Yates (1988) argues, is 'sensitive, differentiated understanding'. However, explorations of what this means and might mean for the classroom are only just beginning in the discourse which seeks to encourage girls into 'non-traditional' areas (see, for example, Collins and Matyas, 1985; Baran, 1987). Meanwhile, one gets a sense from some that perhaps working-class girls should go into trades while girls from more privileged classes should move into more prestigious areas. The following comment from Johnson (1990) sums up rather well the points I have been making:

> Strategies of gender inclusiveness have [thus] tended to become pre-occupied with identifying the female experience in education as a pre-given and unitary experience. Hence, while challenging the dominance of masculine norms, they have left untouched the abstract oppositions of masculinity and femininity upon which these norms rely. We need an approach which gives recognition to those repressed values with which

women have historically been associated, such as a concern with personal relationships, with helping others and with the practical, social implications of what we do. But at the same time we need to recognize the way in which our identities are multiple and historically determined.

Interestingly, some writers question the popular assumption that girls largely perform inadequately in the 'non-traditional' subjects. They do so either by asking questions of the statistics which allow matters associated with change and with specific educational systems, structures and locations to emerge in, say, mathematics (see Willis, 1989), or by questioning the very notion of performance itself. The lines of argument which are developed in the first instance raise questions about the accuracy of the titles 'traditional' and 'non-traditional'. Alternatively, in a challenging article about the discursive production of both femininity and performance, Walkerdine (1989, p. 268) argues that 'femininity is *equated* with poor performance, even when the girl or woman in question is performing well'. In developing such a view, Walkerdine draws on the data from the *Girls and Mathematics Project* at the University of London Institute of Education. In *Girls and Mathematics* (Walden and Walkerdine, 1985) she and Rosie Walden show that it is the *masculine* model of a good learner that many teachers work with, which permits them both to define girls' achievements negatively and to discourage their progress along esteemed mathematical pathways — that is, teachers' perceptions *actually produce* gendered patterns of success and failure. In an attempt to build on the notion of an inclusive curriculum and on Walden and Walkerdine's work, Johnson (1990) suggests that the above problems and those associated with the essentialism of the inclusive curriculum might be avoided if 'non-traditional' subjects for girls

> . . . make explicit the models of the good learner which underlie many of the taken-for-granted practices of teachers as well as many of the organizational features of the school itself — such as assessment procedures, school timetabling and classroom organization.

This explicit pedagogy 'would seek to specify clearly . . . what skills and capacities should be *acquired* by learners and it would seek to teach these'. This suggestion has a strong resemblance to so-called 'genre theory' which has had a powerful recent influence on language and literary education,[3] and the possibilities and limitations of such a theory for this field may well be worth pursuing.

This leads me to an associated concern. The calls from certain educators for interactive, co-operative, intuitive and holistic ways of learning, in the interests of 'girl-friendly' curriculum and pedagogy, are remarkably similar to aspects of humanist and progressive educational discourses. Indeed, they are practices which many educators believe constitute good teaching. From these points of view, such educational practices are not only 'girl friendly', but of benefit to all student's learning, in all school subjects. The acknowledgment of this point not only allows a certain transcendence of the dualism problem, but also creates the possibility of strategic alliances between feminist educators and certain other sections of the educational community. Yet there is too little recognition of this point in the literature (see, however, Kahle [Chap.3] in Kahle, 1985b). An additional point to be made here is that the methods associated with attempts to persuade girls to take 'non-traditional' pathways are too frequently based on a 'banking' model of pedagogy (see Freire, 1972). Such a model fails to engage adequately with the complex issues of reception and identity or even with where students are and want to be. It assumes that students will respond rationally to a well-reasoned case, ignores the importance of fantasy, desire and even romance in girls' lives, and may well generate resistance (see Yates, 1985). However, some recent developments in this area borrow techniques from the youth culture industry — seeking to work through and beyond the interests and desires which this medium helps to construct (for example, the *Poppy* and *Razz* magazines produced by the Tasmanian and Queensland Education Departments respectively). Whether such approaches work any better than their predecessors remains to be seen.

The Problem of Further Repressing Already Repressed Values

Another set of problems arises from the more simplistic and conservative dimensions and interpretations of the discourse. When such slogans as *Maths multiplies your choices* and *Switch on to Science* are accepted uncritically, there are a number of unfortunate and unintended ideological consequences. For example, it appears as though some educators and policy-makers are valorizing these particular domains (even in their unreconstructed form) and attracting to them considerably more esteem than they currently deserve, given, in some cases, their connections with, say, the military/industrial complex and their apparent preoccupation with unreservedly controlling and exploiting nature. It also appears as though current gender-inflected hierarchies of valued knowledgeare being underwritten. In apparently esteeming such field and hierarchies of knowledge so highly, the sets of masculinist values which predominate therein are endorsed. These are not necessarily those which make for a humane and compassionate society (see further, Elliot and Powell, 1987). All too often the message comes across that it is only the 'male domains' which are empowering. Those areas which are more conventionally attractive to girls and women are thus implicitly defined as either power-neutral or disempowering and are thus derided in a very sexist fashion. The values and skills most associated with female culture and female experience come to be seen as valuable only for such 'private' spheres as the family or the emotions, and girls are implicitly taught that they should be more like boys if they want to 'get on'. Girls are defined according to a deficit model — other than and less than boys, who are hence presented unequivocally as the norm (see further, Johnson, 1988).

The argument I want to make here picks up on my earlier point about dualisms. Although many women's and girls' *learned* capacities for nurturance and collectivity may have traditionally been harnessed in the process of their oppression, they might well also be regarded as a source of strength for society. As Chodorow (1978) argues, in the domestic sphere, females often function to provide the morality (the Moral Mother) which may be missing from the public spheres of, say, business and government. Others point to the benefits of 'maternal thinking' for the public sphere, suggesting, for example, that, given the threat of nuclear war or environmental destruction, such thinking may well be humanity's saviour (Ruddick, 1980). Rich observes that the dominant 'masculine culture' of the public sphere is characterized by 'depersonalization, fragmentation, waste, artificial scarcity and emotional shallowness, not to mention its suicidal obsession with power and technology as ends rather than means' (Rich, 1980, p. 13).

Now, in making this case, I recognize that I too run the risk of reasserting the dualisms which I criticized earlier. However, I must emphasize that I am not suggesting that 'maternal thinking' is a natural female essence well developed in all women, that it is exclusively a female quality, or that such thinking justifies the practices of socialization which would restrict women to femininity and fecundity: hearth and home. Rather, my argument is that the positive values associated with nurturing are too often missing from those social, cultural and educational arenas which are dominated by men. For many feminists, the cause is not simply concerned with women's access to these arenas. In emphasizing such things as 'maternal thinking', they offer a critique of such fields and suggest how education and society — and indeed men — might be otherwise (see Daley, 1989, p. 11). This leads to the observation that considerable diversity exists within the overall discourse on the matter of masculinity. While at one end of the spectrum the masculinity that is mapped on to science, maths, technology and trades is indeed made problematic, at the other it is barely questioned — girls and women are the problem, and its solution resides in changing them. Either way, though, too few resources are put into a reconsideration of non-traditional pathways for boys or into helping boys explore the implications for them of the changing organization of work, the family and the relationship between the two.[4]

Some Problems Associated with Restricted Understandings of the Labour Market

The tendency in the populist/conservative/male appropriation of the discourse to diminish women's current skills, experience, interests, aptitudes and expertise applies just as much to discussions of the labour market as to knowledge. For example, the *Draft National Plan of Action for Women in Tertiary Education* (CTEC, 1987, p. 78) had this to say: 'Girls in schools need to be provided with information which guides them away from traditional occupations with shrinking employment opportunities.' Evident in this type of argument are a number of problems. The first is the assumption that the evidence about current labour market trends and likely further directions is unambiguous. Yet, despite claims to the contrary, most people with a specialist interest in the field of labour market analysis argue that areas of shrinking employment and skill shortage are by no means clear (see, for example, Kirby, 1985). Rapid technological, cultural and economic changes are making medium- and long-term prediction hazardous, to say the least. While some may argue that the employment growth areas are maths-, science- and particularly technology-related, others ask how capable of expansion that segment of the labour market is and to what extent it is only interested in the mathematical, scientific and technical élites and the 'gifted girls' who might join such élites. The strongest indications in Australia seem to be that the expansion in high-technology industries will result in fewer skilled jobs and more jobs demanding low skill and offering low wages and, overall, they will not be the areas of greatest employment growth anyway. The point is that if Australia is to follow the pattern of the USA, the growth areas are in clerical, retail trade and service occupations — traditionally women's work (see further Watkins, 1989; Department of Labour, 1990, p. 12). Given this, it would seem that the conservative side of the movement to encourage girls into 'non-traditional' areas is placing girls' educational eggs in a rather fragile basket. Further, as the empirical studies of Game and Pringle (1983) and others show, the movement of women into male work domains does not necessarily ensure them high-powered jobs.

The evidence about the horizontal segregation by sex of virtually all fields of work, but particularly the 'non-traditional' domains, is unequivocal (Mumford, 1989). Getting into these fields does not mean, then, that women gain immediate access to their economic and other benefits, and neither does it necessarily mean that they are sufficiently well placed to promote changes which will be sympathetic to members of their sex. The conservative position allows for very little recognition of the fact that gendered power relations in the labour market help to constitute its hierarchies of skill, merit and reward. Indeed, it implicitly accepts such hierarchies as fixed. Historically, women's work has always been considered less worthy — hence the attempts by certain unions to establish 'comparable worth' and therefore comparable pay. Issues associated with the gendered notion of skill and merit are somewhat tangentially on the agenda for the current corporate restructuring of the labour market (another topic seldom discussed in the girls' literature), and while some women believe that this provides a golden opportunity for redefining the value of women's work, others are decidedly less optimistic and show how, again, women are getting the short end of the stick (Junor, 1988). To an extent, of course, this latter case is to be expected: not because women are not in the 'non-traditional jobs' associated with maths, science and technology, but because they do not occupy much space or exert much authority in the world of big unions, big business and big government. What I am implying here is that the movement to empower girls and women by facilitating their access to the 'non-traditional' domains conceptualizes the connection between power and knowledge far too narrowly. Because it has failed to take on board the fact that definitions of skill and merit arise out of unequal relationships of power between men and women (and indeed between other social groups), it also fails to explore the ways in which the subjects which girls *traditionally* take have the potential to equip them with the appropriate skills to challenge such definitions. It thus wants to encourage girls away from the very areas in which employment growth may occur because such areas attract little status and reward. While at one level this makes sense, at another it must be recognized as a line of least resistance.

The Problem of Placing too Much Faith in Certain Credentials

So what are the implications, then, of the more conservative inflection of the discourse under scrutiny? This question taps into a topical debate (see Harding, 1987/88). In moving into the male domains, will women change them? Will they change women? (And does it matter?) Or will women remain the same and therefore largely marginally located within such fields? As evidence varies, answers tend to be more speculative than definitive. From some perspectives it does not seem to matter who or what changes as long as girls and women gain 'access and success'. At the risk of sounding unduly pessimistic, I should like to offer for consideration a possible consequence of such a scenario.

In moving into 'non-traditional' areas, *as they currently exist*, women will also be subject to the preferred values and behaviours of these fields. They will not just move into a male domain but also into a masculinist culture where success may well depend upon taking on board values antithetical to a feminist cause which is concerned about issues beyond job mobility. It is highly unlikely, in the broad educational scheme of things, that women will be exposed to feminist theory or analysis once they enter the 'non-traditional' areas. Supposing large numbers of girls and women do gain access and success in these fields, and supposing that these fields do remain unreconstructed, despite a strong female presence, what are the likely long-term social consequences? More jobs and greater financial independence for women? Maybe, and certainly let us hope so! But if women are not careful, might this not also be accompanied by certain losses, for example of the 'maternal thinking' mentioned earlier? It is possible that a new conservatism will develop among women, one somewhat different from that which currently leads many of us to be, as it is said, complicit in our own oppression. Having learned to be rational, certain, disciplined, impartial, objective, competitive, individualistic and socially mobile, we may also have *un*-learned those lateral and integrative capacities such as sensitivity and empathy, which no civilized society can afford to be without and which are as important to the public sphere as they are to the so-called private. While some women may not be unduly concerned by this scenario, for those of a more radical bent it highlights the importance of the wider-ranging approaches to change which I discussed earlier.

Another possible scenario is that, despite gaining the appropriate educational credentials, women may still not be able to claim the appropriate employment rewards. As I also indicated earlier, the reasons for this likelihood relate to gendered power relations in the labour market and the workplace and have been well and extensively documented (see Curthoys, 1986). However, another important factor is the family. There is no doubt that women's traditional responsibilities for child care and domestic work within the family have had an ongoing debilitating effect upon their participation in paid work (in science, see Birke, 1986). For example, such responsibilities help to explain their over-representation in part-time and casual work and the difficulties which many women experience in taking advantage of training, promotional and industrial opportunities. The domestic ideology associated with the family and the particular 'person skills' which females develop because of this ideology also suggest, in part, why certain segments of the labour market, the caring professions for example, are associated with women. On the other hand, however, this domestic ideology has also been used by employers and male unionists to protect their own interests and to discriminate against women in such a way as to bring into question both their basic right to be employed and their right to fair treatment in the labour market (Curthoys, 1986). Despite the changes in the labour market and the family to which I alluded earlier, this domestic ideology still helps to shape assumptions about the ways in which women should participate in paid labour.

Certainly, the dramatic changes in the family form have not necessarily meant changes in domestic responsibilities. The evidence is that despite women's increased participation in paid work they still characteristically do the 'double shift', with most women still taking major responsibility for child care and domestic work. Further, the often conflicting demands of the family and paid work place considerable stress on the majority of families and, as emerging research shows, this has its adverse 'spill-over' effects in both the home and the workplace (Arndt, 1989). None the less, governments and employers have not fully come to grips with the fact that they 'are no longer dealing with the traditional male workforce complete with a homemaker support system' (Arndt, 1989, p. 2). The world of work and the public sphere generally have made insufficient adjustments to these new family forms. While provisions for child care, flexitime, parenting leave and so forth have gestured towards the problem, provisions in this regard remain hopelessly inadequate. A particularly astonishing feature of the discourse under scrutiny here is its lack of interest in bringing about gender justice in the family itself (see however, Curthoys, 1988). Clearly, many girls' post-school options will remain restricted until such a cultural shift occurs.

The Problem of Co-option

One of the risks that the field has to deal with is its potential for co-option by subtly competing sets of interests. While on the one hand Labor governments in Australia have offered a good deal of financial and moral support, and while there is no doubt that this has added substantially to the momentum of the movement to enhance girls' futures through 'non-traditional choices', there can be little doubt that its interest has been less in 'equity' (however defined) than in the women's vote and in the possibility of harnessing the field to 'national interests'. The current Commonwealth Labor government expresses considerable faith in the capacity of maths, science and technology (and management and Asian Studies and the like) to help rejuvenate our ailing economy and balance our international trade. It is also concerned about an emerging tendency for appropriately qualified students to avoid certain science and technology subjects at the tertiary level. Males, it seems, prefer to study those subjects which pay greater dividends and so tend to combine maths with such fields as commerce or economics (*Improving Science, Maths and Technology Education Base in Victoria*, 1987). It thus seems reasonable to suggest that the government is encouraging women to enter the science, maths and technology subjects precisely because many men are vacating them for more lucrative pastures. That this push overlaps a certain feminist agenda is, therefore, a rather happy coincidence for both parties. But the Second World War experience of women such as those depicted in the film *Rosie the Riveter* should be kept in mind here. These women were encouraged by an absence of men and by national priorities into 'non-traditional areas'; after the war, however, when the men returned and national priorities changed, they were rather cynically encouraged to do their bit for the nation by now returning home and producing babies. The extent to which governmental support extends beyond an expedient and opportunistic endorsement of the most conservative inflection of that movement thus remains very much an open question. None the less, it is undeniable that a number of projects with some radical dimensions to them have been developed with government money, although it is probably also true to say these dominate neither the field nor the general public's perception of it.

Conclusion

Let me conclude firstly by drawing together the various threads of this paper and secondly by outlining its implications for the movement to encourage girls into 'non-traditional' areas, in order to enhance their post-school options. I began with a discussion of the field and identified its central concerns and premises on the matter of employment, knowledge, curriculum and pedagogy. I showed that it is neither static nor unified and, indeed, that it can be conceived on a spectrum from radical to conservative, depending on the extent of change which is envisaged in these four major areas. I then identified a number of difficulties and dilemmas which the field currently confronts. One particular concern was a tendency towards closure: that is, for matters contestable to become 'matters of fact' and thus to apparently close off opportunities for the development of much-needed further knowledge and better curriculum. A second concern was about the apparent popularity of the more conservative inflection of the field and the dangers associated with this. In particular, I identified an unfortunate side-effect, the naive tendency to exaggerate the capacity of the 'non-traditional' areas to enhance girls' futures.

My discussion of the gendered construction of skill and merit, the threat of co-option and the work/family connection suggests there is much more to the matter of post-school options for girls than increasing their credentials in 'non-traditional areas'. *The National Policy for the Education of Girls in Australian Schools* (Schools Commission, 1987) recognizes this and points to the need for the development of new curricula for girls and boys in practical and personal living skills, family and work studies, and so forth. It is these dimensions to the National Policy which, in comparative terms, have attracted little interest, and yet it is these curriculum developments which, in my view, have an enormous capacity to help students adjust creatively and harmoniously to the conditions in which they will live out their adulthood.

Certainly, women require more than credentials in order to claim a fair deal in the paid labour market. At the level of their personal knowledge, skills and capacities, they need an understanding of how and why it is that they have been disadvantaged. They also need to develop the appropriate industrial and government lobbying and workplace and family negotiation skills to bring about redress in the way in which paid and unpaid work are structured. Sufficiently reconstructed, the humanities and the social sciences have much to offer in this regard, both in helping girls to acquire such powerful knowledge and also in helping boys to move away from what must now be regarded as outdated and untenable notions of masculinity.

Boys must learn that their futures as employers, employees, unionists, fathers or whatever should, and will, involve working fairly and equitably alongside women in the workplace and the home. Among much else, this means that boys too can benefit from the humanizing of what, for them, are regarded as traditional fields of knowledge. But it also means that they should not be encouraged by prevailing ideologies of masculinity or work opportunities to avoid those school subjects which seek to develop their important human capacity to be sensitive, imaginative, responsive, empathetic, sympathetic, creative and perceptive. There is no doubt that families would benefit if men as well as women bring these capacities into the home. Perhaps then domestic and emotional labour would be more equitably shared, thus improving women's workforce opportunities. Of course, the demise of those ideologies of masculinity which spill over into exploitation and violence would mean a reduction in the forms of domestic violence which produce battered families and which send many youngsters away from home and out into the streets. It might also make some inroads on our current self-destructive public culture.

Not girls', boys' or society's options are enhanced by allowing current versions of maths, science and technology to dominate our perceptions of useful knowledge. Such perceptions not only downgrade the so called 'soft' subjects, they also steer students away from the values that such subjects — at best — embody and the human questions that they encourage students to ask. Society is so much the poorer when these areas of the curriculum are pushed to the margins. Clearly students of both sexes need an inclusive *and expansive* curriculum and, this suggests, at the very least, some sort of balance in their subject choices. Indeed, in the light of our increasing capacity to destroy the environment, and given that the cult of selfishness threatens to overtake the national psyche, a case could readily be mounted for the hasty inclusion of nurturant, protective, empathetic and co-operative values in all school subjects. The questions here, of course, are: 'What are the tolerance limits of those government and other agencies which fund and promote gender reform in educational institutions?' 'Where does their enthusiasm for "gender equity" stop?' My suspicion is that it stops at the point when the possibility for significant change — on matters of gender — begins.

The broadest implication of what I have said, then, is that those who are producing this discourse should acknowledge very clearly to themselves and others that its conservative inflection is only the bare beginning to a project which is much more radical in its implications for genuine, far-reaching change. They should also acknowledge that the term 'enhancing girls' post-school options' must be conceptualized sufficiently broadly to include issues beyond those associated with women's mobility and relocation in the labour market. The term must embody a challenge to the structure of the labour market and the values and social practices upon which that structure is built. The notion of 'enhancing girls' post-school options' should also encompass the wider economic, social, cultural and environmental conditions in which they will live their lives. Mathematics, science and technology, as fields of knowledge, exert a major impact on such conditions, and hence girls' participation in reconstructed 'non-traditional' subjects is important — not as an end in itself, however, but in order that girls and women may be more actively and critically involved in shaping the future in humane and life-enhancing ways.

Notes

1 Between 1947 and 1987 women almost doubled their participation in the labour force, going from 22.4 per cent to 40.1 per cent. In 1947 married women

constituted 3.4 per cent of the total labour force, and in 1987 they made up 23.7 per cent. Of all the women in the labour force in 1947, 15.3 per cent were married. In 1987, 59 per cent of all women in paid work were married (see Mumford, 1989).

2 Women's entry into the paid labour force has been made both possible and, in certain senses, necessary by changes in the nature of the family. Reliable birth control has had a significant effect on women's patterns of child bearing. Women today are having fewer children, closer together and later in life than their mothers and grandmothers. An increasing number are choosing to have no children at all. The women's movement has contributed to changes in women's aspirations for their future and, in many cases, the high cost of living (particularly high interest rates) and rising expectations have meant that many households 'require' two incomes (see Mathews, 1987).

Another factor of considerable significance here is the dramatic rise in the divorce rate, from 14 per cent in 1971 to 35 per cent in 1986 (McDonald, 1988, p. 41). This has been accompanied by a rise in single-parent households. In 1972 single parents constituted 9.2 per cent of all families, in 1988 they constituted 15 per cent. Most such families are headed by women. On the other hand, the trend among women is towards later marriage: indeed, 20–25 per cent of this generation are expected not to marry at all (see further, McDonald, 1988). The traditional family, with a single income earned by the male, is no longer the dominant family form (see Gittens, 1988, p. 42).

3 The interest in different genres of writing and speaking in schools and elsewhere (see Reid, 1987) has led to the identification of those genres which are most associated with educational and social success in particular fields, and this in turn has led to the identification of what might be called 'genres of power', that is, those with the greatest investment potential in the current power structures. In identifying with and developing particular skill in a narrow set of genres, girls are seen to under-utilize their linguistic capacities and so to fail to convert such capacitites into wide-ranging educational and career success. Alternatively, of course, many knowledge and work domains clearly do not value the particular genres in which girls and women excel, and many 'genres of power' draw on skills and orientations which are most associated with males. The upshot of this set of complexities is that girls are to be encouraged to 'master' a wide range of generic forms at the same time as learning to recognize and resist their gendered dimensions.

4 I am aware, in making this point, that I am touching on the very sensitive issue of who should attract the diminishing educational reform dollar, and whether boys, again, will claim the lion's share. While I recognize such dangers, I also believe that the dangers associated with neglecting boys' re-education are no less considerable. I have no doubt that sensitive and intelligent policy-making can address both concerns.

References

ALCOFF, L. (1988) 'Cultural feminism versus post-structuralism: The identity crisis in feminist theory', in MINNICH, E., O'BARR, J. and ROSENFIELD, R. (Eds) *Reconstructing the Academy: Women's Education and Women's Studies*, Chicago, University of Chicago Press, pp. 257–89.

ARNDT, B. (1989) 'Reconciling work with family responsibilities', *The Age*, 12 July, 2.

BARAN, G. (1987) 'Teaching girls science', in MCNEIL, M. (Ed.) *Gender and Expertise*, London, Free Association Books.

BARNES, M., PLAISTER, R. and THOMAS, A. (1984) *Girls Count in Maths and Science: A Handbook for Teachers*, Darlinghurst, NSW, Girls and Mathematics Action.

BIRKE, L. (1986) 'Toward gender equality in science', in HARDING, J. (Ed.) *Perspectives on Gender and Science*, London, Falmer Press, pp. 184–202.

BLEIER, R. (Ed.) (1986) *Feminist Approaches to Science*, New York, Pergamon Press.

BYRNE, E. (1989) 'Role modelling and mentorship as policy mechanisms: The need for new directions', Brisbane, University of Queensland.

CHODOROW, N. (1978) *The Reproduction of Mothering: Psychoanalysis and the Sociology of Gender*, Berkeley, CA., University of California.

COLLINS, M. and MATYAS, M.L. (1985) 'Minority women: Conquering both sexism and racism', in KAHLE, J.B. (Ed.), *Women in Science: A Report from the Field*, London, Falmer Press. pp. 102–24.

CTEC (1987) *Draft National Plan of Action for Women in Tertiary Education*, Australian Government Publishing Service.

CURTHOYS, A. (1986) 'The sexual division of labour: Theoretical arguments', in GRIEVE, N. and BURNS, A. (Eds) *Australian Women: New Feminist Perspectives*, Oxford, Oxford University Press.

CURTHOYS, (1988) 'Education and the world of work: Studying gender and the social organization of work', *Independent Education*, 18(4), pp. 34–6.

DALEY, J. (1989) 'Feminism is turning green', *The Age*, 30 June, Features, p. 11.

DEPARTMENT OF LABOUR (1990) *Women's Employment Branch, Women Count: A Statistical Bulletin on Women's Employment in Victoria*, 5, January.

EAGLETON, T. (1985) 'The Subject of Literature', Paper delivered to the Annual Conference of the National Association for the Teaching of English, Nottingham, April.

ELLIOT, J. and POWELL, C. (1987) 'Young women and science: Do we need more science?', *British Journal of Sociology of Education*, 8(3), pp. 277–86.

ELLSWORTH, E. (1989) 'Why doesn't this feel empowering?: Working through the repressive myths of critical pedagogy', *Harvard Educational Review*, 59(3), pp. 297–324.

FEE, E. (1986) 'Critiques of modern science: The relationship of feminism to other radical epistemologies', in BLEIER, R. (Ed.) *Feminist Approaches to Science*, New York, Pergamon Press, pp. 42–57.

FREIRE, P. (1972) *Pedagogy of the Oppressed*, Harmondsworth, Penguin.

GAME, A. and PRINGLE, R. (1983) *Gender and Work*, Sydney, Allen and Unwin.

GEMS (1990) 1(2), pp. 2–25.

GILLIGAN, C. (1982) *In a Different Voice: A Study of Women's Contribution and Resolution of Moral Problems*, Cambridge, MA., Harvard University Press.

GITTENS, R. (1988) 'On pursuing your typical family, or how not to be lied to with statistics', *Sydney Morning Herald*, 5 November.

GRIFFITHS, M. (1988) 'Strong feelings about computers', *Women's Studies International Forum*, 11(2), pp. 145–54.

HARDING, J. (Ed.) (1986) *Perspectives on Gender and Science*, London, Falmer Press.

HARDING, J. (1987/88) 'Filtered out or opting in', *Education Links*, 32, pp. 12–14.

IMPROVING THE SCIENCE MATHS AND TECHNOLOGY EDUCATION BASE IN VICTORIA (1987) Report of the Working Group on Education for Science Technology to the Victorian Government through the Honourable Ian Cathie, Minister of Education, August.

JANSEN, S.C. (1989) 'Gender and the information society: A socially structured silence', *Journal of Communication*, 39(3), Summer, pp. 196–215.

JOHNSON, L. (1988) 'On becoming an individual: A reassessment of the issue of gender and schooling', *Discourse*, 8(2).

JOHNSON, L. (1990) 'Gender issues and education', *Australian Feminist Studies*, 11, May.

JUNOR, A. (1988) *Skill Formation Policies: Implications for Women*, NSW Teachers' Federation Research Notes, No. 1, May.

KAHLE, J.B. (1983) 'Gender and science education: II', in P. FENSHAM (Ed.) *Development and Dilemmas in Science Education*, London, Falmer Press.

KAHLE, J.B. (1985a) 'Retention of girls in science: Case study of secondary teachers', in KAHLE, J.B. (Ed.), *Women in Science: A Report from the Field*, London, Falmer Press, pp. 49–77.

KAHLE, J.B. (Ed.) (1985b) *Women in Science: A Report from the Field*, London, Falmer Press.

KELLER, E.F. (1986) 'How gender matters: Or, why it's so hard for us to count past two', in HARDING, J. (Ed.) *Perspectives on Gender and Science*, London, Falmer Press, pp. 168–84.

KELLY, A. (1985) 'The construction of masculine science', *British Journal of Sociology of Education*, 6(2), pp. 133–53.

KELLY, A., WHYTE, J. and SMAIL, B. (1984) *Girls into Science and Technology: Final Report*, Manchester, Department of Sociology, University of Manchester.

KIRBY, P. (1985) *Report of the Committee of Inquiry into Labour Market Programmes*, Canberra, Australian Government Publishing Service.

LEWIS, S. and DAVIES, A. (1988) *Girls and Maths and Science Teaching Project: Gender Equity in Maths and Science*, Canberra, Curriculum Development Centre.

McCLINTOCK COLLECTIVE (1987) *The Fascinating Sky*, Victoria, PEP.

MACDONALD, M. (1979) 'Cultural reproduction: The pedagogy of sexuality', *Screen Education*, No. 32/33.

McDONALD, P. (1988) 'Families in the future: The pursuit of personal autonomy', *Family Matters*, AIFS Newsletter, No. 22, December, pp. 40–7.

McNEIL, M. (Ed.) (1987) *Gender and Expertise*, London, Free Association Books.

MATHEWS, I. (1987) 'Sharing work and family responsibilities', *Fabian Newsletter*, September, pp. 8–13.

MUMFORD, K. (1989) *Women Working: Economics and Reality*, Sydney, Allen and Unwin.

REID, I. (Ed.) (1987) *The Place of Genre in Learning: Current Debates*, Geelong, Centre for Studies in Literary Education, Deakin University Press.

RICH, A. (1980) *On Lies, Secrets and Silence*, London, Virago.

RUDDICK, S. (1980) 'Maternal thinking', *Feminist Studies*, 6(2), pp. 342–67.

SCHOOLS COMMISSION (1987) *The National Policy for the Education of Girls in Australian Schools*, Canberra, Australian Government Publishing Service.

SJOBERG, S. and IMSEN, G. (1988) 'Gender and science education: I', in FENSHAM, P. (Ed.) *Development and Dilemmas in Science Education*, London, Falmer Press.

TUANA, N. (Ed.) (1989) *Feminism and Science*, Bloomington and Indianapolis, Indiana University Press.

WALDEN, R. and WALKERDINE, V. (1985) *Girls and Mathematics: From Primary to Secondary Schooling*, London, Heinemann.

WALKERDINE, V. (1989) 'Femininity as performance', *Oxford Review of Education*, 15 (3), pp. 267–79.

WATKINS, P. (1989) 'Flexible manufacturing, flexible technology and flexible education: Visions of the post-Fordist economic solution', in SACHS, J. (Ed.) *Technology Education in Australia*, Canberra, Curriculum Development Centre.

WEEDON, C. (1987) *Feminist Practice and Post-Structuralist Theory*, Oxford, Basil Blackwell.

WEILER, K. (1988) *Women Teaching for Change: Gender, Class and Power*, Massachusetts, South Hactley, Bergin and Garvey.

WEINREICH-HASTE, H. (1986) 'Brother sun, sister moon: Does rationality overcome a dualistic world view', in HARDING, J. (Ed.) *Perspectives on Gender and Science*, London, Falmer Press, pp. 113–32.

WHYTE, J., DEEM, R., KANT, L. and CRUICKSHANK, M. (Eds) (1985) *Girl-Friendly Schooling*, London, Methuen.

WILLIS, S. (1989) *Real Girls Don't do Maths: Gender and the Construction of Privilege*, Geelong, Deakin University Press.

YATES, L. (1985) 'Is girl-friendly schooling really what girls need?', in WHYTE, J., DEEM, R., KANT, L. and CRUICKSHANK, M. (Eds) *Girl-Friendly Schooling*, London, Methuen.

YATES, L. (1988) 'Some dimensions of the practice of theory and the development of theory for practice in relation to gender and education', in BLACKMORE, J., KENWAY, J. (Eds) *Gender Issues in Educational Administration and Policy*, Geelong, Deakin University, Press.

Chapter 6

Truths About Assessment and the Learning of Girls: From Gender Difference to the Production of Gendered Attainment

Helen Bannister

Introduction

Many feminist initiatives to develop assessment strategies for girls rest on the assumption that there are particular strategies which promote successful learning of girls. This assumption is informed by the research literature of gender difference. This paper reviews a number of studies which claim to reveal differences in cognitive style between males and females. Explanations for these differences are examined, and in particular, feminist readings of object-relations theory. The whole field of gender-difference theory is questioned as an adequate framework for developing feminist interventions in the education of girls. Drawing on the work of Walden and Walkerdine (1985) the paper concludes that a new approach to understanding learning and assessment for girls might come from an examination of the ways in which the social relations and teaching and learning practices in specific classrooms are implicated in the production of patterns of gendered attainment.

Multiple-choice Assessment: Gender Differences in Performance — Content Specific or Mode of Assessment Specific?

Research on the comparative performance of males and females in multiple-choice tests can be divided into two types: those studies which focus on the *content* of what is assessed as the significant variable affecting male and female performance, and those which focus on the *mode of assessment* as the significant variable.

There is a tendency in some of the studies which look to the science or maths content of multiple-choice tests as the site of gender differences in performance, to draw on deficit explanations in accounting for girls' inferior performance on such tests; that is, such studies explain gender differences in terms of what girls lack in relation to boys. Arzi (1986), for example, explains girls' inferior performance on multiple-choice tests in science as a product of girls' lack of confidence concerning their cognitive knowledge, a lack of confidence which she conceived of as learned sex-role behavior and, therefore, a female personality trait. Even on other forms of assessment, such as open-ended questions, she speculates that girls would be less successful than boys. Adams (1984), too, singles out girls' lack of confidence concerning their success in the Australian Scholastic Aptitude Test (ASAT) as a factor contributing to boys' superior performance on this test. Other deficit explanations point to girls' lack of scientific knowledge or, more specifically, their lack of consolidation of the science knowledge which they have learned. Adams also points to girls' lack of mathematical knowledge as one of the factors contributing to their inferior performance on ASAT. Adams demonstrates males' superior performance on the quantitative items of ASAT compared with the girls' superior performance on the verbal items — which he explains as a superior performance in English ability — but an advantage which did not pay off in the production of a final ASAT score. Masters and Beswick (1986) discriminate further the content of items which differentially affected the performance of girls and boys in ASAT. Females' deficiency in relation to ASAT lay in their subject choice, concentrating in the social sciences and humanities. Masters and Beswick argue that females' superior English scores in their school assessments were not reflected in ASAT because the ASAT score as a single measure of so-called 'general ability' was not a measure of the range of abilities required in a subject like English. Masters and Beswick's analysis moves from a deficit framework to a critique of the inadequacy of the unidimensional ASAT score as a summary of a student's performance. They propose a technical solution to make the final ASAT score multidimensional and therefore more inclusive of a student's performance in social science and humanities subjects.

The National Association of Education Progress Report (NEAP) (Harding, 1985) found that girls achieved lower scores in multiple-choice tests in the social sciences as well as in maths and science, but, arguably, the social science items could have demanded mathematical skills, such as the reading of statistical tables. Murphy's research (Harding, 1985) compares the performance of students across a range of subjects employing different assessment techniques, but the report of his research does not indicate the forms of assessment used in specific subjects, so we do not know whether the use of multiple-choice tests was confined to maths and science subjects. Daley (1986), in his review of overseas studies of sex differences in test results, concludes that, regardless of content, multiple-choice assessment favours boys. However, the committee reviewing tertiary entrance scores in the Australian Capital Territory (ACT) questions Daley's assertion:

> In many of these studies it is not clear that the content assessed by the different methods is precisely the same, so it remains possible that what appears as a 'mode of assessment difference' may be in part a difference in performance on somewhat different content areas (*Making Admission to Higher Education Fairer*, 1986).

Those studies examining the use of different assessment techniques within the same subject or similar subject areas appear to provide us with a somewhat clearer picture. Ferguson's research (Harding, 1985) is more illuminating because it explores the effects of different assessment techniques on performance within the same subject: and the science subject which he investigates can be designated as a female subject (that is, a higher proportion of females than males are enrolled in the subject). In the 'female' subject biology, Ferguson found that the girls did better on the long-answer question while the boys did better on the multiple-choice questions. Harding's (1985) research corroborates Ferguson's in the area of science. In the examination results of the six science subjects which she investigated, girls excelled on the essay paper while boys gained higher marks in the multiple-choice papers. Harding's conclusions are specific to science: the success of girls and boys in science is influenced by the mode of assessment used. In another study she researched gender differences in assessment preferences (Harding, 1986a). More boys opted for factual descriptive questions which approximate the nature of items in multiple-choice tests, and more girls opted for over-arching explanatory questions which multiple-choice tests cannot accommodate.

The University of London Schools Examination Board (1985), in reviewing the English research on what the Board describes as sex bias in examinations, and the Committee in the ACT reviewing the studies on sex differences in ASAT drew similar conclusions. From the conflicting evidence the Board concluded that all examinations were culturally biased and that some of the sex differences in examination performance could be explained by subject choice, whereas others were explicable in terms of the mode of assessment used. The Committee reviewing ASAT accepted 'on balance' that 'the major source' of gender differences in ASAT performance lay in the subject choice of the students. However, the Committee conceded that:

> there may be an additional component of sex difference attributable to differences in the mode of assessment used in the current Australian Scholastic Aptitude Test and that used in school assessments. There is evidence that when the same course is assessed by both multiple-choice tests and essays or other open-ended question forms, males tend to do better on the multiple-choice form than they do on the other, whereas females tend to do better on the open-ended forms than they do on the multiple-choice form (*Making Admission to Higher Education Fairer*, 1986, p. 47).

However, the committee saw this as a 'less substantial' effect than the effect of subject choice on tertiary entrance scores.

Gender Differences in Cognitive Style?

From the above research a number of feminist educators have constructed as a 'truth' that boys prefer and excel at multiple-choice forms of assessment while girls prefer and excel in essays and open-ended forms of assessment. In particular, Jan Harding, an influential feminist educator concerned with redressing the low participation and success of girls in science, has constituted the research findings on gender differences in mode of assessment preference and performance in science as evidence of the possibility of 'broad differences in cognitive style' between males and females (Harding, 1986a). As further evidence of such differences, she has looked to studies of gender and science which investigate gender differences among students who choose to study science and in student preferences for particular modes of teaching, learning and problem-solving.

Studies of students who choose to study science have produced a pattern of gender differences in the reasons the students give for choosing science. The girls who choose science choose it primarily for its social implications, that is, its potential to improve the quality of life; a consideration which is only secondary in boys' choice of science. The girls predominantly define science in its social context in contrast to the boys, who define it predominantly in terms of devices and experiments (Ormerod, 1971). An investigation of student entries to a technology design competition found that for the boys the problem to be solved lay in the technology itself, whereas for the girls the problem tended to be social (for example, designing for people with disabilities) and technology was the means of facilitating a solution (Grant, 1982).

In his study of subject choice among adolescents, Head, a psychologist, argues that 'the main differences between those making different subject choices lie in the affective elements of self, in personality differences and the concomitant different beliefs and values' (Head, 1983, p. 55). Of the group of adolescents choosing to study science, Head found a pattern of affective differences between the girls and the boys: the girls choosing science were more mature and balanced, whereas the boys were less mature, rigid, authoritarian and emotionally reticent. Head explains the recruitment of boys into science with these personality characteristics as resulting from the boys handling the emotional conflict of adolescence by foreclosing on difficult issues and seizing on to the beliefs and values acquired from others. He argues that boys acquiring a masculine identity through a denial of the interpersonal and the emotional find a haven from the emotional uncertainty of adolescence in science, which is presented as an impersonal, predictable and controllable domain. The girls who choose science are not foreclosing on difficult issues in making a subject choice which requires that they act in an unfeminine way at a time in their life when they are concerned with acquiring the identity of a young woman. Harding (1986a) argues that these affective differences between boys and girls who choose science may extend to differences in cognitive style, and she finds evidence for this in the famous study of another psychologist, Liam Hudson (1966, 1968). Hudson's distinction between convergent thinkers choosing science subjects and divergent thinkers choosing arts subjects did not hold when his original sample of boys was widened to include girls; the girls who chose science tended to be divergers rather than convergers.

Female students were found to display preferences for particular teaching styles in a study of science classes in the Nuffield Science Project (Dalton, 1981). This study examined the effectiveness of three different styles of teaching observed in biology, chemistry and physics lessons. The three styles of teaching were characterized as the informers, the problem-solvers and the enquirers. The informers' style involved the teacher conveying a factual body of knowledge; the problem-solvers' style was one in which the teacher asked questions which had to be answered by constructing a hypothesis; the enquirers' style was student-centered, with students investigating problems in small groups. Among the male students in the study there was no clear pattern of preferences for one teaching style over another. However, among the girls there was a strong dislike for the problem-solvers' style and a preference for either the informers' or enquirers' style. The problem-solving style was used most frequently in the physical science classes where girls were a minority, and this teaching style demanded that the girls 'go public' in front of the whole class. Harding infers from this study that there may be a different cognitive style involved in the choice of science for boys and girls which may interact with the way science is presented in the classroom (Harding, 1986a).

Harding suggests that further evidence of different cognitive styles may be gleaned from classroom observation. For example, she observed a third-year physics class investigating electrical circuits in which the girls chose to seat themselves at the back of the class. The teacher handed out instructions which were to be read before the apparatus was collected. The boys went immediately to collect the apparatus, while the girls read and discussed the instructions. There were not enough pieces of apparatus left for all the girls, a problem which took some time to rectify (frustrating the girls) and involved the teacher removing some apparatus from the boys (which was met with hostility from the boys). Harding interrogates the observed behaviours of the girls. Did the girls' behaviour indicate that (*a*) the girls assume physics to be more relevant for the boys, (*b*) the girls obey instructions, (*c*) the girls are less confident than the boys, or (*d*) the girls need to understand what they are doing first before they engage in practical work? Finally, Harding raises the question of the relationship of the girls' observed behaviour to gender differences in cognitive style. Does this amount to a difference 'in cognitive style which may operate elsewhere in committing girls to an interest in science in context (rather than in abstraction) and contribute to the greater difficulty they seem to experience with multiple-choice testing?' (Harding and Randall, 1983, p. 44).

Differences in the way boys and girls learn are documented in a Danish study of primary school children using a computer to solve problems; the boys worked independently and quickly to solve the problem, while the girls worked more slowly and collaboratively, exploring verbally the implications of the problem. The preliminary findings of a project mounted by Head to investigate the possibility of different cognitive styles among adolescents corroborates the Danish study (Harding, 1986a), documenting the boys' preference for working individually and the girls' preference for working in small groups and exploring ideas verbally.

The research findings which Harding constitutes as 'evidence' of gender differences in cognitive style call into question the dominant model of child developmental psychology. Head observes how his study of male and female adolescents who choose to study science, and other studies of sex differences, reveal that the conventional stage models of adolescence do not accurately portray the development of all adolescents, and that this is especially so for girls: 'a substantial minority of girls take the tasks of adolescence in a different sequence from that prescribed in the literature' (Head, 1983, p. 58). Head discusses in particular the work of Carol Gilligan, *In a Different Voice: A Study of Women's Construction and Resolution of Moral Problems*, which claims to reveal a 'disparity between experience and the representation of human development in psychological literature' (Gilligan, 1982, p. 1). Psychologists such as Piaget and Kohlberg have equated maturity with personal autonomy, and have interpreted evidence of women's concern with interdependence rather than autonomy as symptomatic of a problem in women's personal development. Gilligan takes issue with Kohlberg's six-stage model of moral development, a model which is derived from a study of 84 males over the age of 20 years. She observes that women are prominent among those groups whose moral development fails to reach the higher stages of Kohlberg's model. Many women do not even reach Kohlberg's stage four of moral reasoning, in which relationships are subordinate to rules, and certainly do not attain the lofty heights of stage six, where rules are subordinate to universal principles of justice. Gilligan argues that stage six represents a morality based on individual rights which reflects the importance of individuation in men's lives. In her study of the moral reasoning of a sample of women she commonly finds a different morality based on responsibilities which, she argues, reflects the greater importance of relationships in women's lives. The two moralities, one universalistic, the other particularistic, are, she argues, the product of two different modes of reasoning:

> When one begins with a study of women and derives developmental constructs from their lives, the outline of a moral conception different from that described by Freud, Piaget or Kohlberg begins to emerge and informs a different description of development in this conception: the moral problem arises from conflicting responsibilities rather than competing rights and requires for its resolution a mode of thinking that is contextual and narrative rather than formal and abstract (Gilligan, 1982, p. 1).

Gilligan's work is, therefore, a contribution to the construction of a distinctive 'feminine developmental route' which arguably more accurately reflects women's experience of the world. Gilligan draws, in part, on a feminist reading of object-relations theory (in the work of Nancy Chodorow, 1978) to explain the two distinct feminine and masculine conceptions of self which appear to be connected to the two different modes of moral reasoning.

Jan Harding also wishes to explain gender differences in cognitive style by drawing on the body of psychoanalytic theory known as object-relations theory (Harding, 1986b). She returns to the work of one of the originators, Winnicott, which is a prescriptive version of object-relations theory. She appears to accept quite uncritically Winnicott's model of infant development and the requirements this places on the caretaker (the mother). Harding is concerned with the differential consequences of this caretaking environment for male and female infants who receive different patterns of nurturing. The differing affective traits of males and females are explained by Winnicott's model, and Harding's reading of this model extends its explanatory power to include differences in cognitive processes.

Harding selects from Winnicott the following account of male and female development. According to Winnicott, in the process of individuation the infant relates to the world through objects, that is, 'objects which are representations created by the individual of people, things and institutions' (Harding, 1984, p. 10). Winnicott prescribes the developmental tasks faced by the infant and describes two distinct ways the caretaking environment may fail the infant, depending on whether the infant is male or female. The two developmental tasks facing the infant involve separation from the caretaking environment to become an autonomous individual, and the acquisition of the capacity to relate interdependently with the objects in the individual's world. The different nurturing experiences male and female infants receive from the mother may deprive boys of experiences facilitating the capacity for concern, while girls may be deprived of experiences facilitating a sense of control and a feeling of reality. For boys, adaptive care may be withdrawn too soon, resulting in a separation anxiety with the infant, 'seeking in other objects certain reliable aspects, abstracting these and relating to them internally by possessing and controlling them' (Harding, 1984, p. 10). Infants who suffer from this separation anxiety find emotional giving very difficult, and indeed Harding interrupts her account of object-relations theory to suggest that these infants may develop the personality characteristics which Head found to be common among adolescent boys who were attracted to science.

Winnicott suggests that the caretaking environment may fail female infants when the protective function persists long after the child is able to take over this adaptive function. A capacity for concern develops in the infant but at the same time a merging anxiety may develop and the child may experience frustration and even hatred for the mother. These experiences may lead to an 'intolerable ambivalence' and 'suppression of the desire to separate and dependency persist with a tendency to conform and "fit in" (Harding, 1984, p. 10). Harding observes that these latter are personality traits more commonly found among girls.

Harding finds in Winnicott's theory an explanation for the differing values and responses which are displayed among male and female adolescents who choose to study science. In extending the theory to account for male/female differences in cognitive processes she argues that infants who are deprived too early of adaptive care (and who will most probably be males) are likely to look for certainty and the suppression of ambiguity and consequently to prefer a 'view of the world which is logically simple and unproblematic' and to ignore peripheral implications. The preference for knowledge which is produced by a process of abstraction and control and a tendency to make contributions to discussion in the form of separate personal statements are, Harding observes, a further consequence of the early nurturing experience which Winnicott describes. For those infants (who will most probably be female) whose desire to separate from the mother is thwarted, Harding argues, external objects will be valued for their externality and the boundaries between the self and the world will not be clearly delineated. Harding quotes Chodorow's distinction between a masculine and a feminine sense of self: 'the basic feminine sense of self is connected to the world, the basic masculine sense of self is separate' (Harding, 1984, p. 11). Harding extrapolates from this a cognitive style in which females draw on a multiplicity of signals from the world (intuition). In discussion, females test what they hear against what they know before they assess whether they have a contribution to make which will be further discussed.

Harding constructs from object-relations theory an explanation of the ways in which women are separated from science and technology, not only by values and emotional responses but also by cognitive style. Science is presented in its rhetoric and teaching, learning and assessment practices in ways which connect with a set of values, emotional responses and cognitive styles, which, Harding argues, along with Evelyn Fox Keller (1983), have their origins in the early nurturing experiences of male infants.

Evelyn Fox Keller's and Carol Gilligan's use of object-relations theory is more developed than is Harding's. Keller, in accounting for the masculine nature of science, emphasizes that she is talking about 'a system of beliefs about the meaning of masculine and feminine rather than any either intrinsic or actual differences between male and female' (Keller, 1985, p. 87). Gilligan, in arguing for the existence of two different modes of moral reasoning, points out in the introduction to her work that these two modes are characterized not by gender but by theme — and that she is not representing a generalization about either sex, as within each sex there is an interplay between the two modes of moral reasoning. However, despite Keller's and Gilligan's disclaimers that they are not talking about actual differences between males and females, their work as well as Harding's is open to an essentialist reading.

The evidence of the research on gender difference has been contested on a number of grounds, especially methodological. For example, sample size and social representativeness are common areas of criticism. In the case of Gilligan, her failure to give a breakdown of her sample on the basis of class, religion and ethnicity has been particularly criticized. One critic has argued that a contextual and particularistic morality might not be confined to women, but as the product of the material conditions of subordination might also be found among black, working-class and other minority groups (Tronto, 1985; Auerbach, 1987). Valerie Walkerdine argues that even in studies which claim 'scientifically' sound methodologies, the findings of statistically significant differences are not self-evident but as much a matter of interpretation as explaining the differences (Walkerdine, 1986). However, it is on one of the effects of the gender differences research and the explanations of those differences that I shall focus my criticism — the effect of naturalizing and essentializing differences between males and females.

Sexual difference is the central focus of object-relations theory, whether the theory takes the form of Winnicott's prescriptive model or the feminist models of Chodorow, Gilligan and Keller. Sexual difference in these theories has a tendency to become cast into a fixed reality which can be interpreted as essentialist. Although Harding and the feminist object-relations theorists do not assume a timeless female essence which is biologically based, but represent the differences between men and women as historically defined, nevertheless, their work can be read as having an essentialist perspective. Michele Barrett sees a lingering essentialism in all feminist writings which make:

> . . . assumptions about women's language, culture and personality that rest on psychic, social and cultural 'separate spheres' for men and women. The essentialism at stake here is an assumed or argued difference between women and men that is held to have very wide repercussions in society generally (Barrett, 1987, p. 31).

In Winnicott's theory (or rather, Harding's reading of it), the acquisition of two opposed gender identities, archetypally masculine and feminine, is presented as the product of failures on the part of the caretaking environment towards the male or female infant. However, these experiences of failure by the caretaker (the mother) towards the infant are not presented simply as aberrations but as the general tendencies resulting from differential nurturing patterns for male and female infants which produce the basic feminine and masculine senses of self.

Harding sees in these two dichotomous concepts of self the origins of two separate spheres of male and female culture. Object-relations theory describes the emotional development of the infant along gender-specific paths and Harding, following Keller and Gilligan, wants to connect this emotional development path to two distinct sets of cognitive processes.

As a result of her reading of Lacan in conjunction with a theory of signification, Jacqueline Rose (1986) argues that psychoanalytic theory is about problematizing sexual difference rather than explaining it, as the object-relations theorists have done. For Rose, a psychoanalytic account represents the acquisition of a feminine identity as a difficult process and one in which femininity is never fully attainable. A similar line of argument is developed by Henriques *et al.* 1984) which attempts to theorize subjectivity by drawing on the work of Foucault and a reworking of Lacan and theories of signification. In both instances, the categories of men and women are deconstructed. However, it is these categories which the object relations theorists do not appear to question. They assume a pre-given unitary subject (a basic sense of self), whereas the theorizing of subjectivity of Henriques *et al.* is an attempt to break with the individual/society dualism and to conceptualize subjectivities as socially constructed; that is, individuals are socially positioned in multiple and contradictory discourses and as a result their subjectivities are multiple and contradictory. The acquisition of gendered identities becomes, on this theoretical terrain, a more fluid, shifting and contradictory process. Discourses (regulated systems of statements characterized as common sense or knowledge) inscribed in social practices position individuals as subjects in shifting power relations of domination and subordination. Such a perspective makes possible the exploration of historical and cultural 'differences within the specific social existences of women' (Barrett, 1987, p. 31). Such differences between women are completely obscured by the work of object-relations theorists.

As we have seen, feminist readings of object-relations theory have been, in part, a critical response to developmental models of psychology. The critique of these developmental models is that they are models derived from the experience of specific groups of males and do not adequately fit the experience of specific groups of women. Harding, Head and Gilligan have read the research on gender differences as evidence that the experiences of many women do not conform to the behavioural ideals of a good learner or a mature adult, norms according to which an individual's cognitive ability and maturity are judged. They propose an alternative developmental path which is taken predominantly by females who acquire a distinct set of values and modes of cognitive and moral reasoning which are not reflected in the developmental literature. In proposing a distinct developmental path for girls, Harding, Head and Gilligan do not question the project of prescribing a universal account of how girls learn or make moral judgments.

The work of Walkerdine and Venn (both contributors to Henriques *et al.*, 1984) is able to indicate the limits of constructing a female developmental path on terrain which uncritically shares many of the taken-for-granted assumptions of developmental psychology. Walkerdine and Venn regard theories of psychology as involved in the production and constitution of subjectivity and in the regulation and administration of social life. Piaget's theories of cognitive development can be understood as productive of normalizing practices such as child rearing and schooling and of child-centred pedagogic discourses. The object of these practices and discourses, the child, is, in effect, produced by developmental psychology as a normal subject; consequently, as Walkerdine has argued, what it means to learn is, in a sense, also produced by developmental psychology. Psychology in its status as a science creates the apparatuses for producing a regime of truth about learning. Psychology produces the evidence about learning and produces children as learners — naturalizing the sequential development of what are assumed to be the pre-given capacities of the child.

From the perspective of Henriques *et al.*, a feminist project to replace the models of Piaget and Kohlberg with 'less distorted' constructs derived from, in the words of Gilligan, 'a study of women's lives' is engaged in producing evidence about how girls learn or make moral judgments, and a new regime of truth is produced which might have as one of its effects the naturalizing and essentializing of the capacities of boys and girls.

The research findings on gender differences informed by readings of object-relations theory have been formative among feminist educators in constituting truths about how girls learn and about which forms of assessment favour girls' cognitive style. However, the limits of these claims to truth about girls, in naturalizing and essentializing the categories of males and females, might also place limits on the success of feminist strategies aimed at enhancing the success of girls. For example, the claim that girls prefer school-based assessment (drawing on Victorian High School Certificate enrolment patterns in school-assessed courses) has been constituted as evidence that school-based assessment always, and across all subject areas, operates more in the interest of girls (McKay, 1986). Two English research studies, which move away from a focus on gender differences among students to examine the teacher's role in assessment, suggest that the operation of school-based assessment is an area for more extensive research. I shall discuss these further in the following section. Suffice it to say here that these studies suggest some new understanding about assessment and the learning of girls precisely because they move away from a focus on gender differences to an examination of the ways in which teaching and learning practices in specific classrooms produce a pattern of gendered attainment.

Classroom Practices and the 'Production of Gendered Attainment': An Alternative Approach to Understanding Assessment and the Learning of Girls

Margaret Goddard Spear has conducted a major study of science teachers' assessment of students' work and personal characteristics (Spear, 1986). In a preliminary study, Spear reports on a marking exercise in which science teachers gave lower marks to girls' work than to boys' work. In the follow-up larger study, 306 science teachers from a range of 86 schools in Britain assessed six pieces of work in the form of two samples from each of three 12-year-old pupils. The first sample was a practical report of an experiment on distillation, and the second was an essay entitled 'What I think about science and scientists'. The samples were presented to one-half of the teachers as the work of a girl and to the other half of the teachers as the work of a boy. The teachers were instructed to assess the work by grading it and to say what criteria they were taking into account in their assessment. In addition, they were required to assess the pupil's aptitude for science, attitude towards science, interest in science and suitability for 'O' level and CSE physical science courses. The results of this study found that

> . . . regardless of the standard of the work, the teachers generally rated the work and personal attributes of boys more highly than those of girls. The only work characteristic on which girls tended to be favoured was the amount of effort which had been expended in producing the work (Spear, 1986, p. 33).

The sex of the teacher also appeared to have an effect upon the marks awarded: female teachers gave higher marks than the male teachers in 31 of the 45 comparisons. Spear commented on the consequences of this finding for the success of girls in science:

> the combination of a boy's work marked by a female teacher was most likely to produce a generous assessment, whereas girls' work marked by a male teacher was most likely to produce a severe assessment. The outcome of the latter combination of pupil sex and teacher sex gives grave cause for concern, as it suggests that girls could be discouraged from studying science and could be at a disadvantage when they do so. The fact that the majority of physics teachers are male exacerbates the problem (Spear, 1986, p. 38).

Spear concluded that the results of the study pointed to the possibility that boys' superior achievement in science might be 'maintained by the biased expectations, perceptions and judgments of teachers'. The significance of Spear's study lies in the move away from a focus on differences between male and female students to an examination of the role of the teacher in the learning process. A certain line of inquiry is suggested by Spear's work: an exploration of the ways in which classroom practices might produce gendered attainment. Walden and Walkerdine's *Girls and Mathematics: From Primary to Secondary Schooling* (1985) adopts such a perspective. Spear interprets her research within the framework of teacher expectation studies: teachers' 'distorted' and 'biased' perceptions of males and females result in teachers' differential expectations and treatment of male and female students. Walden and Walkerdine, in their examination of the social relations of specific mathematics classrooms, reject the notion of distorted or biased perceptions on the part of teachers. Teachers, in their analysis, make judgments about their students' behaviour on the basis of discourses or understandings available to them about masculinity and femininity and, in the case of mathematics, theories of cognitive development.

The initial problem which Walden and Walkerdine's research addressed is the apparent gap between girls' good performance in mathematics at age 11 and their failure relative to boys to perform well in 'O' level maths at age 16. The qualitative data of the study consists of case studies of teachers and students in the last year of primary school and the first and fourth years of secondary schooling (fourth year was the time when students were selected for entry to 'O' levels or the CSE). What is at issue in the analysis of the case studies is the basis on which teachers' judgments of student performances in maths are made. Walden and Walkerdine question the theories of cognitive development which produce the categories through which student performance in maths is evaluated. They conceptualize these theories as knowledge which is productive; having power in the sense that they produce 'real effects' in determining the life chances of individuals through the claims of these theories to be telling the 'truth' about student maths attainment.

In the teaching of the 'new maths', success is understood not in terms of rote learning but of individual discovery and understanding of mathematical concepts. Walden and Walkerdine argue that on the basis of understanding about how children acquire mathematical concepts (from theories of cognitive development) teachers interpret certain attributes which students display in the classroom as evidence that *real* understanding has occurred. The challenging of mathematical rules, flair, activity, divergence, confidence and articulateness are read by teachers as evidence that proper learning has occurred. These attributes of the successful learner are also attributes which are associated with masculinity. Displays of what is commonly understood as female behaviour are 'pejoratively' evaluated by teachers as a lack of *real* understanding. Walden and Walkerdine observe that the female students in their study were engaged in a struggle to attain femininity and, therefore, were more likely to display behaviour which is regarded as typically feminine, such as being responsible and hardworking, passive and rule-following. Teachers judged students displaying such feminine attributes as lacking the flair and confidence of a successful learner, and were inclined not to push these students. In the fourth year, teachers wished to protect the students who lacked the confidence from the stress of the top 'O' level stream (which was externally assessed) by placing them in the (less prestigious) school-assessed CSE stream in a special maths programme which allowed students to go at their own pace. Walden and Walkerdine do not wish to suggest that the attainment of femininity and academic success are mutually opposed, as does research in the tradition of Horner's 'fear of success' model, but that 'Femininity is not antithetical to success, though what is understood as feminine behaviour is also understood as antithetical to "real learning"' (Walden and Walkerdine, 1985, p. 81).

Walden and Walkerdine conceptualize the social relations of classrooms as relations of domination/subordination and of power/resistance and argue that classroom practices position girls in both powerful and powerless positions. In primary classes, for example, girls can become powerful by being positioned as a sub-teacher. Teachers in primary schools are predominantly female and girls are able to share the teacher's authority by being feminine (that is to say, helping and responsible) and clever at the same time; however, at the same time girls can be powerless in relation to the teacher's judgment of their performance in maths. Walden and Walkerdine do not understand boys and girls as 'unitary and distinct categories' but, rather, conceive of boys and girls as subjects having both masculine and female positionings available to them, and therefore 'Girls can occupy positions which are related to masculinity, for example, challenging the procedural rules of mathematics. Yet such positions are never unambiguous nor gender neutral because of the effects of other positionings on the girls in question' (Walden and Walkerdine, 1985, p. 102). Walden and Walkerdine suggest that the phenomenon which their research initially set out to explain (that is, girls' relatively poor performance compared to boys at 'O' level maths) is the product of specific classroom practices. The quantitative data of their study in the form of the results of maths tests on students in their sample demonstrates that girls are still performing successfully even in the fourth year of secondary school. Walden and Walkerdine found very few statistically significant differences between the results of boys and girls in their data, and these differences were not as large as the differences in test results between schools and tutor sets. They conclude from this finding that 'the social relations, teaching and learning in *specific* classrooms are of considerable importance in accounting for test attainment' (Walden and Walkerdine, 1985, p. 46).

Walden and Walkerdine's study is very suggestive for feminist educational practice, and in a concluding section the authors point to a number of the implications for practice which their research raises. I wish to note the aspect of their discussion which relates specifically to assessment. Spear and Walden and Walkerdine come to similar conclusions about the power of teachers' assessments of students in producing gendered attainment. Walden and Walkerdine observe that 'Our analysis certainly suggests that in the current system the power and effect of teacher evaluation and judgment of pupil suitability and performance is immense' (Walden and Walkerdine, 1985, p. 108). The authors support the replacement of the English two-tiered examination structure of 'O' levels and the CSE with a common certificate: a reform which has now taken place and which will stop the channelling of girls into the less prestigious CSE maths stream. However, they are not so sure that increased school autonomy in assessment accompanying the common certificate is in the interest of girls: their study suggests that such a move 'would not increase girls' chances of success, despite the best intentions of teachers to promote the welfare of their less confident pupils' (Walden and Walkerdine, 1985, p. 108).

Conclusion

Walden and Walkerdine (1985) provide a theoretical framework which might produce new interpretations of the gender-difference research reviewed in the first part of this paper. In one study of gender differences in performance on multiple-choice questions, Jan Harding was unable to explain why a sub-group of girls did not fit the general pattern of girls not performing as well as boys on multiple-choice questions: the girls who performed well on multiple-choice questions were girls in mixed-sex schools doing Nuffield Chemistry and girls doing Nuffield Physics (Harding, 1985, p. 32). Walden and Walkerdine's work suggests that the specific social relations and teaching and learning practices of these Nuffield Science classrooms might have produced these girls' good performance on multiple-choice questions and that it is the specificity of their classroom practices which require further examination. The study of gender differences in student preferences for three teaching styles in the teaching of science produced the finding that the girls in the sample consistently disliked the problem-solvers' style and preferred either the informers' or enquirers' style. This finding was interpreted as further evidence that girls who choose science have a different cognitive style from boys who choose to study science. However, what was a passing observation of a commentator on this study could become a starting-point for further research: namely, that the problem-solving style was used most frequently in physical science and demanded that girls 'go public' in classes where they were a minority (Dalton, 1981). Such an observation could be interpreted as evidence that the social relations of physical science classrooms produced girls' dislike of the problem-solvers' style, and points to the need to investigate the ways in which specific classrooms position girls in more powerful positions than other classrooms.

Spear's and Walden and Walkerdine's work is suggestive of many new directions for research. In particular, the ways in which classrooms maintain masculine and feminine practices is a crucial area for investigation, along with analyses of the specificity of discourses or understandings available to teachers in different subject areas, understandings which produce the categories according to which a student's learning is evaluated. More research needs to be undertaken of science and maths classrooms and their role in the exclusion of girls from maths and science.

However, what is also required, given the enormous power of classroom practices to discourage or enhance learning in students, are analyses of class-room practices in subject areas where girls consistently perform well. Such analyses would provide us with new insights into the ways in which the specific social relations and teaching, learning and assessment practices can positively produce successful learning for girls.

References

ADAMS, R.J. (1984) *Sex Bias in ASAT?*, Australian Council for Educational Research Monograph No. 24.

ARZI, H.J. (1986) 'Gender differences in science achievement: A matter of knowledge or confidence?', Paper presented at National Association for Research in Science Teaching, San Francisco, March 28–31.

AUERBACH, J. *et al.* (1987) 'On Gilligan's "In a different voice"', *Feminist Studies*, 11, 1.

BARRETT, M. (1987) 'The concept of "difference"', *Feminist Review*, 26 July.

CHODOROW, N. (1978) *The Reproduction of Mothering*, Berkeley, University of California Press.

DALEY, D.J. (1986) *Different Sex Differences from Different Modes of Assessment: Common Experiences in Three Countries*, Canberra, Dept of Statistics, Institute of Advanced Studies, Australian National University.

DALTON, M. (1981) 'Differential treatment of boy and girl pupils during science lessons', in KELLY, A. (Ed.) *The Missing Half: Girls and Science Education*, Manchester, Manchester University Press.

GILLIGAN, C. (1982) *In a Different Voice: A Study of Women's Construction and Resolution of Moral Problems*, Cambridge, MA., Harvard University Press.

GRANT, M. (1982) 'Prized projects', *Studies in Design Education, Craft and Technology*, 15, 1.

HARDING, J. (1984) *Values, Cognitive Style and the Curriculum*, Girls and Science and Technology Conference (GASAT) 3, England, April 13–18

HARDING, J. (1985) *Switched Off: The Science Education of Girls*, London, Longmans.

HARDING, J. (1986a) 'Increasing the access of girls to science and technology', Report of Seminar at the Victorian Insitute of Secondary Education.

HARDING, J. (1986b) 'Girls and science seminar', Transcript, Melbourne, Age Education Unit.

HARDING, J. and RANDALL, G. (1983) 'Why classroom interaction studies?' Paper, GASAT 2, Norway, September 5–10, in *Contributions to the Second GSAT Conference*, Institute of Physics, University of Oslo.

HEAD, J. (1983) 'Sex differences in adolescent personality development and the implications for science education', Paper, GASAT 2, Norway, September 5–10, in *Contributions to the Second GSAT Conference*, Institute of Physics, University of Oslo.

HENRIQUES, J., HOLLWAY, W., URWIN, C., VENN, C. and WALKERDINE, V. (1984) *Changing the Subject*, London, Methuen.

HUDSON, L. (1968) *Contrary Imaginations*, London, Methuen.

HUDSON, L. (1966) *Frames of Mind*, London, Methuen.

KELLER, E.F. (1983) 'Women, science and popular mythology', in ROTHCHILD, J. (Ed.) *Machina ex Dea*, New York, Pergamon Press.

KELLER, E.F. (1985) *Reflections on Gender and Science*, New Haven, CT., Yale University Press.

MCKAY, L. (1986) 'A preliminary analysis of final enrolments in the 1985 High School Certificate Assessment Program', *Victorian Insitute of Secondary Education (VISE) Council Notes*, Melbourne.

MAKING ADMISSION TO HIGHER EDUCATION FAIRER (1986) Report of the Committee for the Review of Tertiary Entrance Score Calculations in the Australian Capital Territory, Canberra.

MASTERS, G.N. and BESWICK, G.D. (1986) *The Construction of Tertiary Entrance Scores: Principles and Issues*, Melbourne, Centre for the Study of Higher Education, University of Melbourne.

ORMEROD, M.B. (1971) 'The social implications factor in attitudes to science', *British Journal of Educational Psychology*, 41, 3.

ROSE, J. (1986) *Sexuality in the Field of Vision*, London, Verso.

SPEAR, M.G. (1986) 'Sex bias in science teachers' ratings of work and pupil characteristics', Paper, GSAT 5 Conference, Israel.

TRONTO, J.C. (1985) 'Beyond gender difference to a theory of care', *Signs*, Summer.

UNIVERSITY OF LONDON SCHOOLS EXAMINATION BOARD (1985) *Sexism, Discrimination and Gender Biases in GCE Examinations*, March.

VENN, C. (1984) 'The subject of psychology', in HENRIQUES, J. *et al.* (Eds) *Changing the Subject*, London, Methuen.

WALDEN, R. and WALKERDINE, V. (1985) *Girls and Mathematics: From Primary to Secondary Schooling*, London, University of London Institute of Education.

WALKERDINE, V. (1986) 'Some issues in the historical construction of the scientific truth about girls', Paper, GSAT 5, Conference, Israel.

WALKERDINE, V. (1984) 'Developmental psychology and the child-centred pedagogy: The insertion of Piaget into early education', in HENRIQUES, J. *et al.* (Eds) *Changing the Subject*, London, Methuen.

Chapter 7

Ethical Practice in an Unjust World: Educational Evaluation and Social Justice

Gaby Weiner

Background

This paper is a response to the question asked of me recently: 'Is there such a thing as feminist evaluation?' As an educational researcher in the late 1970s and early 1980s, I had begun to argue that gender issues — not at that time feminist issues — should be addressed by educational researchers. I was accused then of being a 'conviction' researcher and of allowing my politics to intrude into the process of neutral enquiry which should be the main goal of all educational researchers. Times and understanding about the research process have, thankfully, moved on since then, but the memories linger on. However, this question revived my anger at having been thus accused. So I decided to explore further, and presented my findings as a preliminary paper for a small seminar. I realized there, however, that I could not just address gender issues in my presentation. The small number of black participants at the seminar served to remind me that educational and work experiences were shaped as much, if not more, by colour than by class or sex.[1] This paper, then, is a revised (and retitled) version of the conference paper.

Social Justice and Educational Evaluation

Why the concern now about evaluation? In fact, educational evaluation has been an issue for teachers and other educational personnel for some time; since the well-publicized curriculum evaluations of the larger Schools Council projects in the late 1960s and early 1970s (Tawney, 1976). However, evaluation has moved up the educational agenda in recent years, accompanying shifts in state policy towards technocratized perceptions of curriculum development and pedagogy. As a consequence, more people are doing educational evaluation than ever before, whether as formal evaluators, for instance in the context of government programmes such as Technical, Vocational and Educational Initiative (TVEI) in England, or more informally, as teachers contributing to the development of new educational initiatives at school or local authority levels.

However, as Bates (1988) points out, evaluation involves bringing together knowledge and power in quite specific ways, and it is this complex relationship which provides the basis for this paper. It has proved particularly important to those with an explicit commitment to achieving increased social justice within the context of education. How might the ethical principles which inform the practice of anti-racists or feminists[2] in their workplaces inform their approaches to evaluation? Is there such a thing as social justice evaluation?

This paper provides a preliminary discussion of these issues and is divided into four parts. First, it (briefly) provides a critical appraisal of what might be described as the white, male milieu of educational evaluation in Britain and the United States. Second, more importantly, it discusses education theories which offer challenges to conventional perceptions about educational research and evaluation. Third, it attempts to outline principles and procedures for educational evaluators who see the reduction of social and educational inequalities as one of their main professional goals. The fourth section considers the strategies currently available to educational evaluators (for example, within TVEI) or in equal opportunities programmes or educational policy initiatives. The paper concludes with the suggestion that in certain cases, particularly where programmes include equal opportunities dimensions, 'social justice' evaluation may well be both desirable and feasible.

Education Evaluation: A White, Male Milieu?

Before looking briefly at the ethos of educational evaluation, I first wish to introduce a quote from an American historian, J.H. Hexter. He was attempting to defend conventional history against the criticisms of feminist historians who argued that women had been rendered invisible by the writers of history:

> Do not blame male historians for the omission of women. We know who was behind those trends and developments and movements. For better or for worse it was men. On occasions in which they happened to find women they usually noticed the exception; but through no conspiracy on the part of historians, the College of Cardinals, the Parliament of England, the expeditions of Columbus, Vasco de Gama, and Drake must have been pretty much stag affairs (Hexter, 1946).

Historians today will, of course, recognize that if a different perspective of history is taken to that of Hexter — if, for instance, they investigate struggles for political emancipation, historical changes in family life, social and economic history; or working-class women or girls' education or the development of black communities — then women and other hitherto invisible groups will emerge as important historical actors (Arnot, 1986). History is shaped by the subjects, events and interpretations that historians take to be important. The same might be said of educational evaluation and evaluators; educational evaluation is shaped by the subjects, events and interpretations that evaluators, and perhaps their sponsors, take to be important.

Further, it could be argued that, in England, the United States and Australia, educational evaluation is also pretty much a 'stag' affair. It seems to be done mainly *by* white middle-class men, *on* all kinds of educational groupings, *for* white, middle-class men. Certainly, in my view, a specific culture of educational evaluation has emerged, particularly in the context of the Centre for Applied Research in Education (CARE) at the University of East Anglia in Norwich. Its main features can be characterized as follows: high profile, intellectually adroit, street-wise, pragmatically and policy orientated, upwardly mobile, transatlantic, committed to political neutrality and freedom from bias, male and white. A culture, moreover, which is highly exclusive and which has displayed little sympathy with educational theories which address gender or 'race' issues.

What aspects of educational evaluation have attracted most attention? Most of the early debates in Britain challenged the behavioural objectives approach which had been adopted widely by evaluators in the United States. Key features of the discussion were concerned with the methodology and technology of evaluation (quantitative versus qualitative, technocratic versus illuminative), relations between evaluators and sponsors, clients, and the community, and also the ethics and politics of evaluation. These issues have also been of considerable concern to feminist researchers, as I shall show later. Evaluators have also been seen as political actors but not, unfortunately, in relation to oppressed groups or in relation to the power of the state.

MacDonald (1976), for example, argued that evaluators not only live in the real world of educational politics but they actually influence its changing power relationships. He described three distinct types of evaluation study: bureaucratic, autocratic and democratic. Bureaucratic evaluation 'is an unconditional service to those government agencies which have major control over the allocation of educational resources. The evaluator accepts the values of those that hold office'. Autocratic evaluation 'is a conditional service to those government agencies which have major control over the allocation of educational resources. . . . Its values are derived from the evaluator's perception of the constitutional and moral obligation of the bureaucracy'. Democratic evaluation 'is an information service to the whole community about the characteristics of an education programme' (quoted in Bates, 1988, pp. 67–8).

Accordingly, the responsibility of the democratic evaluator, MacDonald's preferred type, is to adopt a neutral judgemental stance in informing various groups about the worth of something.

> In a pluralist society, *he* [the evaluator] has right to use *his* position to promote personal values, or to choose which particular ideologies *he* shall regard as legitimate. *His* job is to identify those who will have to make judgements and decisions about the programme, and to lay before them those facts of the case that are recognized by them as relevant to their concerns (MacDonald, 1975, my emphasis).

There have been criticisms by other evaluators of MacDonald's position. For instance, Elliott (1986) argues that democratic evaluation in education is a form of social criticism involving a critique of educational policies and courses of action in the light of principles of 'equal liberty' and 'fair distribution of social and economic advantages' — what he calls the principles of justice. According to Elliott, the democratic evaluator cannot be neutral. His (*sic*) responsibility is to the general public and not to a plurality of audiences. Promising though it is, Elliott's argument only goes as far as discussing such aspects of evaluation as 'right to know', confidentiality and audience.

MacDonald nevertheless allows that values are increasingly entering into the considerations of evaluators as the boundaries between social and educational programmes become blurred, and that some of these values might be incorporated into his notion of democratic evaluation. In fact, as Codd (1981) points out, evaluation would have little point if it were not related to questions that arise within a particular social context:

> ... evaluation is not a neutral enterprise. Depending on the context, it will focus on some aspects of a situation to the exclusion of others, *it will serve some people's interests rather than others*. As with any form of research activity, evaluation must always operate within specific political and community frameworks. These provide a social context without which the activity itself would have little point (Codd, 1981, p. 8, my emphasis).

This particular position is a little more helpful to those wishing to address social justice issues within the educational evaluation context. What, it seems, we must do is frame each evaluation in the interests of social justice. It is with this in mind that I now want to explore how social justice concerns might be incorporated into the practice of evaluation and also the educational theories that might inform this project.

Educational Theories and Social Justice

I should like to consider here two sets of theories: critical theory which emerged in particular from the Frankfurt School, and theories concerned with research on social justice issues. First I want to use *critical theory* to illuminate the gaps in current thinking about educational evaluation. Briefly, critical theory emerged as a challenge to the emphasis on scientific rationalism in academic discourse and research. It offers a justification for 'deliberative' (or 'conviction') research, that is, research designed to generate changes in social and economic relations. It is not aimed at uncovering irrefutable 'truths' about human relations. Lather (1986) argues that we have now moved into a post-positivist era, in which there has been a 'decline of the absolutes' (Lecourt, 1975):

> Broadly speaking, post-positivism is characterized by the methodological and epistemological refutation of positivism ... much talk of paradigm shifts ... and by increased visibility of research designs that are interactive, contextualized, and humanly compelling because they invite joint participation in the exploration of research issues.... Post-positivism is marked by approaches to enquiry which recognize that knowledge is 'socially constituted, historically embedded and valuationally based' (Lather, 1986, p. 295).

Fundamental to critical theory is the production of emancipatory knowledge (through empirical research or 'critical enquiry') which increases awareness of the contradiction hidden or distorted by everyday understandings (Carr and Kemmis,

1983). In undertaking critical enquiry and reflection, people will become aware of the possibilities for social transformation available to them and develop a discourse of, and strategies for, emancipation. Put another way, taken-for-granted assumptions about research and knowledge need to be subjected to scrutiny and understood in relation to historical and philosophical enquiry and context. According to Giroux (1983), critical theory has laid the foundation for a dialectical framework by which institutions and activities of everyday life and the greater social and historical totality can be understood in relationship to each other.

Further, according to Lather (1986), for 'praxis' (practice informed by theory) to be possible, theory must illuminate the lived experience of progressive social groups and be illuminated by their struggles. For educationists, critical theory offers a framework for analysis of existing assumptions about education. It can also provide the theoretical basis for the development of a more enlightened view of knowledge that is concerned with the emancipation of subordinated groups, and for the creation of new pedagogical forms.

Lather likens the search for ways to establish critical enquiry to a journey into uncharted territory. In a useful, though sometimes awkwardly written and somewhat patronizing, article 'Research as Praxis' (1986), she suggests five criteria for critical enquiry. First, that critical enquiry is a response to the experiences, desires and needs of oppressed people; second, that it inspires and guides the dispossessed in the process of cultural transformation; third, that it focuses on the contradictions which helped the dispossessed to see how poorly their 'ideologically frozen understandings' (Comstock, 1982, p. 384) serve their interests; fourth, the validity of a critical account can be found, in part, in the participant's responses; and lastly, critical enquiry stimulates a process of critical analysis and enlightened action. The problem is now, of course, how to translate these high-flown ideals into feasible practice. *Can* critical enquiry be applied to educational evaluation? As far as I can ascertain, educational evaluators have not yet attempted to redefine their roles in terms of applying critical theory to existing education paradigms. Perhaps, they might argue, that is not their job. But evaluators concerned with challenging the sexual and racial injustices of the schooling system are obliged to do just that.

In attempting to formulate research and evaluation practice that incorporates critical and social justice perspectives, the following principles might provide a useful start:

1 Exploring gender, racial and other social divisions should be central to social science and educational research.
2 Social justice research should be concerned with addressing inequalities generally.
3 The experiences and lives of black communities as well as girls and women should be made more visible in research.
4 Social justice research need not necessarily focus on black communities and/or girls and women but should illuminate their lives and experiences.
5 New interactive methodologies need to be considered. Methods associated with conventional research, such as quantitative, scientific, positivist methods, may be inappropriate for those concerned with social justice issues.

Additional ethical considerations to those raised by MacDonald emerge in the creation of a social justice perspective on research and evaluation. As always, questions about objectivity and validity emerge. For example, how can feminists and anti-racist researchers reconcile their partisanship with objectivity? What role (if any) should white (and/or male) researchers play in anti-racist (and/or feminist) research? What role should research play in promoting equality in educational access, treatment and outcome? To what extent should the educational research act itself actively challenge common-sense racist and sexist beliefs and perceptions? Can anti-racist and/or feminist principles be reconciled with the need for external sponsorship or funding? What steps can be taken to restore the balance *and* facilitate reciprocity in the conventionally unequal relationship between the researcher and the researched? (adapted from Troyna and Carrington, 1989). Feminist researchers have already begun to confront these issues (see, for example, Bowles and Duelli Klein, 1983; Stanley and Wise, 1983). In my view these questions are also applicable to educational evaluators with a commitment to social justice, and they need exploring more fully.

It seems possible, therefore, to envisage the establishment of principles for a social justice perspective which will offer the means by which teachers, researchers and evaluators can re-create their practice. I should now like to consider what social justice evaluation might look like.

Social Justice Evaluation

In the literature, I have come across several examples of evaluation specifically orientated towards social justice. As a feminist evaluator of the Open University Women's Studies Course *The Changing Experience of Women*, Gill Kirkup (1986) drew on Habermas to argue that (i) social enquiry cannot use the same methods as inquiry into the natural sciences, (ii) social action depends on the individual's understanding of her situation, the understanding and reflection of which is not idiosyncratic but is based on the social context in which she operates, and (iii) the purpose of pursuing knowledge is to emancipate.

Adopting these principles did not prevent her from incorporating quite conventional aims for her evaluation: for example, student satisfaction with the course, effectiveness of course materials, examining the impact of distance teaching on the success of the course. However, the political nature of the course she was evaluating and her intention to provide other women's studies course evaluators with appropriate evaluation skills clearly indicated a feminist dimension to the evaluation. She used a 'flexible' Illuminative Evaluation model (using a wide variety of methods of data collection), and claimed to achieve her evaluation targets. Yet she reported problems with identifying who the clients of the evaluation were — the university or the students — and concerns about lack of involvement of the students/respondents in the evaluation.

Another evaluator of a women's studies programme, this time in the United States, reported additional difficulties in combining her duties as both autonomous outsider and participant evaluator of a project whose aims she was clearly committed to. Unable to sustain both roles, she opted for participation rather than independence (Shapiro, 1988).

What, then, might a social justice evaluation look like? Can social justice evaluation be said to occur when some or all of the following occur:

(a) The programme which is being evaluated is grounded in values of equality and liberation.

(b) The evaluation is informed by critical and other theories and assumptions about the reasons and explanations for the subordination of, for instance, women and black people.

(c) The evaluation methodologies used are designed to illuminate the impact of the programme on under-represented or subordinated groups of students, teachers, administrators, and so on.

(d) One of the stated purposes of the evaluation is to further emancipation and equality of subordinated groups.

(e) The evaluator has a commitment to the values of the programme, and to its improvement.

Concerns about sponsor, client, method of reporting, right to know, confidentiality, and the like will all still be important but will be discussed in the light of the five main criteria for social justice evaluation that I have just outlined.

Where Do We Go from Here?:
Social Justice Evaluation for the 1990s

This is all very well, you might say, but what about the possibilities of social justice living as we do with the inheritance of Thatcher's anti-egalitarian Britain? Even in the more progressive 1960s and 1970s, curriculum planners and educational researchers tended to be white males, pressing their views upon their predominantly female target audience of teachers — both Apple (1986) and Goodman and Kelly (1988) report this. What possibilities are currently open to evaluators? In my view there are two defensible positions: evaluators of social justice programmes, and conventional evaluations undertaken by evaluators with social justice perspectives and commitments.

Evaluators of Social Justice Programmes

If they are fortunate enough to be admitted to the frame-setting discussion of a programme, as innovators as well as evaluators, they will be able to participate fully in the design of the programme, its aims and objectives, and the form the evaluation will take. Thus feminist, anti-racist and other critical theories and understandings will inform the design and the evaluation of the programme and the evaluation approach will most likely be participatory, as in the following:

> Participatory evaluation is interactive in its approach. The model contains both qualitative and quantitative methodologies and is well suited for measurements of subtle and not-so-subtle changes. Participatory evaluation allows the evaluator to function freely as a knowledgeable outsider, without having to deal with also being an impartial outsider

... the evaluator can develop a level of trust that permits the voices of the powerless to be heard (Shapiro, 1988, pp. 197–8).

However, these approaches are unlikely to be possible for most publicly sponsored projects in these times except, perhaps, in the case of TVEI, which has an equal opportunities criterion for funding (Weiner, 1989). It is likely that there will be greater possibilities for mounting social justice evaluations for equal opportunities projects and programmes at individual/institution/LEA level.

Conventional Evaluation by Evaluators with Social Justice Perspectives

They have, perhaps, some room for manoeuvre in the design and methodology of the evaluation and, informed by critical, feminist and anti-racist theory, could provide alternative reports and perspectives for alternative audiences. However, they are likely to be limited by the fact that the aims and content of a programme have already been specified. It may nevertheless be possible for them to offer a critique of the programme at particular stages in the evaluation and to raise awareness about social justice issues.

Notes

1 This paper was given at the annual conference of the British Educational Research Association, University of Newcastle upon Tyne, August 1989.
2 To clarify what I mean by feminism and anti-racism, first, there are many different perspectives on, and forms of, feminism. Most would agree, however, that women are subordinated and oppressed in relation to men, whatever their ethnic grouping, class, culture or sexuality; and that feminism has something to do with seeking to bring about changes in the social and economic position of girls and women.

References

APPLE, M. (1986) *Teachers and Texts: A Political Economy of Class and Gender Relations in Education*, London, Routledge and Kegan Paul.
ARNOT, M. (1986) *Race, Gender and Educational Policy-making*, Module 4, Open University course E333: Policy-making in Education, Milton Keynes, Open University.
BATES, R. (1988) *Evaluating Schools: A Critical Approach*, Geelong, Deakin University Press.
BOWLES, G. and DUELLI KLEIN, R. (1983) *Theories of Women's Studies*, London, Routledge and Kegan Paul.
CARR, W. and KEMMIS, S. (1983) *Becoming Critical*, Geelong, Deakin University Press.
CODD, J. (1981) 'Educational evaluation: Concept and approaches', in CODD, J. (Ed.) *Organizational Evaluation in Schools*, Geelong, Deakin University Press.
COMSTOCK, D. (1982) 'A method for critical research', in BREDO, E. and FEINBERG, W. (Eds) *Knowledge and Values in Social and Educational Research*, Philadelphia, Temple University Press.
ELLIOTT, J. (1986) 'Democratic evaluation as social criticism: Or putting the judgment

back into evaluation', in Hammersley, M. (Ed.) *Controversies in Classroom Research*, Milton Keynes, Open University Press.

Giroux, H. (1983), 'Critical theory and schooling: Implications for the development of a radical pedagogy', *Discourse*, 3, 2, pp. 1– 21.

Goodman, J. and Kelly, T. (1988) 'Out of the mainstream: Issues confronting the male profeminist elementary school teacher', *Interchange*, 19, 2, pp. 1–14.

Hexter, J.H. (1946) *New York Times book review*, 4, 73.

Kirkup, G. (1986) 'The Feminist Evaluator', in House, E. (Ed.) *New Dimensions in Educational Evaluation*, Lewes, Falmer Pres.

Lather, P. (1986) 'Research as Praxis', *Harvard Educational Review*, 56, 3, pp. 257–277.

Lecourt, D. (1975) *Marxism and Epistemology*, London, National Labour Board.

Macdonald, B. (1976) 'Evaluation and the Control of Education', in Tawney, D. (Ed.) *Curriculum Evaluation Today: Trends and Implications*, London, Macmillan.

Macdonald, B., Jenkins, D., Kemmis, S. and Tawney, D. (1975) *The Programme at Two, An Evaluation Report on the National Development Programme in Computer Assisted Learning*, Norwich, Centre for Applied Research in Education.

Shapiro, J.P. (1988) 'Participatory Evaluation: Towards a transformation of assessment for women's studies programs and projects', *Educational Evaluation and Policy Analysis*, 10, 3, pp. 191–199.

Stanley, L. and Wise, S. (1983) *Breaking Out: Feminist consciousness and feminist Research*, London, Routledge and Kegan Paul.

Tawney, D. (1976) *Curriculum Evaluation Today: Trends and Implications*, London, Macmillan.

Troyna, B. and Carrington, B. (1989) 'Whose side are we on? Ethical dilemmas in research on "race" and education', in Burgess, R. (Ed.) *The Ethics of Educational Research*, Lewes, Falmer Press.

Weiner, G. (1989) 'Feminism, Equal Opportunities and Vocationalism: the changing context', in Burchell, H. and Millman, V. (Eds) *Changing Perspectives on Gender: New Initiatives in Secondary Education*, Milton Keynes, Open University Press.

Chapter 8

Equal Opportunity, Integration and Parental Participation: A Gender-critical Case Study of Educational Policy Implementation between Two Schools

Terry Evans

People with intellectual disabilities are among the most vulnerable and marginal of all. Throughout history they have been treated appallingly, although pioneering people with care and compassion have gradually lifted the general standards of provision and contributed to increased self-determination for people with intellectual disabilities. This case study concerns the way Victorian government policy of the late 1980s on the 'integration' of children with disabilities into the school system affected the discourses between and within two school councils. It also concerns the consequences of government policy concerning the increases in school council powers — in effect, to give more local 'community' control and responsibility to the councils. Interwoven throughout, as indeed for any element of social life, is gender. This case study focuses partly on the few men who endeavoured to dissolve a Special Developmental School and immerse its people in a large primary school (Linfield).[1] Apart from the children, these people were the women or their successors, who had, over a period of 25 years, established a school for their children with intellectual disabilities in a country town in Victoria. This case study focuses partly on their resistance to their dissolution.

The present chapter stems from a larger research project into the gender processes and structures in primary schools and their communities.[2] It adopts what I call a 'gender-critical' perspective in that, put simply, matters concerning gender are not ignored or left unproblematic, but rather are sought out, presented and articulated — in this case, to show the effects of gender on the ways educational policies are interpreted and negotiated around school councils and how these processes shaped the decisions and consequences which followed. Apart from drawing attention to some of the gender issues and providing some analysis of events and people, this case study has been left 'open' for the reader's critical reflection. I have given as much detail as possible within the confines of the chapter length. I hope that most readers can find a 'place' for themselves in the case study and arrive at their own judgments of what action they would have taken.

Relocation: Linfield and the Special Developmental School

In late 1983, a directive was sent to the principal and council of Linfield school from their Regional Director of Education. The directive required that the school re-establish a planning committee to prepare for the relocation of the local Special Developmental School (SDS) on to the Linfield school site. A little history is useful here.

The SDS was set on a leased site about two kilometres from Linfield primary school. It was staffed by women, most of whom were high on dedication and low on qualifications. The SDS provided care and education for local children with intellectual disabilities and had a reputation for pioneering teaching programmes, for example, in reading skills. It was only in recent years that places such as the SDS have become 'schools' under the present Ministry of Education. They used to be Day Training Centres in the old Mental Retardation Division of the Health Department. Once in the grip of the educational bureaucracy the role, classification and qualifications of SDS 'teachers' came under scrutiny. The then Victorian Teachers' Union also cast its eye in their direction.

In the early 1980s, the Education Department (the Ministry's predecessor) adopted a 'normalization' or 'mainstreaming' policy to 'integrate' children with disabilities, where possible, into 'normal' schools. At this time, Linfield primary school was linked with the SDS by the Education Department for the purpose of implementing the new policy. This original link was established mainly because Linfield possessed the largest site of any primary school in the town. When the Labor government came to power in Victoria in 1982, a two-year pause occurred while the new government developed its own policy (*Report of the Ministerial Review of Educational Services for the Integration of the Disabled*, 1984).

The relocation issue was resurrected in 1983 when it was known that the lease for the SDS site would not be renewed on its expiry in 1984. The regional office of the Education Department hoped to solve the problem by *relocating* the SDS on the Linfield school site. Hence, the *integration* policy was not the concern, rather the practical problem of finding a replacement site for the school. Only a few of the school buildings were owned by the Education Department and could be relocated, and some new buildings were therefore required at any new location. A planning committee was formed and, in line with new government policies for community participation, it comprised staff and parents from both schools and was chaired by the local Senior Education Officer (SEO).

At both schools there existed a resigned reluctance towards the relocation. However, at Linfield there were several senior (male) staff, including Ted Symes, the principal, who were always responsive to new developments in education. They influenced the school to set about the task of establishing a planning committee with a willingness which belied the previous reluctance. The council selected Brian Garden, the president, and Andrew Masters, who was eventually to become president the following year, as the parent representatives. During the council discussion about the membership of the planning committee it was stated that these people (men) were necessary because of their (perceived) abilities to cope with the anticipated 'hard' negotiations over the issue. Masculine notions of 'tough decisions' and 'hard fights' were expected and, thus, a 'masculine' agenda was being constructed. Miriam Tate, a staff representative on council, was selected as the teacher representative and was the only woman member. Miriam Tate also had a reputation for being a 'strong' person on the school council as she was the one who usually argued the staff case on matters of concern at council.

It is difficult to point to the genesis of any particular social process: each seems to have roots extending well back into history. However, the establishment of the planning committee for the relocation of the SDS at Linfield was certainly a key event. The emerging construction of 'masculine' discourses over the relocation was mostly fostered by concerns over dealing with the regional educational bureaucracy and had little to do with any possible disputes with the SDS. If the concern had been for the beneficial relationships between the staff and children of the two schools then, perhaps, different representatives would have been chosen. The only female parent on the school council, Jane Peters, the Parents' Club representative, was a reluctant contributor at school council meetings. She was regarded as hesitant and, thus, not a contender for a place on the planning committee with such a 'masculine' task. However, she had the best links with parents, especially mothers, and also knew most of the SDS staff. Steve Weston, a staff representative on the council, was a gentle and sensitive person who may well have proved successful at forging links between the school staffs and in developing the educational and social benefits for the children.

The formation of the planning committee was followed by another formative step. The planning committee was established to work on the relocation of the SDS to Linfield, and at the same time a few senior staff at Linfield, especially the principal, began to study the rationale behind the Education Department's policy on *integration* which was fuelling the integration issue in other parts of Victoria. They sought information from other schools with similar experiences. The SDS staff, particularly through the work of the principal, Prue Cameron, already knew these details from their own professional networks and contacts. They were opposed to these developments for children with intellectual disabilities, not because they rejected the rationale, but rather because they believed the practice would not match the policy. In Prue Cameron's words, 'the philosophy is fine, the practicalities are a concern'. In particular, the SDS staff believed that children with intellectual disabilities would have less attention paid to their personal, social and educational development within larger schools, mainly because the government would not provide sufficient funds and also because any extra funds there may be would be partly redirected to 'normal' schooling. The staff also recognized that their vulnerability would increase enormously in a large school, such as Linfield, where they would be confronted by a male-dominated hierarchy.

The Linfield school planning committee members visited the SDS to see it at work and to talk to the principal, staff and parents; goodwill was soon established. Both schools discussed their reservations about the relocation, though the Linfield representatives were forming the opinion that these could be solved. Gradually, a few of the senior staff at Linfield became convinced that integration was good for all children. This represented a significant development, because it not only meant that Linfield was willing to proceed with the *relocation*, but also was becoming interested in some measure of *integration*. Eventually the term 'integration' began to be used interchangeably with 'relocation' in the various discourses within Linfield. Such a willingness for integration was neatly within Education Department policy and received affirmation from the SEO chairing the planning committee — who was to be seen often at Linfield and rarely at the SDS.

Relocation versus Integration

The discussion of integration caused alarm at the SDS. They thought they were planning a relocation of their school on to the Linfield site where they would maintain their separate identity and, maybe, some educational links with Linfield. Integration was a much bigger threat and it came at a time when the Victorian Teachers' Union was becoming involved in discussion with the Education Department over the status of the many 'unqualified' SDS teachers in Victoria. Only one of the five teachers (there were also usually four teachers' aides) at the school was qualified as a primary school teacher; in particular, the principal had no teaching qualifications, although she was a BA graduate. Prue Cameron's fear was that she would be employed as a teacher's aide at an integrated school which would represent a denial of nearly 25 years of work, experience and commitment.

Linfield school arranged for a group of staff and parents, including Alan Masters, Miriam Tate and Jane Peters from the council, to take a day and a half visit to another country town school where a similar relocation had taken place. This visit marked a watershed in Linfield's understanding. By all accounts, the school they visited was a battleground of acrimony and antagonism between the antecedent institutions. In the opinion of the Linfield people, this severely detracted from the children's schooling and the working lives of the staff. Reports were given to a Linfield staff meeting attended by the SEO. Some staff, especially the male senior staff, began calling for written and explicit agreements between the schools on administration, staffing, resources, and so on before proceeding further. Ted Symes and Miriam Tate tried to moderate these demands by pointing to the current good relationships between the schools. However, the deputy principal, James Porter, who was probably the most influential person in the school, insisted that it was unworkable to have two principals of one school and, thus, all the proposed administrative and organizational changes had to be agreed in advance, including the principalship. Clearly, the Linfield staff were debating the integration of the two schools and not just the SDS relocation.

By now the concerns of the SDS were becoming reality as the Linfield school began to use its power to ensure its interests were served in any new integrated structure. Recognizing the contentious nature of the issue, the SEO assured the staff meeting that 'no decision will be made without consultation' and that 'the situation is very fluid'. The discourse became firmly masculine as the men took their positions to debate power and resources, not educational principles, children's lives or the livelihoods of the SDS staff.

At the council meeting six days later, Miriam Tate attempted to shift the discourse to matters of principle and people. She said it was important for the staff and community to understand the principles of the integration of children with disabilities into 'mainstream' schooling, and she recommended the school council undertake to explain these principles to parents. She also raised the matter of staffing and the 'tagging' of positions in relation to the teaching of children with intellectual disabilities. The principal then raised the matter of the qualifications of the staff at the SDS. He believed that the Education Department would allow people until 1987 to improve their qualifications to the minimum required for primary school registration. There was some discussion of the implications of this for the SDS staff, during which the principal said that he believed that 'they would be OK'. However, Hilda Stone, who was representing the Parents' Club in Jane Peters' absence, said she believed that at least two of the SDS staff would have difficulties because of their lack of formal teaching qualifications. She was the only Linfield person to explicitly recognize the concerns of the SDS staff for their own futures. Unlike Linfield, the SDS was entirely staffed by local people: women who had grown up in the town or lived most of their lives there. Linfield parents like Hilda Stone and Jane Peters had known them, or about them, for many years, and current local knowledge included an understanding of the concerns of SDS staff. The men of Linfield had no idea or, if they had, they ignored it.

What was now at stake for the SDS women was not only status and job satisfaction, and being forced to add study to their busy lives, it was also the *disintegration* of a small, close-knit, caring community for children with intellectual disabilities. A community which was established through a 25-year struggle against the massed ranks of professionals, bureaucrats and prejudiced public.

A week after the Linfield council meeting, the SDS arranged for the school council to meet the SDS staff and management committee. Ted Symes opened the discussion, and it was soon clear that the visit to an integrated school and the subsequent meetings at Linfield school had added some circumspection to his approach. He raised several problems to do with the administration of the integration of the two schools. His choice of the term 'integration', instead of 'relocation', was to prove significant. The SDS people raised several questions concerning the operation of the two schools. It was stated by the SDS that, although there could be a shared administration block, 'to help overcome any personality problems and communication breakdowns', there needed to be two separate schools, 'because the needs of the children are different'. It was argued by Linfield school that a single school council was necessary, which the SDS questioned on the grounds that there may be insufficient recognition of their children's special needs in the allocation of resources and equipment. The SDS people were surprised at the commitment that Linfield was applying to fulfilling the regional office's relocation directive. The SDS expected a good deal of reluctance from Linfield, but were witnessing relatively speedy progress on their part. This, and the fact that integration was now the issue, prompted the SDS to give much more serious attention to the matter.

They began to debate the issue on Linfield's terms, that is, by explicitly recognizing that Linfield was pursuing integration. The energies which had sustained the school over the years were directed to the task by Prue Cameron, she was also beginning to understand what the changes to school council powers meant for the SDS (see Education Department of Victoria, 1983). They were currently headed by a management committee on which the staff had little say or representation; however, their recent new status as a school in the Education Department meant that in 1984 they had to abide by the new regulations for school councils. This not only meant more power but also all the staff would have to be members of the council in order to comply with the composition requirements. Ironically, these same changes to the composition and powers of school councils meant that, if integrated into a single school, they could well have little say on a council with more power over their work.

A week after the meeting with the SDS, the Linfield school council held an extraordinary meeting devoted to the SDS issue. The SEO attended the meeting. The president asked for reports on the meeting with the SDS and on the visit to the integrated school. These were led or presented by male council members. Miriam Tate, who had visited the 'integrated' school, and Jane Peters, who attended both, said nothing at this stage; the president did not ask for their thoughts and they did not assert them. In addition, Miriam Tate, as at previous meetings, was asked by the president to record the minutes. She always resisted such requests, partly because she felt she was being asked because she was a woman. With the SEO present, however, she acceded in spite of her visible reluctance. This restricted her opportunity to contribute, because she needed to concentrate on recording others' comments.

Ted Symes talked of the integration as amounting to a shared administration 'block' (that is, a building), 'preferably housing all staff with intermingling as much as possible'. Since the visit to the integrated school, integration policy was now becoming problematic for both schools. The council meeting was dominated for the first 45 minutes by three men: the president, the principal and Andrew Masters. Later, the matter of the two principals was raised and the SEO entered the debate. He said that the principal of Linfield school was 'an A-grade [the most senior grade] principal and more senior to the principal of the SDS'. The council discussion, substantially maintained by these four men, then centred on the notion of a single hierarchy with a 'super principal' or 'el supremo' at the top. These men could conceive of no other way to administer the integration of the two schools other than within a single hierarchy. Ted Symes was reluctant to be an 'el supremo' — and there was no doubt he could have worked amicably with Prue Cameron in any shared direction of an integrated school — but he offered no alternative.

The men then raised the question of resources for the new school. The president and Andrew Masters endeavoured to haggle with the regional office, through the SEO, in order to obtain the 'cyclic' maintenance work for the school in exchange for the council's compliance with the proposed relocation and integration of the SDS. 'Cyclic' maintenance was an issue at the school because, due to government spending cuts, this periodic maintenance of school buildings had been deferred and the condition of the school was deteriorating. The concern was that the SDS would have new buildings on the Linfield site while the original primary school fell further into disrepair without its maintenance. The SEO quickly dispelled any ideas of such a deal; however, he assured them that 'there should be no diminution of the resources available to this school'. Andrew Masters, the main haggler, said, 'We do not want to see the Education Department maintain the SDS in pristine condition when doing this place [Linfield] in the eye . . . it is necessary to bring the school up to a reasonable standard'. He later stated to the SEO: 'Before we go in we want to know what the Education Department is going to put into it.' To which the SEO replied, 'If you want to win races you've got to realize that you are not going to get cyclic maintenance just because you are being integrated with a SDS.'

The SEO later suggested that the new SDS building may have 'a low maintenance requirement' so that 'maintenance money may be directed' to the primary school. It was interpreted that a new administration block for both schools would be a physical gain in space for Linfield, because it would enable the existing administration areas to be used in other ways. The SEO offered a thinly veiled inducement to the staff by suggesting that the new administration building may include a new staffroom. Apart from one contribution, the whole of this debate about resources, which lasted for 40 minutes, was conducted by four men: the president, principal, SEO and Andrew Masters. This was exactly the type of debate that the council had anticipated some weeks earlier when the planning committee was established.

The meeting continued for another two hours dominated by the same four men. Towards its conclusion there was considerable debate about the power of the school council to veto the relocation and to refuse to join the planning committee. In essence, they were demonstrating the tension between different government policies: in this case, between a policy leading to greater autonomy for local school councils and another concerned with integrating children with intellectual disabilities into the 'mainstream' of schooling. The SEO produced a written motion, prepared prior to the meeting in consultation with the regional director, which expressed the council's compliance with the directive to relocate the SDS at Linfield and which also requested the regional director to form a planning committee for the new school. The president objected to the unquestioning compliance of the motion. After some discussion it was agreed to add the words, 'to consider all matters pertaining [to the relocation of the SDS at Linfield]' to the motion requesting a formal planning committee be established by the regional director. These additional words allowed the planning committee to consider the broader resource, administrative and educational aspects of the relocation, together with the usual matters of buildings and grounds.

The debate over the wording of the motion took 44 minutes, after which the president observed: 'The three people who have discussed this motion are the three people who have no right to do so.' What he meant was not that they could not discuss the motion, but rather that the three men who dominated the discussion, the president, the principal and the SEO, could not propose or second a motion at a council meeting. It was necessary to find council members to do this. At first no one would volunteer to propose the motion. Then Steve Weston offered, but a seconder proved even harder to find. It was only after the president said that the motion would lapse if it was not seconded, that Miriam Tate agreed to second the motion. She was later to say in an interview that the only reason she did this was to curtail the meeting.

The motion was passed at 10.15 p.m.; most people were tired and keen to leave. The membership and composition of the planning committee was covered before the meeting finished at 11.00 p.m. The preceding three and a half hours were crucial to the formulation of the council's policy and procedures concerning the relocation of the SDS. It was dominated by four men and at no stage was Jane Peters involved, even though she was one of three people present who had attended both the visit to the SDS and to the integrated school. Linfield, like primary schooling in general, is run by women — in 1984, 72 per cent of Victorian state primary teachers were women — and yet it is dominated by men — in 1984, 81 per cent of principals were men (Education Department, Policy

and Planning Unit, 1984). However, the real male domination of primary schooling is related to the sort of interconnections between men seen at Linfield, not to
a simple measure of numbers or percentages. At the staff meeting, James Porter,
the deputy principal, led the debate in response to the issues aired by other senior
men. On the council, the way the SEO, president, principal and Andrew Masters
shaped and controlled the discourse about the 'relocation' to this point is clear.
Women, with the partial exception of Miriam Tate, had little influence, neither
did Steve Weston, although he was the first to 'toe the line' with his proposing of
the motion at the meeting. Significantly, Jane Peters sat without responding
throughout the embarrassing silence followed by the president's cajoling to find a
seconder.

Three weeks later, at the first meeting of the planning committee, chaired by
the SEO, it was emphasized by both schools that they had not agreed to the relocation, but were merely considering it. The meeting aired many of the schools'
concerns and both wanted further consideration of what was at stake. Prue
Cameron began to use her tactical skills and she argued that it was necessary to
consult all the SDS parents before a decision could be made. Knowing full well
that the SEO could hardly refuse such consultation which was part of government policy, Prue Cameron said that this could not be done properly until the
1984 school year. This SEO acquiesced, but was visibly irritated by it all. Prue
Cameron hoped that by stalling for time she would be in a position to argue, if
necessary, for a further delay in 1984 to await the election of their new school
council. This would give her and the SDS staff greater power and representation
in any final decision. Prue Cameron endeavoured to maintain and extend the
school's relationship with the SEO and so she invited him to spend a day at the
school and work with the children: this he did, acting as a *de facto* teacher's aide.

The Christmas school holidays passed with little happening on the relocation
matter. Early in the new school year a meeting was held at the SDS to discuss the
implications of moving to Linfield. The 38 parents and 10 staff who attended the
meeting engaged in a spirited discussion ranging over eight or so points which
they felt were likely to affect detrimentally the education of their children if the
relocation, and possible integration, went ahead. The regional office, and more
generally the Education Department and government, were seen as the SDS's
opponents rather than Linfield itself, although there were also many reservations
expressed about the difficulties of working with a large primary school like
Linfield, especially when the present staff left the school and were replaced with
others who may be less amenable. There was a sense at the meeting that they had
some power to resist or influence the proposed relocation, partly because of their
understanding of the government policy (and rhetoric) of community participation and responsibility for schooling. In addition, they were disgruntled
because the debate about the relocation had shifted the concern of everyone,
especially the regional office, away from considering what the SDS felt were their
pressing needs for better facilities at the school. The meeting culminated in passing unanimously a motion: 'That the community of the Special Developmental
School expresses the wish that the school remain on its present site and the
buildings be extensively renovated.'

Linfield school decided to forget the relocation issue over the holidays and
see what the SDS decided. After the SDS motion was passed they waited for the
regional office to respond before considering the matter further. It came as a

surprise to both schools when the regional office announced that the SDS could stay and, after all, the lease could be renewed. Prue Cameron began immediately wresting from the regional office some of the half a million dollars which had been allocated to the SDS relocation which she wanted for renovations to the school. She had some success. Linfield school forgot the matter entirely.

Postscript

In 1992 the SDS remains a separate school and the debate has continued in educational circles about the strengths and weaknesses of the integration of children with disabilities. Staff were required to improve their qualifications and they now have the equivalent of four or five years of teacher education. Prue Cameron obtained her private pilot's licence, retired from teaching in 1987 and took to the air to see some of the country. She now lives in Queensland.

Notes

1 The names of people and schools are fictitious in order to preserve anonymity.
2 This study was entitled 'Gender Processes and Structures in the Primary School'. It was supported by a grant from the Australian Government under the Projects of National Significance Program of the Commonwealth Schools Commission. The views expressed here do not necessarily represent the views of the Commission. The fieldwork was carried out by the author and Rosemary Langmore, who was the research assistant. An outline of the methodology can be found in a report of some findings by the author (Evans, 1987a). Additional findings are reported in Evans 1987b. A detailed discussion of the project and its implications are to be found in Evans 1988.

This chapter is a slightly revised version of the paper presented at the *National Conference on Gender Issues in the Theory and Practice of Educational Administration and Policy* held in November 1897. In the light of events and debates which have occurred in the intervening years a whole new chapter could be written, but that is another story.

References

EDUCATION DEPARTMENT OF VICTORIA (1983) *Ministerial Working Paper Number 4: School Councils*, Melbourne, Education Department of Victoria.
EDUCATION DEPARTMENT OF VICTORIA, POLICY AND PLANNING UNIT (1984) *Women in the Education Department of Victoria*, Melbourne, Education Department of Victoria.
EVANS, T.D. (1987a) 'Gender and primary schooling in Australia: Some classroom and curriculum findings', *Journal of Curriculum Studies*, 19, 2, pp. 183–6.
EVANS, T.D. (1987b) 'Gender and primary schooling in Australia: Shaping policies and making decisions', *Journal of Curriculum Studies*, 19, 3, pp. 271–3.
EVANS, T.D. (1988) *A Gender Agenda: A Sociological Study of Teachers, Parents and Pupils in their Primary Schools*, Sydney, Allen and Unwin.
REPORT OF THE MINISTERIAL REVIEW OF EDUCATIONAL SERVICES FOR THE DISABLED (1984) Melbourne, Victorian Government Printer.

Political and Administrative Theory: Some Feminist Challenges

Chapter 9

Contemporary Issues for Feminism: The Politics of the State

Anna Yeatman

The premise of what follows is the proposition that as political actors feminists are involved necessarily in the politics of the state. At least they are involved in the contemporary politics of the Australian state which I have discussed at length in my recent book *Bureaucrats, Technocrats and Femocrats* (Yeatman, 1990). I advance this proposition for the following reasons. First, comparatively speaking, Australia is a state-centric society, that is to say, the state is relatively centralized rather than dispersed. In this regard Australia is closer to Sweden than it is to the United States, the latter being a state-society where the state is relatively dispersed. A relatively centralized state structure is conducive to the rationalized social reform orientations of the new class, the class which makes its political, cultural and economic claims on the basis of its cultural capital, its knowledge claims. Second, the new class, wherever it is, tends to view the state as the vehicle of its claims to power as social planners and rational policy-makers. When the state is a relatively centralized structure it is a ready site for the political culture of the new class. Third, in Australia the new class is, via the current political hegemony of the Labor Party at the federal level and in four of the states, in control of the state administrative apparatus. This does not mean that it is in control of all the political agendas that require to be addressed by the state's administrative staff: this is clearly not the case with regard to economic public policy. It is in control of how the state as an administrative apparatus operationalizes political agendas even if they are set by forces external to the state and to the Labour Party. Moreover, there are some agendas which may have party political support, especially from new class elements within the parties, but which are distinctive new class agendas: for example, access, equity and participation agendas are driven by the meritocratic, universalistic and participative values of the new class. Gouldner (1979) characterizes the 'culture of critical discourse' as the culture of the new class.

In this context, and where the ethos of the public sector has not been eroded by wholesale privatization and by the renewed ideology of the free market, progressive politics is largely centred on the state. For feminism this is certainly true. Essentially, all feminist claims impacting on issues of the distribution of social goods and values are made as claims on the state's role in directing or influencing distributive mechanisms and outcomes. Consider, for example, the significance to feminist politics of the public provision of child care. Moreover, most Australian feminists are employed within the public sector: they are public servants, women's shelter workers, teachers and academics. Accordingly, a politics centred on the state, and indeed the fate of the public sector itself, are central to most feminists. Finally, feminism may be viewed as an ideology of incorporation of women into the new class, and in this sense as an ideology of upward mobility for women. If this is so, it may be doubly so because there are no other vehicles for upward mobility for women as individuals in their own right. Hence, historically, there has been a strong affinity between the culture of professionalism and feminism, and access to education, especially higher education, has been a central vehicle of mobility for women. Accordingly, when the new class is able to exercise its platonic illusion because the state as a principle of intervention and social direction still enjoys legitimacy (as it does in Australia), feminists, as other members of the new class, will be particularly drawn to the politics of the state.

The fragility of this state of affairs is worth underlining. It is clear that even in this relatively state-centric society there can be, in the near future, a profound de-legitimization of the politics of the state if either the Labor government continues with its privatization policies or if the Liberal Party come to power and are able to set the terms of the overall political agenda. Both parties seem attracted to policies associated with the free market. It is not that the state's sphere of influence actually dwindles under the orientation of the free market politics of the Thatcher type of neo-conservatism. The principal change is that it becomes no longer legitimate to view the state as a vehicle of progressive social change and as an instrument of redistribution. (This point is well made in Preston's article in this collection.) In this context the substantive politics of the new class become irrelevant to the business of the state: social planners in the larger sense of the terms social planning, and policy-makers who are oriented to the principles of public policy and the participative process of public policy-making are no longer required. The platonic ideal of the new class has to subside.

Accordingly, what I have to say now about a feminist politics centred on the state will hold true only as long as the politics of the state itself continues to enjoy legitimacy. It is my hope that there will be a more successful struggle around this in Australia than there has proved to be in Britain or in the United States. However, if we are to maintain the legitimacy of the politics of the state, it will be because we take on board and deal with the current challenges to the viability of the culture and the structure of the public sector.

What should a feminist state-centred politics look like at this time? By feminist I mean a politics oriented by feminist values, and by these I mean values which promote the integration of women and children into the structures of citizenship. Women and children share an identity in this regard because historically they have both been subsumed under the private patrimonial authority of male individual householders. Integration of women and children into the structures of citizenship means that they are no longer subsumed under patriarchal private property, but have entered into society as individuals in their own right. This process of integration still goes on and is subject to the contingencies of political struggle around the status of women and children. It has become clear that the structures of modern citizenship require changing if women, children and men are to be redefined as individual actors enjoying an equality of status within the same society.

Perhaps because feminists could not appeal to private power and had to look for an alternative source of power which would help them secure their claims, they have looked to the state as the vehicle of conferring on women and children rights against partriarchal private power. This becomes particularly evident in the feminist political discourses concerning domestic violence and child abuse.

In this way the state has assumed a positive aspect for feminists, even those who have come to accept the analysis of the modern welfare state as embodying patriarchal assumptions concerning women and children. For a comprehensive discussion of feminist theories of the state, see Kenway (1991). However, Pateman's (1987) argument is particularly instructive here. She accepts the argument by Elizabeth Wilson (1977) and others that the welfare state reconstitutes women as dependents on patriarchal authority, in this case the authority of the state. She reminds us that feminists, especially first-wave feminist social reformers, fought for many aspects of what later came to be institutionalized as the welfare state, a point that begins to complicate the critique of the patriarchal character of the welfare state. In addition, Pateman argues, firstly, that welfare benefits have helped to make it possible for many women to be independent of individual men, and secondly, that there is one crucial difference between the 'construction of women as men's dependents and dependence on the welfare state':

> In the former case each woman lives with the man on whose benevolence she depends; each woman is (in J.S. Mill's extraordinarily apt phrase) in a 'chronic state of bribery and intimidation combined'. In the welfare state each woman receives what is hers by right, and she can, potentially, combine with other citizens to enforce her rightful claim. The state has enormous powers of intimidation, but political action takes place collectively in the public terrain and not behind the closed door of the home, where each woman has to rely on her own strength and resources (Pateman, 1987, p. 35).

The crucial assumption in Pateman's argument, which is developed more fully in her latest book *The Sexual Contract* (1990), concerns the public status of women's welfare claims and dependencies. This is slightly different argument from the one I have advanced in several places, namely the proposition that in so far as women and children have rights, these are positive rights, and like all positive rights they are instituted as such by the state (see Yeatman, 1988a). Since private right is antagonistic to the rights of women and children they have nothing to gain from the liberal tradition of natural right. It is only the state which can constitute the rights of women and children. The emphasis in this argument lies on the authority of the state rather than on its public character. Arguably, however, the state can intervene with (patriarchal) private right only as it assumes the authority of a public ethical principle.

If these arguments have merit, they would suggest that a feminist politics of the state should be focused on the welfare state, specifically on maintaining and extending welfare entitlements for women and on maintaining and extending the rights which the state confers on women and children. A feminist politics focused on a defence of the welfare state would appear particularly relevant given that the vast majority of welfare workers and clients are women. Indeed, we might expect that the neo-conservative disestablishment of what Marshall (1977) called 'social citizenship', by introducing where possible a user pays principle and by pushing back caring activities on to private family services, would evoke a militant feminist defence of the welfare state.

There are serious problems with this perspective, which probably explain why it is that this militant defence seems not to have eventuated. First, welfare entitlements are not 'rights'. Welfare benefits entail the state's patronage and the client's tutelage (see Donzelot, 1979). In a sense it does not matter that they are located in the public domain because they are still contained within the principle of patronage. Symbolically, welfare entitlements are not associated with the essentialist (natural) foundations of private individual right, and they are instead identified with the contingencies of electorally oriented party politics.

Second, because of this, women welfare beneficiaries have not organized. It is impossible to derive political action from the position of tutelage.

Third, it is worth mentioning that in the current Australian restructuring of the welfare state, a number of reports and reviews have significant implications for the visibility of women as a distinctive class of potential welfare beneficiaries. The intentions of these policy documents are that women are no more assumed to be dependent than men are, and that the norm will become one of women's full integration into labour markets. The effect of this will be to abolish the idea that if a woman is a wife or mother or both she is entitled to economic support from her husband or, if there is no husband present, from the state in exchange for her full-time home-making contribution.

Fourth, there is very little evidence that the highly feminized population of welfare workers are particularly influenced in the construction of their practice by the fact that the majority of their clients are women and children. Or if they are, the point becomes that this can cut both ways: it can lead in conservative as well as progressive directions. For example, it is arguable that the recent orientation of the various welfare departments in the Australian states to child protection has functioned to associate these departments with statutory control roles and to stringently ration the services which case workers can deliver. In short, child protection as a bureaucratic practice has moved the relevant government agencies in thoroughly conservative directions. It has been very difficult for progressive welfare workers to resist this direction, because their own sympathies are all too easily co-opted by the child protection discourse (for discussion, and critique of this discourse, see Yeatman, 1988b). Similarly, the Commonwealth Government Maintenance proposal, which was implemented in 1988, has had strong femocrat advocacy. This proposal concerns the establishment of a national system to collect maintenance from non-custodial parents. Since the vast majority of custodial parents are women, feminists and femocrats are tempted to see this proposal as one in line with redistributing wealth from men to women and children. In fact the proposal works in the direction of privatizing welfare by making welfare benefits conditional on the willingness of women beneficiaries to bring their children within this maintenance collection system. The whole proposal is structured by the logic that, in the first instance, the responsibility for the economic maintenance of children is the private responsibility of their parents. This is private rather than social parenting, the latter being a situation where one would expect all who belong to a political community to contribute through their taxes to the children of that community. The corollary of privatized parenting is the deeply regressive principle stated in the Maintenance proposal, that a child has the right to share in his or her parents' income (see *Child Support: A Discussion Paper on Child Maintenance*, 1986).

Fifth, welfare and, more broadly, human service workers are not bureaucratically powerful in the sense of being able to influence the agenda frameworks which govern state policies and programmes. Indeed, they are among the least powerful sections of the state bureaucracy, and appear to be the first to go when state services are privatized (see Dunleavy, 1986).

Finally, the problem with a welfare state politics is that the 'old' welfare state has become uncoupled in relation to 'the economy'. Neo-conservatives insist on this point by arguing that the welfare state led to an unlimited inflation of claims on the state which only resulted in an ever-increasing public deficit and the development of public service careers for members of the new class. Instead of the state becoming a vehicle for the development of what Marshall (1977) called social citizenship, it became the inappropriate vehicle of interest group claims which were not held in check but, indeed, allowed to proliferate because expansion of the state's power expanded the power of its new class bureaucrats. Hence it becomes logical to force these interested claims out of the state and into the market arena, where they will be subject to the checks of market-place competition.

It is not only neo-conservatives who argue that the welfare state and the economy have become uncoupled. Social democratic corporatists also argue this but in a very different fashion. In Australia now, and under the leadership of the new class in a corporatist Labor government, we are witnessing the building of a 'new' welfare state which is reshaping the structures of entitlement in relation to a highly rationalized and universalistic combination of manpower and human capital investment policies. I have already mentioned the aspect of this which ties state-provided income support for women to labour market participation. Income support for young people is tied to their willingness to participate in education, training and employment.

In effect, this corporatist 'new' welfare state rations claims on the state and insists that if they are to be regarded as legitimate they must be tied into the government's strategy of rebuilding the Australian economy so that it becomes more internationally competitive. This approach maintains the validity of public economic policies and strategies which involve significant government input of various kinds into what is accepted as both real and desirable: a 'mixed' economy. In this respect it is an approach which revalorizes the politics of the state.

There is little in this approach which accommodates a feminist politics which is oriented to women and children as groups which have distinctive claims of their own on the state. The corporatist restructuring of the welfare state is universalistic and economistic. If a feminist politics is to be developed in this context, it needs to be oriented in these ways to the extent, at least, of understanding these mainstream agendas and developing the required competencies to debate them. Historically speaking, this represents unprecedented demands of a feminist politics of the state. It represents the radical loss of the ideology of 'separate spheres' as a point of anchorage for a feminist politics of the state.

Stated differently, this new context for the politics of the state means that feminists can no longer contain their politics of the state within what O'Connor (1973) and Offe (1985) after him have called the legitimation functions of the state. Feminists, in order to be credible, will have to develop a politics of the state that is oriented to both legitimation and accumulation, and which seeks to influence the issues of the state's strategic management of the contradiction between legitimation and accumulation. This means that feminists need to become engaged in the issues of political economy and to become literate in the relevant bases of knowledge.

If the dominant agenda is that welfare and the economy, having become decoupled, have to become re-coupled, and if a feminist politics of the state is to become relevant to this agenda, it is clear that it will have to become linked up to mainstream left, progressive politics. This it must do on its own terms, while maintaining a clear focus on distinctive feminist agendas and input.

At the moment our historical options are not very wide. As I see them, they concern whether we are to be part of maintaining the legitimacy of the politics of the state or of contributing to the delegitimizing of the politics of the state. If the former, then we have to enter into an uncomfortable and critical relationship of support to the Labor corporatist politics of economic and welfare state restructuring. If the latter, then regardless of our intentions or ultimate allegiances, we will be giving support to those who want to displace public in favour of private principles of distribution.

The former maintains a highly state-centric and rationalized set of controls over the 'fit' between the economy and the claims of citizenship. The latter seeks to emancipate the economy from the claims of citizenship.

I would want to insist that there can be a critical and tough-minded action on behalf of the politics of the state. For example, it seems to me that we do no service by an uncritical acceptance of the current Commonwealth Labor government's economic policies. Over recent years this government has sponsored major policy statements or reviews (such as the Kirby Report, the Social Security Review, *Skills for Australia*, the Green and White Papers on Higher Education) which depend on an enormous emphasis on labour market programmes and their integration with training and education programmes. The idea behind all this is that the Australian economy must be shifted from relying overly and uneconomically on primary commodity exports to increased reliance on the export of value-added goods. This, it is thought, demands a more skilled and more highly educated workforce. All of this may be true, but the kind of thinking which operates does so in terms of wholesale assumptions and undifferentiated propositions. There does not appear to lie behind it any genuine economic planning for the short, medium and long term, where the base for such planning would be an alliance between national capital, the trade union movement and the state. The kind of genuine economic planning to which I refer depends critically on the development of a culture of a national polity which regards its own self-determination as central to the modernization of the Australian economy. This culture is not reconcilable with the financial deregulation that the current Labor government has permitted nor with its willingness to attract foreign capital at the expense of maintaining a solid tax base for the Australian national policy and its expression in a vital and creative public sector.

Nor it is possible, in my view, to espouse a politics of the state without being willing to consider and to debate the neo-conservative challenges to the legitimacy of the politics of the state. We need to understand why the public sector has come under such sustained and effective attack. Is it simply a reassertion of the old nineteenth-century ideology of *laisser-faire* and its de-nunciation of the principle of collectivism? Is it a pendulum swing or is it some-thing historically unique — even while, in broad terms, it is suitable within the recurrent debate between a market-oriented possessive individualism and some species of collectivist ideology?

I think it is clearly the latter, depending as it does on the 'crisis' of the welfare state and on how this crisis has unravelled within the context of a chan-ging international division of labour. Those of us who want to maintain the pol-itics of the state and the continued importance of the public sector will need to identify the precise challenges which confront these political commitments in the present. There are two very important such challenges which are still far too in-frequently discussed within progressive and feminist circles. These are respectively:

1 The problem of public asset replacement — where, in the current context of severe restraints on public spending, will the funds come from for the replacement of water and sewerage pipes and other public capital works? Or can this replacement process be turned over to the market? And should it be, bearing in mind the regressive features of private principles of distribution and their notorious indifference to long-term and public needs?

2 Can there be any continuing commitment to full employment — is this a realistic commitment in the context of technological change and global restructuring? Is this a technical or a political question? Do we need to explore the provision of socially valuable work as distinct from employ-ment, and how is the former to be funded and what kind of income provision is it to afford to those who work, as distinct from being employed?

In conclusion I offer the following remarks. I have argued in this paper that historically feminist politics has been tied to the politics of the state, and that any redistributive politics is tied to the politics of the state. This has amounted to a plea for an intelligent and critical defence and development of the politics of the state in the face of the neo-conservative challenge to that politics.

This is not an easy politics to espouse. It demands the combination within the same politics of theoretical critique and constructive policy creation of the practical activities of political debate and of policy implementation. It demands a high degree of tolerance for complexity and for the contradictions which will reside in working within the current politics of the state and in simultaneously working for long-term social change. It demands considerable flexibility, and it demands a pluralistic acceptance of the value of different positions and per-spectives as they come from individuals and groups positioned in different relationships to the politics of the state.

Above all it demands the re-situation of the feminist commitments of the 1970s within new standards of value relevance, that is to say, situating feminist politics within the context of the following: global economic restructuring, the development of the global political and cultural order, neo-conservative chal-lenges to the legitimacy of the politics of the state and of the public sector, the fragility of the bourgeois democratic polity in the face of these challenges, the revalorization of the nuclear family and the pushing back on to the family, and especially on to women in families, of the social responsibilities of caring, and the challenges to a western-centric way of seeing which have come from a post-colonial age and which are especially pressing for the Australian polity given its own multicultural population and its Pacific basin regional setting. Perhaps more than anything else the de-centring of normative politics which has inevitably followed from the multi-vocal character of this post-colonial politics has fragmented and destabilized the traditions of left politics: neither 'red' nor 'expert' can have uncontested meaning in the context of a legitimate plurality of perspectives. Feminism is caught, also, in this crisis of conscience of political traditions which developed within an Enlightenment rationalist commitment to mono-vocal principles of justice and science. At the same time the marginality of feminism with respect to these traditions permits it more give and more resilience in the face of this massive cultural challenge to western-centric progressive values.

Ultimately, a defence of the politics of the state depends on a defence of the existence of the polity itself. Perforcedly, the polity is still a national polity and is identified with the boundaries of a particular national state society. The development of a politics adequate to contemporary challenges means that we must fight to maintain the basic principles and structures of public life and open, public debate. There is nothing inevitable about the continuation of these — far from it. Indeed, if we are still to enjoy meaningful participation in a polity in the twenty-first century it will be because we have been able to revitalize and develop the principles and structures of public life. To a considerable extent this will depend on feminists, and other progressives, giving some of their best energies to an intelligent and critical politics of the state.

References

CHILD SUPPORT: A DISCUSSION PAPER ON CHILD MAINTENANCE (1986) Canberra, Australian Government Publishing Service.

DONZELOT, J. (1979) *The Policing of Families*, London, Hutchinson.

DUNLEAVY, P. (1986) 'Explaining the privatization boom: Public choice versus radical approaches', *Public Administration*, 64.

GOULDNER, A.W. (1979) *The Future of Intellectuals and the Rise of the New Class*, New York, Seabury Press.

KENWAY, J. (1991) 'Feminist theories of the state: To be or not to be', in MUETZELFELDT, M. (Ed.) *Society, State, and Politics in Australia*, London, Pluto Press.

MARSHALL, T.H. (1977) *Class, Citizenship, and Social Development*, ch. 4 ('Citizenship and Social Class'), Chicago and London, University of Chicago Press.

O'CONNOR, J. (1973) *The Fiscal Crisis of the State*, New York, St Martin's Press.

OFFE, C. (1985) *Disorganized Capitalism*, Cambridge, Polity Press.

PATEMAN, C. (1987) 'The patriarchal welfare state: Women and democracy', in GUTMANN, A. (Ed.) *Democracy and the Welfare State*, Princeton, Princeton University Press (the copy used here was in manuscript form and incorporated only the author's revisions).

PATEMAN, C. (1990) *The Sexual Contract*, Cambridge, Polity Press.

REPORT OF THE COMMITTEE OF INQUIRY INTO LABOUR MARKET PROGRAMS (the 'Kirby Report') (1985) Canberra, Australian Government Publishing Service.

SKILLS FOR AUSTRALIA (1987) Canberra, Australian Government Publishing Service.

WILSON, E. (1977) *Women and the Welfare State*, London, Tavistock.
YEATMAN, A. (1988a) 'Beyond natural right: The conditions for universal citizenship', *Social Concept*, **4**, 2, pp. 3–32.
YEATMAN, A. (1988b) 'The politics of child abuse', *Flinders Studies in Policy and Administration*, 5, pp. 9–44.
YEATMAN, A. (1990) *Bureaucrats, Technocrats and Femocrats*, Sydney, Allen and Unwin.

Chapter 10

Privatizing Public Schooling: Its Causes and Consequences

Barbara Preston

'The state aid debate is dead.' That politically powerful assertion may be strictly true, but it serves to disguise a reality which is very much alive — the dynamic relationship between public and private schooling.

The height of the state aid debate in the early 1980s had its social basis in many people's lived experiences of that relationship. It was in large part an accident of the times that the political expression of concern arising from those experiences was the state aid debate. Yet the debate itself tended to focus on the fairly abstract principle of public funding of private institutions, rather than the concrete and complex consequences of that funding — which was the reality of people's experiences.

The state aid debate was destined to be lost by those opposing the public funding of private schools (though in reality the position was lost more than a decade earlier). The focus on 'state aid' kept the focus away from the complexities of the dual schooling system and the strength and consequences of the dynamic of residualization of public schooling. By the mid-1980s the concern with these other matters was coming to the fore — notably in the Commonwealth government's New Schools Policy (Commonwealth Schools Commission, 1985) which was intended to deny public funding to new or substantially changed private schools which were assessed as likely to have a significant detrimental impact on existing government and non-government schools. However, by then the powerful dynamic of residualization of public education was well entrenched, and the New Schools Policy could only ameliorate its worst excesses.

In this paper I shall seek to place the privatization of schooling over the past decade or so in context, both historical and within Australian society as a whole. I want to emphasize the central importance of the privatization of schooling for social justice, to show how it interrelates with general attitudes to the role of the state, and to make it clear that the privatization of schooling is a feminist issue.

Schooling and the Social Position of Children

Privatization of schooling — involving either expansion and strengthening of private schools relative to public schools, or the abrogation of responsibility by governments for aspects of children's education within the public system — has some differences from privatization in tertiary and other forms of adult education because it involves 'children'. Thus it has some characteristics in common with other publicly provided children's services and benefits including child care, relevant health services and family allowances.

Centrally involved is the view held of children: either as the private possessions of their parents, or having citizen rights and with the community as a whole (through governments) taking some responsibility for them.

In the first view children are seen as an optional choice of their parents — if parents chose to indulge their desire to have children then they must bear the financial costs (though a charitable approach consistent with this view would seek financial support for the 'needy' — thus means-tested family allowances). In this view it is inappropriate for those on middle to high incomes to benefit from cash transfers, or free or subsidized children's services — if they do they are 'middle-class greedies'. A classic manifestation of this view of children as the private indulgences of their parents was in an *Australian Financial Review* editorial, 'The case against family allowances' (4 March 1987), in which a US economist was favourably cited as suggesting that 'children should be considered durable goods' with 'certain features in common with a boat or refrigerator — they are costly to acquire initially, last for a long time, give flows of pleasure during that time, but are expensive to maintain and repair, often do not live up to expectations and definitely have an imperfect second-hand market'.

Seeing children as citizens with rights, and for whom the community as a whole takes some responsibility (and seeing that children make their contribution to society currently and when they become adult) involves the notions of 'horizontal' and 'intergenerational' equity. That is, it is fair and equitable to make transfers from those without responsibility for children to those with responsibility for children (general taxation expended as universal family allowances, for example), and that it is fair and equitable to make transfers from those currently in the workforce to those too young (or too old) to gain substantial income from paid work.

These notions of equity are irrelevant if children are just the private possessions of their parents. Such a view was reflected in the British television series *Blind Justice* where two barristers are discussing a colleague. The conversation goes more or less like this: 'He takes a lot of legal aid work,' says the first. 'How does he pay his kids' school fees?' asks the second. 'They go to state schools,' is the reply. 'Aaah . . . the tax-payer pays,' comments the second in the contemptuous tone that is used for middle-class greedies with their snouts in the welfare trough supposedly reserved for the deserving poor. Thus we see public education being represented as 'middle-class welfare'. This view that those who can afford it have no moral right to send their children to state schools is perhaps of less direct relevance in Australia where most private schools are highly funded by the state, but it has a powerful influence all the same, manifest in the increasing view that public education is not the appropriate place for the aspiring middle class, and it is the other side of the coin of then Commonwealth Education Minister John Carrick's 1973 comment that 'government-supported public education exists in order that poor people may obtain an education'.

This thinking resonates through Australian society in attitudes to key aspects of the social wage. This lack of basic support for the social wage — seeing it as only appropriate for the failures of the private market-place, the deserving poor, and not as something of relevance, value and rightful participation by all citizens — is a striking feature of Australia compared with many similar countries.

Origins of the Residual Social Wage

Positions taken by the Australian labour movement have played a central role in the development of the sort of public social wage (and its private competitors) which we have, and in the development of attitudes in the community to the public social wage.

The 'social wage' is public (government) expenditure which directly supports the standard of living (or, more generally, the quality of life) of individuals. Clearly included are cash transfers such as pensions and benefits; expenditure on public education, health, housing, transport, and expenditure on culture and recreation. Public expenditure on private education is also part of the social wage (though more akin to cash transfers to the individuals who benefit than to service provision by the public sector).

In general, people's living standards can be seen as largely maintained (in quantifiable, financial terms) by the industrial wage (wages or salaries paid to them or to a 'breadwinner' on whom they are dependent) and the social wage.

The historical approach of the labour movement in Australia to the support of the living standards of the working glass is a labourist tradition, not a social democratic tradition. That is, people's living standards are to be supported and enhanced through the industrial wage system, not the state (via the social wage).

The formation of the Australian Labor Party arose from the industrial defeats of the 1890s and a belief that the union movement should get involved directly with the politics of the state if it was to adequately serve its members: direct struggle between labour and capital was not sufficient.

The labour movement supported a strong state role in incomes policy and industry policy, usually with the agreement of employers and conservative politicians. This may have seen the state as a legitimate site of trade union activity, but it was still 'labourist'. That is, it was based on the belief that the living standards of all members of the working class (broadly defined) should be maintained by the industrial wage, that the social wage had no significant role to play. Thus there was support for industry (and incomes) policies promoting full employment, but, at least until the human effects of the 1930s depression became apparent, little support for unemployment benefits; there was support for a 'family wage' but little support for child endowment, and so on. A 'social democratic' approach would have given a central place to a substantial social wage. (See Stuart Macintyre, 1986, for a more detailed discussion of the history of 'labourist' and 'social democratic' tendencies in the Australian labour movement.)

For the labour movement there are two alternative models for the support of most people's living standards: either the industrial wage paid on a family wage basis (and women denied equal pay, and the social wage being mean and meagre), or an industrial wage, equal for men and women and for those with and without dependants, plus a substantial social wage. These alternatives could be simply put as 'the family wage versus the social wage'. The family wage has played a central role in the history of Australian wage-fixing, and its influence remains.

Support for the family wage has been the most significant determinate of the labour movement's approach to the social wage. And a consideration of the family wage and its implications most clearly illuminates the nature of different roles the social wage can have in society, whether it is 'residual' or 'universal'. (See Table 1 for a listing of characteristics of more or less universal and residual public social services.) A family wage is a wage paid to a male breadwinner sufficient to support himself, a wife and several children. The family wage (or 'basic' or 'living' wage) is a minimum for all unskilled male workers. By implication women cannot receive equal pay, and those who fall outside the support of a family wage-earning worker are dependent on private charity or meagre state welfare.

In Australia the family wage notion developed through the late 1800s (Hutson, 1971, p. 33), but received its most influential expression in the 1907 'Harvester' judgment by H.B. Higgins, a person powerfully sympathetic with what he believed to be the interests of working people.

The Harvester judgment was not only the key 'family wage' case in Australia, but also arose from an integration of industry policy and wages policy — Deakin's 'New Protection' which matched tariff protection for manufacturers with guaranteed minimum wages for their employees (Rickard, 1984). The Harvester judgment embodied a coherent vision of society: industry was to develop behind protective tariff barriers, and the structure of society was formed by full employment and adequate wages for men and disincentives against women taking up waged work — assuring the proper rearing of children and thus the future of the nation.

The family wage not only implies unequal pay for women and the sex segregation of the workforce (because cheap female labour needs to be excluded from competition with male labour), but it also implies a high level of dependency on individual breadwinners by other individuals, and a lack of citizen rights of and community concern about the responsibility for those other individuals. As Eleanor Rathbone, a leading British campaigner for family allowances in the 1920s and 1930s, noted when commenting on male unionists' support for the family wage, 'Are they not influenced by a secret reluctance to see their wives and children recognized as separate personalities . . . instead of being fused in the multiple personality of the family with its male head' (Cass, 1983, p. 59).

The 1907 Harvester judgment has historically been held up by the trade union movement as a high point among wage decisions. Yet it laid the foundation for formalization and increasing levels of sex segregation in the labour market and unequal pay for women, and of a lack of support for the public sector and its continuing weakness. Thus the legacy of Harvester has created a supportive context for current privatization of social services generally. A weak state which provides meagre services is in itself less supportable, as well as having less political support in the community.

It is important to recognize this history, and its deeply unegalitarian, individualistic, anti-public sector, and patriarchal implications.

Out of this history arises the fact of Australia's more selective (that is, means-tested and otherwise restricted) and residual social wage relative to that of many comparable countries, and the belief that such a more selective social wage is more in tune with social justice. It is such a belief that is the base of much of the scathing attack on so-called 'middle-class welfare', the Commonwealth

Barbara Preston

Table 1   *Universal versus Residual Social Services**

Tending to be Universal	Tending to be Residual
Social Value	
It is considered of value to the community as a whole (it has *collective value*), it is not just seen as of value to participating individuals.	It is only seen as having relevance or value to those individuals actually using it.
It is supported by the full social and cultural spectrum — the wealthy and powerful as well as the weak.	It is not supported by the whole community, even those who use it may not support it.
High-income earners have no objections to 'their' taxes supporting it — it has *financial solidarity*. (This ensures the first point above.)	The wealthy resent 'their' taxes supporting it, and may demand tax rebates or other more direct public financial support for private sector alternatives.
It is generally chosen in preference to private sector alternatives by all strata in society.	It is only used as a last resort. It has stigma attached. Those who can, choose the private alternative.
Funding and Provision of Service	
It is funded by governments at a level sufficient to provide a service of high quality.	It is not adequately funded by governments.
Private alternatives receive little (if any) direct or indirect financial or other government support. .	Governments financially and in other ways support private alternatives which are in competition with the public service.
It is available to all irrespective of means and it is free. Targeting may be according to workforce status or age, or by nature, or location of service, etc.	It is only available on a selective means-tested basis, or it is provided on a user-pays basis (as in the private market-place).
There is sufficient quantity of the service for all who desire access (and are qualified for entry).	Access is rationed (by, for example, competitive exam results beyond determining entry requirements, quotas or simple first in, only one served).
Design and Nature of Service	
The service is provided on a *planned* basis (e.g., salaried doctors in a planned public health system).	It is allocated on a *market* or semi-market basis (e.g., fee for service medicine even if funded by a universal public insurance scheme).
It has a general *preventative* approach to problems (illness, learning difficulties).	It has a post hoc *curative* approach to social problems — attempting to patch them up after the event.

Table 1 (Cont.)

It has an *inclusive* orientation to those most disadvantaged — the content and structure reflect their culture, and thus success is possible without cultural alienation and stigma. The whole service is inclusive, not just a marginal or dead-end ghetto.	It has a *compensatory* orientation to those most disadvantaged, whose culture (etc.) is devalued and who are expected to fit the dominant norms. Where their culture is catered for it is in dead-end ghettoes.
It is *participative* — participants (consumers) have a high degree of control over the nature and operations of the service through involvement locally and centrally.	It is *paternalistic* — participants (consumers) have no control over the service, and are not even consulted.

Social Role

It socially defines and exhibits what is considered 'quality' in the service.	Quality is socially defined by the private sector alternative. The public is seen as inferior (whether or not this assessment stands up to disinterested and more objective scrutiny).
It determines and controls the relationships with and the transitions between it and the other services, institutions and practices.	The private sector determines and controls relationships/transitions, for example, the past control of the school–university nexus by élite private schools.
The public sector is not in any significant competition with private alternatives.	The public and private sector are in competitive relationship, with the private sector having the competitive advantage.
It manifests and promotes citizen rights and collective responsibility for all by all.	It manifests and promotes the view that responsibility for individuals is a private matter — for individuals alone or families.
It provides coherent social infrastructure for wider cultural, social and economic activity.	Services are discrete and play no positive social role beyond the services provided directly to individual users.

* *Note:* Not all characteristics are relevant to all aspects of the social wage. There is a complex and dynamic relationship between various characteristics — for example, there is mutual reinforcement between social value characteristics and funding and provision of services. Changes in one characteristic (whether or not resulting from government policy or intentional) can then influence other characteristics. Thus can be set in motion a 'vicious circle of residualization'.

government's decision to means test family allowances in 1987, and generally 'tighter targeting' of benefits and services.

Yet in fact a more universal and less selective orientation is generally more equal in final outcome in terms of income and wealth (as well as citizens' rights). This is because of the greater 'financial solidarity' of universal systems. That is, the community as a whole, especially the middle class, is more willing to pay taxes to fund a universal system than they are to fund a selectivist system with which they have no identification and from which they gain no benefit (see Saunders, 1987, and Table 1).

The selectivist, residual model for the social wage, complemented by an industrial 'family wage', powerfully reinforces the financial dependence, political powerlessness and denial of citizen rights of women and children.

Now, to return to the privatization of schooling.

Origins of Strong Private Schooling

Compared with similar countries, Australia has a very large private school sector, the origins of which are several. First, there is the ideological climate and general social wage model already outlined. Second, there is the size of the Catholic population and its generally quite justified distrust of the Protestant-dominated state at the time schooling systems were established over a century ago. Third, the option of Catholic schools within the public system was never taken up as has happened elsewhere (a problematic and perhaps increasingly less feasible option); at the time the Catholic system's viability was most threatened (the early to mid-1960s), the resolution was public funding with negligible strings attached, Finally, for the non-Catholic sector, the wealth of individual families around the middle of the last century and the difficulty for the state in establishing schools (especially secondary schools) for a rapidly expanding population led to the establishment of many independent schools (Sherington *et al.*, 1987).

Once the private sectors were well established they used their political power to restrict public education and thus to enhance their own competitive position. It was well recognized that the advantages of one type of school were at the expense of others and their clientele. Victoria in the decades around the turn of the century provides an interesting example — a little more extreme than most other states, but there are certainly parallels elsewhere. In Victoria the independent school sector and other private schools (Catholic and schools for profit) were much stronger relative to the public sector right from the beginning. The wealth from the gold-fields and the developing grazing, manufacturing and financial industries led to the establishment of twice as many still existing independent schools in Victoria before 1872 as compared with New South Wales (Sherington *et al.*, 1987). Victoria continues to lead New South Wales and the other states in size of the private sector relative to the public sector. In Victoria currently only 67 per cent of students attend public schools, whereas nationally it is 72 per cent.

At the turn of the century in Victoria it was only the independent schools which provided a secondary education at matriculation level, a monopoly they jealously and forcefully guarded. The then Director-General of Education, Frank Tate, fought for the provision of full secondary education accessible to all with ability. Tate recognized that strengthening and broadening public secondary education was crucial because access to full secondary schooling was 'locked against the mass of people and can only be entered by the private stairways for which a heavy toll is charged'. In his 1905 annual report, Tate claimed that those who rejected full state secondary schooling did so 'because they regard such an extension as an attack upon their own class interest and privileges' (Selleck, 1982, p. 15), a frankness that is rare today. His attempts at opening up full secondary education in the public system were limited to agricultural high schools in the country and a teacher training school in the city. The power of the independent and other private school lobbies ensured that until the passing of the 1910 Victorian Education Act there was no formal and open establishment of public secondary schools which provided an education through to matriculation level giving access to university.

Even after the passing of the 1910 Act, the interests of the private schools ensured only the very gradual establishment of public high schools, barely keeping pace with population growth, and the complete exclusion of public high schools from the inner south-eastern region of Melbourne until around the Second World War — the area where many of the most powerful middle and upper class still live. That 'interest' in restraining the strength of the public system continues. As Lyndsay Connors said in her excellent paper, 'A national framework for public schooling' (1989), 'Those who pay what they see as a higher personal price for private schooling will feel a vested interest in talking down and keeping down the value of what is provided publicly, in order to keep up the value of their own investment.' It is an interest which is seldom explicitly expressed, but that does not diminish its impact.

The more recent history of public–private school relations has seen the relative strengthening of public schooling to the mid-1970s, then, under the impact of public funding to private schools, a quite dramatic fall in the public sector's relative strength.

The government sector's share of enrolments hovered around 80 per cent until the mid- to late 1970s. In 1890, 83 per cent of Australian school students attended government schools. In 1900 it was about 80 per cent, 1940 79 per cent, 1950s around 78 per cent; some further dropping back took place in the early 1960s to 76 per cent, and then a strong growth to 78 per cent in 1970 and gradually moving through to about 79 per cent in 1977. Then we have a dramatic falling away: by 1980 it was down to 78 per cent, 1985 74 per cent, 1990 72 per cent, and in Victoria it is down to 67 per cent, with only 64 per cent of all students at the secondary level in government schools.

There is no doubt that it has been the financial support of non-government schools provided by the Commonwealth (and to varying degrees the states/ territories) which has been the major factor leading to the decline in the share of enrolments held by government schools (see, for example, Williams, 1985).

Consequences of Privatization: Residualization

Such a change in enrolment share, combined with other factors, leads to an increasing lack of social coherence, a lack of understanding and appreciation of those from different backgrounds, and to greater social divisions and gaps between the more and less privileged. It undermines the quality of education received by the large majority of students (those in government schools), and makes less viable the further development and public understanding of schooling as a vital and effective social infrastructure for the economic, cultural and social future of Australia.

This is not a particularly radical view. The 1985 Report of the Panel of Commonwealth Schools Commissioners noted that 'to some extent, competition between schools is an inevitable outcome of a [publicly supported] dual system of schooling', and if there is strong competition 'based on economic, cultural or religious differences, then there is a risk of serious community conflict' (para. 38).

The effect on enrolment share of Commonwealth recurrent and capital grants for non-government schools was anticipated, in fact intended, by the Interim Committee for the Australian Schools Commission. In their May 1973 report, *Schools in Australia*, known as the Karmel Report (Interim Committee, 1973), the Committee explicitly gave as a reason for substantially increasing recurrent grants and providing significant capital grants the expectation that such funding would turn around the then declining share of school enrolments held by the non-government sector (particularly the Catholic sector).

To turn around the then trend of increasing share of enrolments held by government schools was a major task, but one in which the Whitlam government, in implementing the Committee's recommendations, was eventually successful. That trend was reinforced by the changes in the programmes wrought by the Fraser government, and by the real increases in grants provided by the Hawke government (with some countervailing effect from the New School's Policy).

While the 1973 Karmel Committee sought a reversal of the non-government sector's declining share of enrolments it also noted that

> there is a point beyond which it is not possible to consider policies relating to the private sector without taking into account their possible effects on the public sector whose strength and representativeness should not be diluted. . . . As public aid for non-government schools rises, the possibility and even the inevitability of a changed relationship between government and non-government schooling presents itself (para. 2.13).

It is unfortunate that this position was not further developed, and that the warning has been so little heeded.

The changes we have seen in enrolment share have been accompanied by complex changes in relationships between the sectors and changes in clientele and social role. Other factors enter into the dynamic: the individual competitive pressures arising from youth unemployment and unmet demand for many higher education courses; the impact of overall declining enrolments during the 1980s; community attitudes, and so on. A vicious circle is created, with a complex of mutually reinforcing elements. It could be termed the 'residualization of public education' (Preston, 1984a).

This analysis is reflected in the 1985 Report of the Panel of Commonwealth Schools Commissioners, *Planning and Funding Policies for New Non-Government Schools*. The Commissioners commented that:

> Government schools have a unique legal obligation to provide high-quality education services for all children of school age in Australia, now including the full range of secondary schooling. A continuing significant decline in the government school sector's share of overall enrolment is likely to change substantially the social composition of the student population in government schools, with potentially significant negative consequences for the general comprehensiveness of public school systems. The cumulative effect of these financial, educational and social consequences could, in the long term, threaten the role and standing of the public school as a central institution in Australian society (Commonwealth Schools Commission, 1985).

The threat has already become manifest. The problem is one for the present, and will intensify if not seriously addressed.

Privatization of the social wage, including schooling, moves us more power-fully towards the family wage model, with that which makes up people's living standards being purchased in the private market place with the earnings of a breadwinner. Even where there is public subsidy it has attached to it little public responsibility. Children are the sole responsibility of their parents: they are at their parents' whim, they are commodities with no independent rights as citizens, and the community as a whole takes no responsibility for them. There is no collective community responsibility for the young, the old, the sick — or all of us for each other. The purchase of schooling, child care, health care — all so neces-sary for the support of children — places an extraordinary financial burden on families with children relative to families without children. The old pressures in support of the family wage model will intensify, and the pressures on women in families with children (whether one parent or two) will escalate. The abrogation of responsibility for the social wage by the state places the burden on women.

The state-facilitated privatization of schooling creates burdens much greater than financial ones alone because of the importance of schooling in individual children's lives, its importance to various social groups (who may have their access to social power facilitated or restricted by their relationship to the insti-tution of schooling), and its importance to the community as a whole.

In closing, I want to draw upon the writing of Lyndsay Connors. She has argued that 'the definition of "public" requires that public schools belong to, concern and serve the public — the people as a whole', and she noted that 'access to public schooling is one of the practical ways in which our society recognizes the status and value of children; with a range of their own entitlements, as human beings, independent of their parents' positions or behaviour'. She then went on to say that

> One function of public schooling is to protect the coherence of society
> by transmitting and shaping the core of common principles which hold
> us together as a civilized society. Public schooling requires the support
> and protection of the majority to fulfil its true, democratic purposes. The
> irretrievable breakdown of marriage requires only one of the two
> partners involved to withdraw. The 'opting out' of public education by a
> sizeable section of the public can cause irretrievable breakdown of the
> public school system (Connors, 1989, p. 11).

'Opting out' is not limited to choice of school for enrolment, but to commit-ment and support in many ways. The aggregation of many seemingly isolated individual choices (and withdrawals of support) creates the social and political climate which forms the cultural and institutional structures within which future choices must be made — the choices of some in the past determine the choices available to others in the future.

Australians have before them an imperative to prevent the irretrievable breakdown of public education, through the options they choose within families and through positions taken in the public social and political arenas. The respon-sibility lies with us, but that is not to say that solutions and choices are easy.

Barbara Preston

References

CASS, BETTINA (1983) 'Redistribution to children and to mothers: A history of child endowment and family allowances', in BALDOCK, CORA V. and CASS, BETTINA (Eds) *Women, Social Welfare and the State in Australia*, Sydney, Allen and Unwin.

COMMONWEALTH SCHOOLS COMMISSION (1985) *Planning and Funding Policies for New Non-Government Schools* (Report of Panel of Commonwealth Schools Commissioners) Canberra, Commonwealth Schools Commission.

CONNORS, LYNDSAY (1989) 'A national framework for public schooling', *The Australian Teacher*, 22, April, pp. 10–14.

HUTSON, J. (1971) *Six Wage Concepts*, Surry Hills, NSW, Amalgamated Engineering Union.

INTERIM COMMITTEE FOR THE AUSTRALIAN SCHOOLS COMMISSION (1973) *Schools in Australia*, (the Karmel Report), Canberra, Australian Government Publishing Service.

MACINTYRE, STUART (1986) 'The short history of social democracy in Australia', in RAWSON, DON (Ed.) *Blast, Bludge or Bypass: Towards a Social Democratic Australia*, Canberra, RSSS, ANU.

PRESTON, BARBARA (1984a) 'Residualization: What's that?', *The Australian Teacher*, 8, May.

PRESTON, BARBARA (1984b) 'Women and the accord: Reassertion of the family wage, and the need for a new industrial strategy', Paper presented at the Women and Labour Conference, Brisbane, 13–15 July.

RICKARD, JOHN (1984) *H.B. Higgins: the Rebel as Judge*, Sydney, Allen and Unwin.

SAUNDERS, PETER (1987) 'Past development and future prospects for social security in Australia', in SAUNDERS, PETER and JAMROZIK, ADAM (Eds) *Social Welfare in the late 1980s: Reform, Progress or Retreat?*, SWRC Reports and Proceedings, no. 65, June.

SELLECK, R.J.W. (1982) *Frank Tate: A Biography*, Melbourne, Melbourne University Press.

SHERINGTON, G., PETERSEN, R.C. and BRICE, I. (1987) *Learning to Lead: A History of Girls' and Boys' Corporate Secondary Schools in Australia*, Sydney, Allen and Unwin.

WILLIAMS, ROSS (1985) 'The economic determinants of private schooling in Australia', *The Economic Record*, 61, 174, pp. 662–8.

Chapter 11

Equal Employment Opportunity and Corporate Planning[1]

Clare Burton

This chapter offers different ways of thinking about organizations and, in so doing, places the concept of corporate planning into a meaningful context. The intention is to facilitate a better understanding of the language and the basic assumptions of the corporate planner in a way which will provide a direction to take equal employment opportunity strategies that make sense within a corporate planning model without compromising some of the values which lie behind EEO legislation — values relating to equity and social justice as well as a fuller utilization of the skills and qualities of members of target groups within work organizations (for critical reviews of equal opportunity in corporate Australia see Burton, 1987a; 1991; Poiner and Wills, 1991).

The idea of corporate planning is based on a set of beliefs about organizations and the methods by which they attain their goals. It is couched in a particular *language* which reflects and contributes to those beliefs: language which implies the system-like character, the logical–rational nature of organizations. The organization is, in one way or another, conceived of as an instrument designed efficiently and effectively to achieve its particular mission, purpose or goal. The language of corporate planning is technical, and the achievement of the corporate plan is seen as depending upon rationally devised systems and techniques.

Corporate planning, then, is presented as a systematic, ordered process, constituting ways of bringing together the strategic and operational goals of an organization through the devising of programmes all of which make their contribution to the broader organizational effort. It involves the harnessing of all resources to this end, including human resources, and thus requires integrated systems linking individual performance with programme and organizational performance, measured in output terms. Management information systems are set up to direct, control and monitor performance at each of these levels. A range of subsystems might be brought in as means towards the overall effort. For example, performance appraisal systems might be linked to a management by objectives scheme so that the organizational goal is broken down into its programme and individual manager components, again with the emphasis on output which is, as far as possible, specified in measurable form.

There are variations in practice on this general theme (see Burton, 1987b). What I want to do now is demystify the idea of corporate planning to some extent, to make practitioners in educational organizations dealing with corporate planning feel more comfortable with the idea and the language used to present the idea. Not so comfortable that they will uncritically embrace or endorse it, but comfortable enough that they will be able to work with it in productive ways to produce more equitable outcomes.

It is not as if, once corporate planning arrives at your organization, you are all of a sudden in a new environment with activity around you driven by, and determined by, a corporate plan and its constituent systems. This would be like saying that all you have to do is design the Opera House or the new Australian Parliament House, and it will be built without any problems and we can proceed to be entertained in them. Sometimes the idea of a corporate plan makes us think it is there, all around us. Remember that it is not and that it has to be put into practice. Indeed, its practical details have to be worked out, and it is here that your contributions are essential.

But you cannot make such contributions unless you can enter the dialogue, and for this you need an understanding of the overall structure of the corporate plan and the assumptions lying behind it. You need to know the code, the language that is used to set up the plan, a language which directs or shapes the way it will be implemented. The way something is designed shapes what can and cannot be done with it. The same is true of an organization, a piece of kitchen equipment, or a corporate plan. It shapes, it never determines activity. We can, in some circumstances, reject the design and find another, or redesign something to suit our purposes better. But the point here is that the language used by corporate planners, tied as it is to concerns with the efficient use of scarce resources, is powerful; it helps to legitimate certain actions, it exerts normative pressure on people to act in certain ways, it shapes practices. The language used has an effect on how the plan is implemented.

Let me quickly illustrate the importance of language in shaping our practices and understandings. You have heard how trivial the issue of non-sexist language is: what does it matter if one is called a spokesman or a spokesperson? A chairman or a chairwoman? Yet we know how often we have caught ourselves forming a picture of a male doctor or a male manager in our heads when we hear a news item about a manager or a doctor — even while many women practise as both. The example I shall give is, I think, a very important illustration of the shaping effect of the language of the corporate planner.

When I first talked to a group of students about the work I had done, with others, on selection processes, I pointed to the shift we felt was necessary in job descriptions and selection criteria, from task specification to outcome specification. This was intended to produce particular effects on the selectors and on the applicants. By shifting the emphasis, there was a greater likelihood that selectors would take a wider range of backgrounds, qualifications and experience into account and applicants would be encouraged to demonstrate the relevance of non-traditional qualifications and experience to performance in the job. One of my students, from the private sector, said they had already implemented such a system. He was referring to their management by objectives (MBO) scheme and the emphasis this places on achievements, or job outcomes, as a measure of task performance. But in fact the student, with his systems approach, and the associated language of inputs, transformation processes, outputs and feedback, was concerned only with *outputs* whereas I was concerned with *outcomes*. A small difference, you might say. But the dictionary does not think so. Outcomes are defined as 'the consequence or the result of' something else. Outputs are defined as 'quantity produced; for example, data from a computer in printed or coded form'. The latter is quantifiable, the former not necessarily so and allows for qualitative results; one is measurable, the other not necessarily so; one appears as an objective result, the other could be more subjectively perceived. He and I were not talking about the same thing. Although 'outcomes' is an acceptable term for corporate planners (particularly in so far as 'unintended outcomes' are monitored) the pressure is there to make as many of them as possible fit into the measurable box of outputs.

Those of you who have dealt with EEO management plans are already prac- tised in the use of the language of the corporate planner. The format of EEO plans is based on a rational organization model (for recent critical reviews of EEO and EO in Australia, see Burton, 1991; Poiner and Wills, 1991). You identify a problem, set objectives to be achieved to deal with it, break them down into component parts, develop strategies and action plans to reach them, set targets to be achieved within a specific time frame, identify officers responsible for their achievement and determine appropriate monitoring and evaluation procedures. What you do not do, on paper, is identify all the resistances, the interests you will not be serving, the delicate processes of negotiating and bargaining you know will be involved in order to achieve your desired outcome or goal, which is not necessarily desired by everyone around you. On paper it looks like a rational, means–end relationship. In other words, the politics of the situation and the value judgments that will be brought to bear on it are not formally acknowledged, even though they may selectively be commented upon in the annual EEO report. It is no different for a corporate plan.

The language of corporate planning can mystify and give the impression of an apolitical process. People often talk in acronyms, so that you know you are ignorant when you do not know to what they are referring: PPBS (programme planning and budgeting system), MIS (management information systems), SWOT (strengths and weaknesses of the organization, opportunities and threats in the environment), PERT (programme evaluation review technique). The corporate plan also has the appearance of neutrality, of not being based on any particular set of values. The language of corporate planners leads one to believe that there is certain knowledge about means–ends relationships in organizations, about cause–effect relationships, about the measurability of the important com- ponents of organizational work, about the relationship between organiza- tional structures and organizational performance. Indeed, it implies there is an organizational goal as an uncontested fact, to which all organizational work must be directed, in partial fulfilment of it.

If you understand the language and also understand that this language does not reflect reality as much as it attempts to shape it, to direct people's activity and ideas in certain ways, then you can more confidently enter into dialogue with corporate planners, borrow some of their vocabulary, add to it in ways consistent with it and contribute to the shaping of the practice of the corporate planning exercise. While you are mystified by it you are not in a position to do this. But there are limits to what can be done within the orthodox corporate planning framework, which is why I also want to give you some keys to opening it up in ways that will allow some of your concerns on to the corporate agenda.

The rational model of organizations, and variations of it, continue to inform organizational restructuring, change, and reform processes. We could be forgiven for quoting a writer who referred to 'the recycling of warmed-over recipes for reform' (Heydebrand, 1983, p. 112). Corporate planning is not new, although much of the language is new. Neither is it based on a new or innovative image of what organizations could be like.

I want to now address the use of metaphors to describe organizations and emphasize the important point that ways of seeing are at the same times ways of not seeing; that the metaphor chosen to describe organizations is necessarily selective, and what it obscures from view is as important as what it admits. With the use of any metaphor (this man is like a lion) attention is drawn selectively to some features (his lion-like qualities) at the expense of others (Morgan, 1986, pp. 12–13).

Rationality has been described as the myth of modern society (Morgan, 1986, p. 135). To be rational is to be endowed with reason. Organizational belief systems emphasize its importance, and with it the associated concept of efficiency. It is a powerful form of legitimation of the organization's existence and activities. Metaphors used to describe organizations (as if organizations were machines, organisms, cybernetic systems), which retain this central idea of rational processes, hide from view the importance of human agency, ethical accountability and political community (Brown, 1978, p. 375). The language of rational models is not the language of human action. What is obscured is the important role of judgment, dialogue, morality, and the role of creativity, intuition, and other essentially human characteristics (Ferguson, 1984). Does this mean they are written out of organizational life, that we are supposed to leave these aspects of ourselves outside the door of our work organization? Not entirely. The idea of a corporate culture, which establishes the place of values, traditions, norms, language, ritual and myth in organizational life, allow them in but in a curtailed form. The human characteristics we value appear to be driven by our rational (for rational, read administered and socialized) selves in such a way that we, the human resources of the organization, have reasonably aligned our personal goals with that of the organization, so that we 'fit in' and the individual and the organization benefit from the association. In order to be sure that this alignment is secured, the corporate planning process sets up various systems of monitoring, evaluation, and feedback, so that if we err, we are put back on course. If we cannot fit in (and remember, all cultural systems have their exclusion processes, particularly where minority values, interests, and experiences are concerned) we do not benefit from the system's rewards.

The technocratic strategies which are deployed in a corporate planning context are presented as the rational, economically efficient, administrative solutions to organizational problems (Heydebrand, 1983, p. 97). Questions within a rational paradigm are posed as technical rather than social in a broad sense (Bolman and Deal, 1984, p. 251); they do not direct attention to underlying structural arrangements. Rather than 'Who gets what?' or 'Are there different ways of organizing with entirely different outcomes?' we have 'What is the best way to do X?', X being the predetermined goal which is frequently not subject to debate.

Rather than having multiple organizational rationalities, and multiple, complex and contradictory organizational goals (Heydebrand, 1983, p. 100), and competing and conflicting interests and interpretations of what the goals mean in practice, we have, from within this framework, people's interests and those of occupational and structural groups coinciding with those officially defined as the organization's (Heydebrand, 1983, p. 109). All organizational problems, whether they be problems of equity, or resource allocation, or power, are provided with technical–rational (that is, depoliticized) solutions (Heydebrand, 1983, p. 97; see also Alvesson, 1985).

This is why it is hard to fit EEO readily within the corporate planning process, with its emphasis on technical–administrative solutions. The concern with techniques, with 'the efficient establishment of systems', Marcuse argues, has the effect of 'removing from reflection the total social framework of interest in which strategies are chosen' (Habermas, 1970, p. 82, cited by Bryson, 1987). Further, there is a denial of the role of values in the solving of administrative problems, so that when value questions arise, such as the equitable distribution of reward structures or the issue of redress under affirmative action programmes, they cannot be handled readily. The problems for which there are no ready solutions get downplayed, 'to create time for solutions to emerge, or in the hope that problems they pose will disappear' (Morgan, 1986, p. 90). It is useful to think of what is going on as a set of strategies, rather than as a unified, coherent system, so that you can see the potential for resistance and challenge, you can see ways to influence the process (Heydebrand, 1983, p. 102). Moreover, it is important to recognize that they are, to use a phrase from Bourdieu, 'officializing strategies', 'their object being to transmute "egoistic", private, particular interests into disinterested, collective, publicly avowable, legitimate interests' (1977, p. 40).

The metaphor of organizations as political systems opens up a set of questions it is difficult to pose from within the models of organizations as machines or other scientifically, rationally designed systems. Rationality here becomes a resource to be used in organizational politics (Morgan, 1986, p. 195). The idea of rationality justifies actions in terms that appear reasonable from an organizational standpoint or from the standpoint of an interested and strategic or powerful public. As one author has put it, PERT charts and critical path analysis and other management methods are as effective technically as rain dancing, but they can be effective politically. A reputation for managerial efficiency makes it difficult for anyone to challenge to corporate plan (Sapolsky, cited by Pfeffer, 1981, p. 337).

The political perspective views organizations as 'political arenas that house a complex variety of individuals and interest groups' (Bolman and Deal, 1984, p. 109). Bolman and Deal present some propositions which summarize this perspective. First, the most important organizational decisions involve the allocation of scarce resources. Second, organizations can be viewed as coalitions, composed of a number of individuals and groups with different values, preferences, beliefs, information and perceptions of reality. Third, organizational goals, far from being set and uncontested, emerge from processes of bargaining and negotiation. Finally, because of the scarcity of resources and the fact of enduring differences among individuals and interest groups, power and conflict are central features of organizational life (1984, p. 109). Of course, the parties to organizational situations are not equal in their bargaining power, and their values and beliefs are not equal in status. This is where a more developed concept of the politics of organizational life would take into account the broader social context within which the bargaining process takes place. It would also connect the powerful language of rationality to dominant value systems (including ideas about the positive relationship of science, technology and progress, and the negative relationship of women and work value) in the wider society.

But we know how awkward people feel about discussing the politics of organizational life. It appears to raise uncomfortable questions about the organization's mission and the effectiveness with which it is being pursued. The acknowledgment of diverse interests and values appears to be an acceptance that the organization is performing at a less than optimal level. Yet the political perspective suggests that these are the facts of organizational life, so to speak of optimum performance as relying on their absence is to speak nonsense. In addition, the political perspective would argue that contest and debate, conflict and negotiation are not only inevitable, but productive of new ideas and of change (Pfeffer, 1981, pp. 334–42). The problem is that to acknowledge these processes undermines the legitimating facade of the rational, efficient pursuit of organizational objectives. It raises the difficult questions of 'Efficiency for whom?', 'Rational from which point of view?' and 'Whose interests are being protected or pursued?'

A useful metaphor which is not a radical departure from orthodox thinking about organizations, which has elements of the scientific in it, yet allows scope for challenging what is going on around you, is that of the organization as a brain, or as a cybernetic system (Morgan, 1986). Here we have the idea of a machine again, but one with the adaptive capacities of organisms, a machine which is flexible and adaptive like a living thing, like a brain. Let me say that not all metaphors are used to their full capacity. You will find the language of cybernetics used by corporate planners without the full implications of the metaphor drawn out or practised. This, of course, is the political aspect of metaphor use, of the application of models and frameworks.

Cybernetics has as its base the self-regulating behaviours of organisms and the development of mechanisms by which machines incorporate this self-regulating process (Morgan, 1986, p. 85). The core insight of early cybernetics was that the ability to self-regulate is derived from information exchange involving *negative feedback* (Morgan, 1986, p. 85). Did you know, for example, that when you go through the process of picking up a mug of coffee, what you are doing is avoiding not picking it up? Cybernetics suggests that this action occurs through a process of error elimination whereby deviations between hand and object are reduced at each and every stage of the process so that in the end no error remains (Morgan, 1986, p. 85).

In organizational terms, negative feedback is part of the process of measuring and comparing actual results with a standard: checking the effectiveness of an output with a standard and correcting for the error by altering the input in some way so that the difference between the output and the standard is reduced (O'Shaughnessy, 1976, p. 201). This is a simple system, called by Morgan 'single-loop' learning. This is because the standard is given. The negative feedback is on the discrepancy between output and standard. There is no capacity in the machine to question or change the standard.

Double-loop learning, which cybernetic systems such as advanced computers or the brain can perform, can detect and correct errors in *operating* norms and thus influence the standards that guide their operations. Learning to learn, we might say. It requires reflexive activity, a double look at the appropriateness or relevance of the operating norms (Morgan, 1986, p. 88). In organizational terms it involves a corporate philosophy with encourages the continuing review of and challenge to norms, policies and operating procedures by encouraging continuing debate and innovation (Morgan, 1986, p. 89). In other words, it opens up the possibility of asking questions from the political framework in the technical language of the rational framework.

Some of the technical–scientific language can be used as resources in your attempt to challenge prevailing values, attitudes and practices. You can speak about innovative and progressive policies as consistent with a corporate planning process which is flexible and adaptive enough to be taking into account the rapid social changes occurring around and within the organization in which you work. While you are remaining consistent with the language of the corporate planner you are pushing the conception of such a planning process more into the direction that is suitable for an equal employment opportunity environment. For an organization which aims to present itself as rapidly reorganizing and adapting to be more effective and efficient in a changing set of economic and social circumstances, your contribution cannot so readily be ignored. Part of your argument, and this is consistent with the language of the corporate planner, is that affirmative action is an integral component of a progressive and innovative human resource management system, at least in the forseeable future. But remember the difference between regarding what you do within a corporate planning framework as an end in itself, and what you use as a strategy for reshaping practices and thus people's understandings of what the ends might be.

Remember, too, that organizations are, as well as other things, political entities — they are constituted by activities which represent competing values, conflicting interests, competition over scarce resources and the exercise of power. Your adoption of the language of the corporate planner is to facilitate the process whereby your employment equity concerns are put on the corporate agenda. You need to concentrate on opening up the terms on which the corporate plan is discussed, terms which tend to close off options and possibilities for alternative management practices. This is a dynamic process, and you cannot afford to lose sight of the underlying values of EEO and the broader equity issues which prompted a concern for EEO programmes in Australia over a decade ago. But Kathy Ferguson reminds us, and this is perhaps the entry point to a more radical critique of the corporate planning exercise, 'feminism is not compatible with bureaucracy, and like all forms of opposition, it is endangered by too-close contact with bureaucratic linguistic and institutional forms' (1984, p. 180).

Note

1 This paper is a revised version of one presented to a seminar on EEO and Corporate Planning sponsored by the NSW EEO Co-ordinators' Group, 19 August 1987. See also, Burton, 1987b.

References

ALVESSON, M. (1985) 'A critical framework for organizational analysis', *Organization Studies*, 6, 2, pp. 117–38.
BOLMAN, L.G. and DEAL, T.E. (1984) *Modern Approaches to Understanding and Managing Organizations*, San Francisco, Jossey-Bass.

BOURDIEU, P. (1977) *Outline of a Theory of Practice*, Cambridge, Cambridge University Press.

BROWN, R.H. (1978) 'Bureaucracy as praxis: Toward political phenomenology of formal organizations', *Administrative Science Quarterly*, 23, September, pp. 365–82.

BRYSON, L. (1987) 'Women and management in the public sector', *Australian Journal of Public Administration*, 156, 3, pp. 259–72.

BURTON, C. (1987a) 'Equal employment opportunities — a future? The consequences of government policy on EEO in the public service', *Canberra Bulletin of Public Administration*, October, pp. 77–81.

BURTON, C. (1987b) 'Merit and gender: Organizations and the mobilization of masculine bias', *Australian Journal of Social Issues*, 22, 2 (May), pp. 424–35.

BURTON, C. (1991) *The Promise and the Price: The Struggle for Equal Opportunity in Women's Employment*, Sydney, Allen and Unwin.

BURTON, C., HAG, R. and THOMPSON, G. (1987) *Women's Worth: Pay Equity and Job Evaluation in Australia*, Canberra, Australian Government Publishing Science.

FERGUSON, K. (1984) *The Feminist Case against Bureaucracy*, Philadelphia, Temple University Press.

HABERMAS, J. (1970) *Toward a Rational Society*, Boston, Beacon Press.

HEYDEBRAND, W.V. (1983) 'Technocratic corporatism: Toward a theory of occupational and organizational transformation', in HALL, RICHARD H. and QUINN, ROBERT E. (Eds) *Organizational Theory and Public Policy*, London, Sage.

MORGAN, G. (1986) *Images of Organization*, London, Sage.

O'SHAUGHNESSY, J. (1976) *Patterns of Business Organization*, London, Allen and Unwin.

PFEFFER, J. (1981) *Power in Organizations*, Boston, Pitman.

POINER, G. and WILLS, S. (1991) *The Gifthorse: A Critical Look at Equal Employment Opportunity in Australia*, Sydney, Allen and Unwin.

Chapter 12

Educational Leadership as Emancipatory Praxis

Shirley Grundy

In this chapter I wish to consider the possibility of alternative forms of educational leadership; that is, alternatives to the hierarchical, bureaucratic approaches which characterize most of our experiences. I do not wish specifically to claim that these alternative forms of praxis are exclusively feminist, although I would want to claim that they are essentially so. One of the abiding contributions of feminist discourse is that it has opened up to both men and women the possibility of challenging the 'taken-for-granted' world and has exposed hitherto unrecognized interests in domination. Through this discourse the anti-democratic nature of so many of our social institutions, educational institutions among them, has also been exposed.

This exploration will be grounded in an analysis of human work and educational practice which draws upon Habermas's (1972) conceptual framework of 'knowledge-constitutive interests'. The importance of the theory of cognitive interests for educational practice has been explored in some depth in *Curriculum: Product or Praxis?* (Grundy, 1987b) and will not be rehearsed in detail here. Rather, the nature of technical, practical and emancipatory interests will be briefly sketched. What these theoretical constructs mean for the work of those who elect to take on positions of educational leadership will be explored in more detail before I address the question of whether it is actually possible for educational leadership to pursue emancipatory goals.

Knowledge-constitutive Interests

Habermas argues that there are three fundamental human interests which constitute, or shape and determine, what we are willing to call knowledge. These are the technical, the practical and the emancipatory interests.

The task of the empirical–analytic sciences incorporates a technical cognitive interest; that of the historical–hermeneutic sciences incorporates a practical interest; and the approach of critically oriented sciences incorporates the emancipatory cognitive interest (Habermas, 1972, p. 308).

The technical interest exhibits itself through the methodology of positivism which aims to produce knowledge of the world which is grounded in 'positive' (that is, objective) observations and experience. It is the programme of the empirical–analytic sciences to work out the objective 'rules', by which the universe operates. Once science has discovered the 'rules' technology will be able to utilize that knowledge to enable persons (significantly, usually designated 'mankind') to control the environment for their (specifically 'his') well-being. The technical interest, then, is 'a fundamental interest in controlling the environment through rule-following action based upon empirically grounded laws' (Grundy, 1987b, p. 12).

While the fundamental orientation of the technical interest is towards control, that of the practical interest is towards understanding. This is not the technical understanding of principle formulation for the manipulation and management of the environment. Rather, it is a subjective understanding which recognizes the source of human life and society in the interaction of humans with the environment (both physical and social) rather than in competition with that environment for survival.

This fundamental human cognitive interest exhibits itself through the agenda of the historical–hermeneutic sciences where 'access to the facts is provided by the understanding of meaning, not observation. The verification of lawlike hypotheses in the empirical–analytic sciences has its counterpart here in the interpretation texts' (Habermas, 1972, p. 309). Acknowledging that such knowledge is subjective not objective by its very nature (in other words, knowledge of and by 'subjects' not of 'objects' in the universe), is not to devalue such knowledge. It is to recognize that not all human knowledge has as its source an interest in control. Knowledge which is constituted by a practical interest is knowledge which is grounded in 'a fundamental interest in understanding the environment through interaction based upon a consensual interpretation of meaning' (Grundy, 1987b, p. 14).

These two kinds of knowing have, of course, long been recognized and have been identified as objective *v.* subjective knowledge, or quantitative *v.* qualitative methodologies. The value of the work of critical social scientists, such as Habermas, however, has been to show the shortcomings of both of these forms of knowledge. Habermas argues that there is another, even more fundamental human interest,[1] the interest in emancipation, which will shape and determine yet another form of knowing. This is the knowledge of the 'critically oriented sciences'.

Knowledge constituted by an emancipatory interest is knowledge which recognizes the fundamental importance of freedom for being human and also recognizes that freedom is inextricably linked with truth and justice. Moreover, emancipatory knowledge clearly provides a basis for the critique of empirical–analytic science because the very claim to objectivity and value freedom masks a fundamental interest in control and domination. However, the emancipatory interest also exposes problems with interpretative, hermeneutic ways of knowing. It turns out that the interpretations or meanings we are able to make in any situation are socially constructed, and hence susceptible to being hegemonically determined and once again serve interests in domination, not liberation. What is needed is a form of critical discourse which will open up the potential for the recognition of the overt control exercised by technical relationships and the covert domination consequent upon the hegemonic production of meaning. Such a form of discourse will be informed by 'a fundamental interest in emancipation and empowerment to engage in autonomous action arising out of authentic, critical insights into the social construction of human society' (Grundy, 1987b, p. 19).

The feminist movement and feminist discourse is, of course, a powerful example of a critical social science which is grounded in an emancipatory interest. Feminist discourse also provides many examples of how our meanings are socially constructed so that our way of interpreting the world continues to serve rather than challenge unrecognized interests in domination. For instance, one interpretation of the meaning of liberation is that women must learn to be like men. Ferguson (1984, p. 94) exposes the relation which this interpretation has with hegemonic power relations when she insists, 'women will not be liberated by becoming "like men" but rather by abolishing the entire system that allocates human potential according to gender'.

Forms of Action

The theory of knowledge-constitutive interests is not just a theory about knowledge, it also has important implications for action. All of the summaries of the meanings of the various interests provided above link the form of knowledge to a form of action. The technical interests generates rule-following action grounded in empirical laws. Interaction is both the source and consequence of knowledge informed by a practical interest, while autonomous action is the hallmark of emancipatory knowledge. Let us examine, however, a little more closely the nature of these various forms of action, for it is only by understanding the nature of human action that the possibilities for alternatives can become evident.

Technical Action

Technical action has been recognized as a fundamental form of human activity since the Greeks. The Greeks called this sort of action *poietike* (or 'marking' action) and Aristotle identified it as the action in which artisans and poets engaged. Such action has a number of components. The first is the guiding *eidos*, that is, the action plan, pattern, objective, the 'image' of what is to be done. The *eidos* for technical action will be informed by empirical–analytic knowledge of what it is objectively possible to achieve. This *eidos* is then transformed into a material outcome through the skill (to the Greeks *techne*) of the actors. Once again, skill will be determined by empirically grounded rules of operation which will ensure that the actors produce the outcome envisaged by the *eidos*. It will be possible to make specific judgments about the adequacy of the work of the actors by comparing the outcome with the specifications in the *eidos*.

This technical operation is a familiar one within our society. The language of skills and outcomes dominates industrial and educational discourse alike. It is the hegemonic discourse of late-twentieth-century capitalism. As such, it is also the characteristic discourse of bureaucracy. Note how many of the characteristics of the above analysis of the technical interest are present in Ferguson's (1984, p. 7) description of a bureaucracy:

> The modern bureaucracy is usually described as an organization having the following traits: a complex rational division of labor, with fixed duties and jurisdictions; stable, rule-governed authority channels and

universally applied performance guidelines; a horizontal division of graded authority, or hierarchy, entailing supervision from above; a complex system of written record-keeping, based on scientific procedures that standardize communications and increase control; objective recruitment based on impersonal standards of expertise; predictable, standardized management procedures following general rules.

Educational leadership practices which are informed by a technical cognitive interest will conform to this bureaucratic model. Leadership will operate hierarchically. Leaders will be expected to exercise control so that the objectives of the organization, clearly defined and articulated, will be achieved. There will be a division of labour between the leader who plans (or who receives and interprets plans imposed from elsewhere) and the practitioners who implement the plans. The language of administrative planning will be 'end–directed', with criteria for the achievement of the objectives being articulated along with the plans. It will be the leader who will be responsible for the training of the practitioners, and such training will be oriented towards the development of skills. It will also be the responsibility of the leader to motivate and enthuse practitioners to embrace the specified objectives and work for their achievement.

The technical or bureaucratic administrator will be responsible for the evaluation of the outcomes of the practitioners' work. Outcomes will be assessed by processes of measurement and the leader will be concerned with the development of appropriate instruments for assessment.

From this analysis we can identify some characteristics of the technical leader. She will be one who:

- sets unambiguous short-term goals
- pre-selects the strategies for the implementation of institutional objectives
- structures and sequences implementation strategies clearly
- anticipates problems and prepares alternative strategies
- as far as possible supplies answers to staff questions
- is well prepared for staff meetings
- runs orderly, task-oriented staff meetings
- enthuses practitioners through her charisma
- defuses conflict and redirects dissatisfaction
- identifies areas of staff weakness
- arranges staff training opportunities for the development of skills
- rewards staff success.

It is not, however, the behaviours alone which indicate the technical interest. Rather, it is the interest in control and the unequal distribution of power within the institutional setting which are indicative of a bureaucratic consciousness. Thus, while all of the above actions may result in an efficient system of education, each act operates to vest control in the hierarchical system through the leader. Control of the system as a whole, and, ultimately, of practice itself, does not lie with the practitioners who, nevertheless, must carry out the purposes of the system through the direction of the leader. The meaning of these leadership behaviours can be appreciated more fully as they are juxtaposed with other forms of leadership.

Practical Action

That which we now call 'practical action', that is action informed by a practical cognitive interest, was a form of praxis to the Greeks. Praxis (literally meaning 'action') was the sort of reflective action in which the politicians (that is, all male citizens) engaged. It was the sort of deliberative action requiring the exercising of judgment that was necessary for decision-marking in a democracy. Praxis was informed by an *eidos* of 'the Good', that is, a shared consensus of what was in the best interests of the city-state.

This is the sort of action which is characteristic of the practical interest because it is essentially interactive and deliberative. An interpretation of a situation provides the knowledge basis for this kind of action rather than a set of empirically grounded rules.

Its interactive nature means that this form of praxis requires a more democratic form of organization for decision-making. As I argued elsewhere (Grundy, 1987a), the importance of judgment in the process of deliberative action indicates that the practical interest opens up possibilities for professional practice that the technical interest denies.

This will mean that the educational leader whose work is informed by a practical interest will be concerned to engage staff in the joint planning of goals. These goals will be formulated within considerations of 'the Good' of the client group for which the institution is responsible. Judgment will clearly be central to a determination of that 'Good'. Moreover, educational plans will not simply be concerned with outcomes, but will also entail a concern for learning processes by clients, and indeed for the quality of the decision-making processes of the staff as a whole. The educational leader will, therefore, become a facilitator of deliberating processes more than a designer of plans.

The division of labour between the developer of action plans and the practitioner who enacts the plans will not be as distinct when a practical interest is informing action and organization. The leadership role in developing organizational structures which facilitate understanding of all facets of the work of the organization will be crucial.

The leader will also be concerned with the evaluation of the outcomes of action, but not in a way that utilizes external measurement criteria as an indicator of success. The professional leader will want to set up evaluation processes which are themselves interactive and which centralize deliberative judgment-making. Concern will centre upon the meaning of the work of the institution rather than upon the products of the labour.

From this analysis of the characteristics of administrative work which is informed by a practical interest, it follows that the 'practical' educational leader will be one who:

- has an overriding concern for the welfare of staff and clients
- encourages staff to pursue broad professional development options
- assists staff to set broad, long-term goals
- involves staff in decision-making
- facilitates the use of deliberative processes for decision-making
- shares leadership roles among staff
- encourages staff to adopt an experimental approach to their work

- recognizes a variety of evidence of achievement of goals
- arranges for shared reflection on and analysis of the outcomes of action.

Beyond Practical Action

The question which needs to be asked at this point is whether this form of practical action is the alternative to bureaucratic control that many feminists and others concerned with exploring the possibilities for more just and equitable ways of working are seeking? In some ways it is. Following Ferguson's (1984) critique of bureaucracy she enunciates a vision of feminist praxis which is consistent with and builds upon the experience of women as 'caretakers, nurturers and providers for the needs of others' (p. 158). Ferguson argues that 'a feminist restructuring of work entails rejection of the hierarchical division of labor of bureaucratic capitalism and the reintegration of the planning and performance of tasks' (p. 205). The form of educational leadership which is informed by a practical interest meets this criterion, for participatory decision-making is its hallmark.

The restructuring of work to allow for participation by all members of the institution will allow for the sort of deliberative approaches that are characteristic of the practical interest. Ferguson describes this possibility as follows: 'Active, participatory citizenship is a process through which individuals create themselves with others through the shared processes of speaking, deliberating and judging, ordering their collective lives through institutions they have designed and in a language they have made their own' (p. 174).

Again, the sort of action associated with the practical interest seems to fit well with this aspiration. We have noted above the importance of deliberation, judgment and interaction. However, the stipulation which Ferguson makes regarding the ownership by participants, not only of the problem to be addressed, but also of the very language through which deliberation will proceed and indeed of the institution itself, suggests that practical action may not be quite the alternative form of action we are seeking. Indeed, reflection upon ways in which institutions co-opt participants to work towards institutionally designed and directed goals by introducing ways of working that are seemingly participatory, will suggest that another alternative is desirable. The use of the Nominal Group Technique (Hegarty, 1971) for goal setting within institutions is a case in point. This process engages seemingly democratic and participatory methods of problem identification. Input is derived from each participant and action priorities are decided upon by voting procedures. By applying this procedure, however, while a form of consensus is achieved, conflict is defused and along with it any argumentation through which critique and alternative interpretations of meaning could also be achieved.

And here is the crux of the problem with this form of praxis. Our meanings are often hegemonically determined. When we deliberate about what is 'Good' for our clients we are all too likely to accept traditional definitions of worthwhile practice which are embedded in the traditional practices of our profession. For instance, does the aspiration for individualized instruction in schools serve the interests of students (especially working-class or Aboriginal students)? Is individualized instruction 'good' for ruling-class students? What group or groups' interests are served, then, by this traditional educational 'good'? What does it really mean to have a school welfare policy built around the concept of rewards for acceptable behaviour? Is it possible that the tradition of positive reinforcement by teachers of student behaviour really masks a system of authoritarian power relationships?

It is not, therefore, that there is anything undemocratic about the practices of educational leadership informed by a practical interest. If these practices are engaged as authentic expressions of power sharing, then they provide a useful starting-point for alternative forms of educational leadership. However, these practices need to be situated within a framework of critical social theory if they are to be emancipatory.

Emancipatory Praxis

The first thing that distinguishes emancipatory praxis from other forms of reflective practice is its critical nature. By 'critical' here I do not mean negative criticism, rather I refer to a propensity for critique which is constantly entertaining the possibility that things could be otherwise. The search for alternatives is not, however, simply a yen for novelty. Not any old alternative will do. The critique which opens up the possibility for emancipatory praxis is one which recognizes that the way things are perceived to be may, in fact, be the way they are being made to appear so that some existing unequal relationships and unjust practices may not be recognized for what they are. This is, of course, how ideology works through the development of a hegemonic meaning system, as Apple (1979, p. 5) notes:

> Hegemony acts to 'saturate' our very consciousness, so that the educational, economic and social world we see and interact with, and the commonsense interpretations we put on it, become the world *tout court*, the only world. Hence hegemony refers not to congeries of meaning that reside at the abstract level somewhere at the 'roof of our brain'. Rather it refers to an organized assemblage of meanings and practices, the central, effective and dominant system of meanings, values and actions which are lived.

The purpose of critique, therefore, is to reflect upon this assemblage of meanings in order 'to determine when theoretical statements grasp invariant regularities of social action as such and when they express ideologically frozen relations of dependence that can in principle be transformed' (Habermas, 1972, p. 310). Within the term 'theoretical statements' here we can include traditions and meaning systems.

But what is to be the basis of such critique? Habermas would argue that it is that most fundamental of human interests, emancipation. Furthermore, emancipation means freedom from domination, and such freedom is possible only within communities in which justice and equality are the fundamental determinants of action.

Thus the educational leader who seeks to work in emancipatory ways will engage in a similar set of practices to those which were characteristic of a leader whose work was informed by a practical interest. However, all those practices will be situated within a socially critical framework. Participation in decision-making, therefore, will extend beyond participation by practitioners to encompass participation by all those who are affected by the action, including, in the case of educational institutions, students. Negotiation of goals and institutional purposes will be the hallmark of emancipatory practice. Such negotiation will not seek to defuse conflict, but will regard contestation as a legitimate aspect of critical planning. Plans will be developed out of processes of critical self-reflection which will take account of the social construction of knowledge. Planning will specifically encompass goals of justice and equality. Planning will be a process of problem-posing, that is, a process of recognizing the potentially problematical nature of all social action and interaction. In this way planning processes will confront the taken-for-granted.

Action which follows from planning will be collaborative, once again with every person encompassed within the field of action being responsible for the taking of action. Action will not necessarily be a process of problem-solving, but rather of further problem-posing which will be fruitful for future critical reflection.

Evaluation will also employ critical self-reflection so that judgments about the worthwhileness of action will be made on the basis of criteria of justice and equity. The scope of any evaluation will encompass the social context of action as well as the action itself, given a recognition of the social construction and situation of all human action.

Approaching the organization and conduct of educational institutional life in this way is to engage in forms of critical pedagogy (Freire, 1972). This will mean that, along with staff and students, emancipatory educational administrators will become students of their own work and that of their institution, recognizing the hegemonic social construction of that work. Giroux (1986, p. 39) calls such people 'resisting intellectuals':

> Central to the category of resisting intellectuals is the interplay of the languages of critique and possibility. Utilizing the language of self-critique, resisting intellectuals employ the discourse of self-criticism as well as forms of critical analysis that interrogate the ideological and material practices of domination. . . . The language of critique unites with the language of possibility when it points to the conditions for new forms of culture, alternative social practices, new modes of communication and a practical vision for the future.

It is not so easy to list a series of characteristics of the educational leader who seeks to work in such emancipatory ways. First it must be recognized that institutionalized leadership is, in general, antithetical to emancipatory praxis, grounded as institutionalized leadership is in hierarchical power relationships. There are, however, some possibilities, and these encompass what Habermas (1974) has called the 'organization of enlightenment' and the 'organization of action'.

The development of a critical consciousness which is the basis for emancipatory praxis is a process of enlightenment. Habermas has used the analogy of the therapeutic discourse as a means to understanding the process of enlightenment. In that form of discourse life experiences are reconstructed in the light of critical theorems. These theorems do not have explanatory power for the client, however, unless they are authenticated in her/his self-reflections. It is, then, for the therapist to organize situations which open up the possibility of enlightenment, but strong professional sanctions must operate to ensure the autonomy of the client.

Of course, there are problems with seeing educational leadership as a therapeutic discourse, but the analogy has reflective potential. If the development of emancipatory praxis is consequent upon critical reflection then processes of enlightenment will be important. The educational leader whose work is informed by an emancipatory interest will work in ways akin to the facilitator of emancipatory action research.[2] In general this will involve:

1 Providing access to critical theorems for participants in reflection. The designated educational leader will have flexible working arrangements which provide the opportunity and obligation for reading and discussion not available to other members of the educational community. Such theoretical knowledge should not be hoarded to empower the leader, but should be used for the empowerment of the whole group.

2 Ensuring symmetrical communication. Emancipation is dependent upon the equalization of power relations within and between groups. Symmetrical communication between participants in a discourse is an essential component of equality. The group facilitator can work towards symmetrical communication on a number of levels:
— by assisting the group to develop a common language (this will not be jargon that only the group understands, and which, therefore', excludes potential participants; rather it will be a concern that meanings are common and understood by all);
— through the development of group processes (this will entail bringing to consciousness unequal interaction patterns in the group, particularly gender- and status-related patterns of talk, and generally encouraging reflection upon decision-making processes);
— redistributing power within the group (this will entail sharing responsibility for group organization among members of the group).

3 Providing an institutional and social context for the work of the group. This may involve the establishment of links with other institutional groups who have similar aspirations and keeping the group informed of wider institutional constraints and possibilities.

In all this it becomes obvious that the action of the educational leader who works in emancipatory ways is more educational than managerial. So in the realm of action it is support that is needed for emancipatory praxis, not direction. The notion of the leader being 'above' or 'in front' of the practitioners who comprise the organizational unit is anathema to emancipation. The emancipatory educational leader will see her work as being enabling and supportive of the action of the practitioners. This will, of course, also entail a fundamental reorientation of the values assigned to different types of work. The value of the work of the practitioners must be acknowledged as being central to the educational enterprise and hence to the institution. But the work of the educational leader must also be recognized as comprising a set of practices and, as such, being amenable to investigation, evaluation and improvement.

Is Emancipatory Praxis Possible?

Emancipatory praxis is not a set of behaviours in which an educational leader can be trained. This form of praxis is grounded in a critical consciousness which will manifest itself in action that will always be becoming emancipatory. The question for the educational leader is not, 'Am I emancipated and how can I emancipate my staff?' but, 'How can I engage in forms of critical, self-reflective and collaborative work which will create conditions so that the people with whom I work can come to control their knowledge and practice?'

Of course, emancipatory educational leadership is antithetical to bureaucratic forms of organization. This means that it is likely that the educational leader who seeks to work in these ways will come into conflict with other levels of the bureaucratic hierarchy which may demand certain leadership styles. Furthermore, staff of educational institutions may resist collaborative work, believing that the administrator is failing in her responsibility by not providing a traditional leadership role.

Bureaucracies are not monolithic, however. Participatory worker involvement is now regarded as a respectable management strategy, the theory being that workers who feel involved in setting and achieving corporate goals will be more productive. The fashionable management strategy is to set up shop-floor 'quality circles' which allow workers to develop their own strategy for improving production. In many ways such strategies merely co-opt practitioners into supporting corporate goals as if they were their own and, by the illusion of participation, further mask exploitative power and labour relations. However, such officially sanctioned practices also provide cracks within the bureaucratic structures which can be exploited for emancipatory purposes.

School-based curriculum development is a case in point. Encouraged as a strategy for making schooling more relevant to the needs of particular populations, SBCD, in many ways, serves hegemonic interests of maintaining unequal power relations in society. The opportunity to engage in curriculum development, however, also affords opportunities to become engaged in curriculum critique and to take control of an aspect of the educational enterprise. An educational leader whose work is informed by an emancipatory interest will be able, perhaps very gradually, to transform the process of curriculum development into a process of critical pedagogy with emancipatory potential.

Postscript: A Personal Reflection

This paper was written as part of the discourse which Habermas (1974, p. 32) would call 'the formation and extension of critical theorems'. It is essentially a theoretical discourse about leadership practices, which is informed by a critique of generalized, but reified practices. It is not a description or critique of any specific practice. Coming back to the paper with some distance between the original writing and a renewed reading, I am happy with the way in which it stands up as a theoretical discourse which, I would hope, could and would 'be applied and tested in a unique manner by the initiation of processes of reflection carried on within [appropriate] groups' (Habermas, 1974, p. 32): specifically, groups of educational leaders.

Since I began writing this paper, however, I have taken on a more demanding educational leadership position than had hitherto been my experience. I have been head of a university department, consisting of some twenty academic staff (approximately 50 per cent of whom are women), two administrative assistants (both women), various part-time staff and post-graduate research students. It seems appropriate, therefore, to engage in some personal self-reflection on the meaning of educational leadership as emancipatory praxis.

I will use as a focus for this brief reflection the three areas of work noted above as characteristic of an emancipatory leader: that is, providing access to critical theorems; ensuring symmetrical communication; and providing an institutional and social context for the work of the group.

I was[3] not happy about the way in which I was personally able to foster the intellectual growth of the department. My own reading and research were seriously neglected. I was not disciplined enough to set time aside for my own intellectual well-being. On the other hand, this was one area where the principle of our being a 'collective' not a set of individuals became evident. My being head of department did not mean that I had to exercise leadership in every area. There are a number of members of the department who are able to take leadership in this area, fostering collaborative research and sharing their research experience with others. All I had to do was not block such activity and be a learner along with the rest of the group.

I saw the task of ensuring symmetrical communication and equalizing power relations within the group as central to my work as an educational leader. In many ways that was not difficult because it is a department staffed by very experienced, highly competent and professional people. I was very much aware of my role as servant of these people, and facilitator of their work. This feeling of equality may have been enhanced by the fact that I was on the same salary scale as the majority of members of the department. Salary can be used to provide tangible evidence of equality or lack thereof.

However, the administrative structure of the institution has designated me as the 'supervisor' of this group of people and given to me the official responsibility for organizing, monitoring and approving many aspects of the work of these colleagues. I saw my task, therefore, as being to facilitate this work, not to be its judge.

Living this principle, however, required moment-by-moment vigilance, constantly positioning myself in relation to members of the department (including administrative assistants) as colleague, not as superior. I adopted a number of strategies to symbolically enact this principle. I rearranged the head of department office so that I was not sitting behind a desk whenever anyone entered; I would vacate my high desk chair to sit beside visitors in a chair of the same size; when colleagues indicated they wanted to see me while I was busy, I would visit them in their rooms as soon as I was free, rather than waiting for them to revisit me. I believe that it is most important to keep the symbolism of our interaction patterns constantly under critical review and to find ways of symbolizing equality.

I have focused upon the minutiae of power-equalization strategies, for it would require a much longer reflection to discuss other power-sharing aspects of this form of leadership. But let me say that I found and still find that sharing power is constantly problematic (as it should be). As soon as we find a power-sharing formula which can be applied successfully we will have technologized rather than liberated democratic leadership.

Let me finally comment briefly upon the third area identified above, that of providing an institutional and social context for the work of the group. I believed that it was essential that as a department we were all informed about the institutional context of our work. This was especially important since we were engaged in an institutional and faculty amalgamation. I therefore believed that it was essential that I involve myself as widely as possible in university administration, in order to be well informed. I had to be careful, however, that my own desire to be informed, albeit for the benefit of the department, did not exclude others from opportunities to participate. I did not always strike the right balance in that regard.

Sharing information became problematic for me. Although it is relatively easy to distribute or circulate material, if information is to be empowering, it needs to be interpreted, challenged and its significance noted. Sometimes this can happen individually, but it also needs to happen collaboratively. So departmental meetings became important information-sharing times. This meant that they were inevitably longer than we ever hoped or tried for, but there was little talk about meetings being something that should ideally be avoided.

I do not know if I shall ever feel completely comfortable in a position of leadership — I want it always to remain problematical, for only then is improvement possible. But that also means that I seldom feel satisfied with my work. Exercising educational leadership as emancipatory praxis is a difficult aspiration. In so many ways the terms are contradictory. Working out these contradictions in ways that are truly empowering requires constant vigilance, for it is easy to generate a state of unproductive frenzy through making every decision a major participatory event. On the other hand, it is also too easy to relieve hard-worked colleagues of the necessity of participation, and maternalistically disempower. The answer is not achieved through balance, but through moment-by-moment strategic decision-making about what it means to empower and emancipate at any given time.

Notes

1 That the emancipatory interest is the most fundamental of human interests, Habermas argues, is discernible through an analysis of the act of speech which exists both for and on the basis of freedom to mutually agree upon truth (cf. Geuss, 1981, p. 65).
2 I consider the role of the facilitator in action research at some length in Grundy, 1984.
3 Since this is a reflection, I write in the past tense. This reflection looks back over the first year of leadership.

References

APPLE, M. (1979) *Ideology and Curriculum,* London, Routledge and Kegan Paul.
FERGUSON, K. (1984) *The Feminist Case Against Bureaucracy*, Philadelphia, Temple University Press.
FREIRE, P. (1972) *Pedagogy of the Oppressed*, Harmondsworth, Penguin.

GEUSS, R. (1981) *The Idea of a Critical Theory: Habermas and the Frankfurt School*, Cambridge, Cambridge University Press.

GIROUX, H. (1986) 'Curriculum, teaching, and the resisting intellectual', *Curriculum and Teaching*, 1, 1/2, pp. 33–42.

GRUNDY, S. (1984) 'Beyond professionalism: Action research as critical pedagogy', Unpublished PhD thesis, Perth, Murdoch University.

GRUNDY, S. (1987a) 'Critical pedagogy and the control of professional knowledge', *Discourse*, 7, 2, pp. 21–36.

GRUNDY, S. (1987b) *Curriculum: Product or Praxis?* Lewes, Falmer Press.

HABERMAS, J. (1972) *Knowledge and Human Interests*, London, Heinemann.

HABERMAS, J. (1974) *Theory and Practice*, London, Heinemann.

HEGARTY, E. (1971) 'The problem-identification phase of curriculum deliberation: Use of the Nominal Group Technique', *Journal of Curriculum Studies*, 9.

Section 4

Feminist Praxis

Chapter 13

The Theory–Practice Relationship in Schooling, Academia and Feminist Theory[1]

Lyn Yates

Everyone, of course, is involved in both practice and theory. For people like me, the practice includes not just teaching and administration and equal opportunity battles in the politics of the institution, but the practice of writing and theorizing. It is important to remember that these latter activities are a practice, because the conditions of that practice affects what is done in them. Some of the conditions of the practice of theorizing in universities, for example, require that the academics take account of what is being done in their areas of interest throughout the world, rather than simply attending to local matters; require that they formally attend to other people's arguments (or, rather, to the arguments of other academics); require that they be looking to be recognized as having something *new* to say. In the past, at least, academics in universities have been given rewards (tenure, promotion) in a way that says the most important theorizing is that which is most abstract, most general, and is least specific to a particular local practice. (I say 'in the past' here, because governments in a number of countries are attempting to reorganize universities towards narrow economic objectives, and this brings with it a new set of problems).

There are other conditions of academic practice too, of course, such as the historically developed forms of disciplines or subjects, and how the boundaries regarding ways of knowing are drawn. This issue has been the focus of an extensive discussion by feminist theorists, and includes a continuing debate about the nature and form of women's studies as an appropriate challenge to traditional disciplines (see for example, Bowles and Duelli Klein, 1983; Magarey, 1983; Sheridan, 1986). But in terms of thinking about the relation of the theorizing that academics do to the problems being addressed in schooling, I want particularly to draw attention to the fact that initial appointments, promotions, tenure reviews, all give greatest weight to theoretical originality rather than practical usefulness, and to international reputation and international publications. So the conditions of academic practice in many ways have worked against being sensitive to local conditions — that is, it is acceptable to deal with local problems such as girls and mathematics, provided you can do so in a way that sees this simply as one case of a problem which is the same everywhere. The colonial cringe of Australian academic practice also makes it difficult for Australian educational or feminist theory to be recognized as having any distinctive form or questions, or any status comparable to overseas work.

Teachers and politicians have often criticized 'ivory tower' academics for producing the very theories that the conditions of their practice are set up to produce. But the conditions of academic work are not simply distorting ones. The time and material conditions available, as well as some of the imperatives (the desire to get the big picture, to canvas a range of arguments, to be critical, to present material in a certain way) have an enabling quality, too, which we begin to become more aware of now that it is under threat.

While academics who theorize are involved in a practice, those who work in schools, and administrators and policy-makers in education departments, are all involved in theory. Their actions and decisions presume philosophical positions on the nature of sexism, the processes through which equal opportunity will best be achieved, not to mention major issues like the nature of good education, the foundations of knowledge, the relations between education and the state. However, the conditions under which people in these situations theorize those questions are constrained in different ways from my own. The conditions are not simply the obvious material differences of time and resources, though these clearly shape the solutions that are found. People are also working to different imperatives.

For example, at one stage I was involved in a case study of a school which was attempting to develop a 'sexually inclusive curriculum', and it was decided that each of us would produce an account of how we had come to think about this issue and what our understandings and concerns about it were. The statements produced by the teachers told a story of incidents and speakers who had made them aware of sexism, and showed that they were trying to develop the 'sexually inclusive curriculum' by working on particular lessons and attending in particular to how the students reacted to these; above all, they were concerned about language and classroom dynamics. My statement referred to my interest growing out of previous work on core curriculum and curriculum theory, and trying to address the issue of what range and content of curriculum would do equal justice to girls; I did not mention language. Our responses in those statements were good examples of the effects of different conditions of theorizing gender and education. School-based initiatives have been sensitive to reforms needing to work in concrete circumstances, and have been exploring insights of feminist theory in doing so. But because of the conditions of their activity, they give less attention to the big picture, or what is happening and what should happen *overall* in education. On the other hand, my failure to mention language in that example was not because I did not think language is important. It was because I had first started reading the new feminist analyses of language a few years earlier and at that time had been excitedly raising them in every class, every staff-room conversation, everything I wrote. By the time of the school case study, these issues had lost their newness and theoretical excitement for me, so I was focusing my attention on an issue which I felt had not yet been given enough attention (where there might be a chance to say something new?), namely, given the new insights of feminist theory, where does that leave the range of fundamental knowledge that schooling should deal in?

The point of all this is that the search for more complex understandings and the academic attempts to address new aspects of the problem are important and do need to go on, but the search for bigger and better critiques can be insensitive to the needs of practical reform (see Williamson, 1981–2; Yates, 1986b). Nevertheless, while the conditions of work in academic institutions and the conditions of work in schools and bureaucracies each have their own constraints, I would argue that it is to their mutual benefit to preserve and use some of these differences. To illustrate this, we might consider the concern of the 1970s to persuade girls to take on non-traditional jobs, and the concern in the 1980s with the Participation and Equity Program (PEP).[2]

What gave the 'non-traditional jobs' and the PEP projects life was not so much formal theoretical propositions about how education worked and what it could do, but beliefs, slogans, rallying ideas: 'Girls Can Do Anything', 'Who Does the Talking?', 'Democratic Decision-Making', 'Access and Success'. The alternative jobs campaigns and PEP were important practical experiments, and it was valuable to see what could be achieved by pushing these. As a result of these practical initiatives and practical research, the idea that in principle women have the capacity to be competent workers in a wide range of areas is now more clearly acknowledged than it otherwise would have been; and the idea that the schooling process involves listening to what girls and women say about their needs and interests, and experimenting with ways to meet these, was similarly boosted through PEP. But it was also valuable to have continual theorizing by those not in the field *which was not simply directed to how we could best get girls to take on a different range of jobs,* or how we could best achieve PEP. Recurrent theorizing on gender and class helped to explain why the initial jobs campaigns did not work as people had hoped that they would, and also to show up class biases and insensitivities in the strategies being pursued (see, for example, Newell, 1985: Franzway and Lowe, 1978; Yates, 1985).[3] With PEP, the use of the literature of educational evaluation and of feminist social theory to raise questions like, 'Might this be a diversionary tactic of the state?', or 'What about outcomes?' These questions are useful in enabling people involved in 'participation and equity' to be self-critical about continuing approaches. They also prepare the ground for when the policy is inevitably dumped for a different sort of emphasis (compare White, 1984, 1985; Yates, 1986b). (This, incidentally, is why it is not even in the Government's interests to have all tertiary research narrowly directed to its own questions — it will be left bereft when policies are seen to be failing, or conditions change and it wants something else.)

Next let us consider the conditions of practice of another form of theory that informs and is used by those involved in gender and education, namely feminist theory. (Feminist theory is the product of a movement and does not simply consist of what is written down, but here I do want to refer to the identified writings and theories we tend to refer to when we are looking for new understandings and approaches to gender and education.) 'Feminist theory' is written for adult women (and sometimes for adult men); it is not usually written to address girls or boys who have not reached adulthood and who are engaged in schooling. Feminist theory is addressed sometimes to a wide and popular readership, sometimes to those who are part of a particular movement, sometimes for specifically academic discourse. For the work to be published and circulated, it will need to be seen to advance the existing state of a particular discussion: it will need to be 'new' either in its content or in the catchiness of its presentation; but it is not a condition of its success that it take account of the concerns of those working in a particular practice, such as schooling, which is not simply about theory.

Consider too that feminist theorists all have specific life histories and associations which inform the work they produce. For example, Mary O'Brien's experience as a midwife gave rise to a new social theory centred on human reproduction as the basis of culture and patriarchy (O'Brien, 1981), while Julia Kristeva is able to write highly abstract and difficult analyses of subjectivity and to pour scorn on simpler feminist programmes, from the position of one who has a track record of outstanding academic success and honours and who is working in a country where such intellectuality is valued and where the material conditions for such theorizing, in the form of certain journals, exist (see Moi, 1986). Similarly, it is hardly surprising that those who are actually employed as psychoanalysts see the core of feminist action in a liberating psychoanalytic practice, and those who work in media see theories of representation as the key to understanding ideology.

Now, much as it may seem like it, I am not trying here to argue some very crude determinist position regarding people's material being determining their ideas, but I am rather trying to draw attention to the fact that those of us working in education are trying to deal with some particular concerns which on the whole feminist theorists have been fairly insensitive to, because they are working in other conditions and responding to other imperatives. And the point of this is that, in so far as we want to talk of 'the theory–practice relationship', it is not simply a matter of feminist theory providing the answer which our practice in education then tries imperfectly to live up to. It is also that, if we consider the practice of education, we should be critical of those theories which inadequately take account of this.

One thing that theories such as Mary O'Brien's (1981) *Politics of Reproduction* or Michelle Barrett's (1980) *Women's Oppression Today* or Kathy Ferguson's (1984) *The Feminist Case Against Bureaucracy* have in common is the tendency to write off institutionalized schooling as a field for feminist practice. And in doing so, of course, they say many useful things about the ideological tasks schooling performs in moulding girls to the purposes of 'the state', that is, to accepting and perpetuating forms of inequality and social division, to accepting non-feminist definitions of what is important knowledge and what is a valued way of life. But the mistake these theorists make is in suggesting that women working in schooling are simply caught up in this inexorable process in a quite different way from the theorists themselves who do presumably see their own ideas as something other than ideology and who expect their ideas to have some effect on the people who listen to them and read them.

Feminist theorists, themselves usually the products of high levels of formal education, generally fail to acknowledge that this education may have contributed to their ability to criticize or 'see through' the sexist forms of contemporary society. If ideology is all there is (or if discourse is all there is), why are their views any good? Why are they able to write what they do? Why do they attack other feminist theories in terms of the content of those theories, rather than by talking about the limited conditions under which such theories were produced (the favoured form of attack on male theorists)? It is because ideas matter, because they are not totally reducible to a determined ideology or to a discursive realm in which individuals play no part. And the formal process of education has some value in understanding things, that new insights are not *simply* the product of being in particular situations (though the reverse does not apply either).

In terms of theory, I would suggest that neither feminist sociological accounts of education, nor feminist post-structuralist theories have produced theories which satisfactorily deal with the question of how they themselves are able to write what they do, and they are too critical of schooling and too limited as a basis for action in relation to schooling as a result.

In this first section of the chapter, then, I have argued that theorizing in different contexts is subject to different constraints and is likely to come up with different emphases and solutions. For those working in educational policy and administration, at times it may be most useful to concentrate on getting a particular movement going and at other times to stand back and draw from other fields of theory. Those working in the conditions of academic practice have the luxury of some more extended and distanced reflections on educational practice, but may be drawn to abstraction and novelty and insensitivity to local conditions and the conditions of actually producing change as a result. Those working in the area we call 'feminist theory' have undoubtedly been a source of new insights about women in society and the nature of ideology, but they have rarely taken institutional education and the problem of action in it as a central problematic, and this has been some limitation of their social theory as well as for attempts to develop their ideas in the field of educational practice.

In the second part of the chapter I outline what I see as three continuing dilemmas which confront those attempting to theorize and also those attempting to act in education with regard to non-sexist or feminist ends.

Education as Selection versus Education as Learning

Dilemmas for policy and practice are often talked about as differences between political positions ('liberal' as compared with 'radical' feminism; changing the shares of the cake, compared with changing the cake) or, sometimes as dilemmas between long-term and short-term objectives. In fact, mixed up in this is something about the nature of institutionalized education that both educational theorists and feminist theorists have found very hard to put together. This is that state systems of education always have some involvement in selecting and certifying people to take their places in the incessant division of labour and some involvement in teaching them things. Further, understanding what is involved and what is possible in relation to teaching and learning requires more than seeing this merely as the ideological branch of the selection–allocation process, while, equally, working on attempts to feminize the teaching–learning process does not make selection-allocation disappear. And to make things additionally complicated, we have to deal with something which is having an immediate and compulsory impact on children and adolescents but which also has an important but complicated and unclear relationship to post-school life. Let me give some examples of some of the dilemmas that have arisen here.

In terms of practice, those who are putting their efforts into increasing the proportion of women in higher positions, or in increasing the numbers of girls succeeding in mathematics, are sometimes portrayed as limited reformers, concerned with changing shares of a cake, while leaving the unsatisfactory nature of the cake untouched. Those who are working on a 'feminist curriculum', on the other hand, on changing classroom processes and developing alternative science, mathematics or the newly instituted Victorian Certificate of Education courses, are seen as having properly feminist approaches. But because of education's complex relation to the wider society I would suggest that there are problems in both approaches, or, equally, there is some value in both. For example, in Victoria in 1983 there was a move towards a policy change to remove the competitive graded assessment of the compulsory English subject at Higher School Certificate level. Doing away with the competitive graded assessment is seen by many people as one way of beginning to 'change the cake' in schooling.[4] But as Fomin's (1984) and Tyler's (1984) work shows, because the proposal to remove grading was beginning with only one subject, and because this happened to be a subject where girls did well, it would work to the short-term detriment of girls. And indeed, such an approach might serve to reinforce rather than undermine the difference between 'hard sciences' and other forms of knowledge, and to further entrench the former as the benchmark of what was important.

Or again, we might consider the Victorian move to decentralize the selection of principals in schools. This had been supported by many as a fundamental move towards a more democratic education and against bureaucratic hierarchies which in the past had worked to the disadvantage of women. But because of the composition of the supposedly 'democratic' local committees (which rarely had more than a single token woman) and because of ingrained cultural assumptions about what authority and the dynamic personality looks like, fewer rather than more women were chosen. And again this is not just a matter of concern because of the frustrated career aspirations of a few women teachers; it is of concern because it is indicative of a continuing culture of schooling whose assumptions about women's and men's roles and rights have failed to be changed.

Another way in which the dilemma of concentrating on getting girls to succeed versus trying to get students to think about themselves and the world differently is a difficult one, relates to the complex matter of how people begin to understand discrimination and to want change. There is some evidence that schoolgirls do not necessarily see themselves as discriminated against and do not necessarily appreciate teachers trying to teach them 'women's studies' to show them that they are; there is also some evidence that women's experience of discrimination increases as they get older, and even as they reach higher positions in employment. For example, a study of women academics in Australia found a greater proportion of those in senior positions expressed a belief in discrimination than those at lower levels (see Cass *et al.*, 1983; Eisenstein, 1981). This suggests that there are limits to what a changed curriculum and pedagogy will accomplish in relation to young people's consciousness, and that, given that schooling is involved in the processes of selection and allocation to further education and to the workforce, it is not simply a limited and reformist approach to be concerned about 'who gets what', about what basis girls will have for not living in poverty and to what extent whole professions will be able to be organized around the interests and assumptions of men.

Nevertheless, what is taught in schools is important too: 'who gets what' can be overrated, and in any case who eventually does get what is clearly related to what is taught in schools. Elshtain (1981), Ferguson (1984), Franzway and Lowe

(1978) and a host of other writers have been right in pointing out the selfishness and limited impact involved in focusing too heavily on 'women and careers' in the context of a society with greatly unequal jobs and unemployment. On a purely pragmatic note, it has become increasingly clear that concentrating on getting girls and women a bigger share of success is hard to do without recognizing that the process and content of education will have to be changed; and that improving the situation of women and employment will be related to what they (and men) learn about themselves at school, and not simply whether they get the right qualifications. To take one example, attempts to encourage girls to go on with mathematics and science by themselves have had remarkably little success in proportion to the amount of equal opportunity resources devoted to this issue. Altering the numbers who do so may require some fundamental reworking of the cultural context, not to mention the content and pedagogy of the subjects. In addition, that women's entry to paid employment is not attacked simply by increasing their success in education is shown by a host of facts, such as women's lower retention rates to the higher education courses they have been qualified for (Powles, 1987), their lower retention to higher education notwithstanding their success in their first degree (Burns, 1984), and the fact that the relative wage gap between women's earnings to men's is actually widest among those with higher education (Commonwealth Department or Education, 1985).

So both 'who gets what' and what is taught in school matters; neither is easily changed and, given the complexity of the short-term and long-term effects of schooling, there are plenty of dilemmas about which strategies of change to put one's energies into and which research problems to pursue.

There is a further dilemma which arises in relation to these complexities which could be termed a 'big policy/local approach' dilemma. Two good examples of this are the question of whether and in what way 'women's studies' should be taught in schools (and in tertiary education, for that matter), and the single sex/coeducation debate. Certain things can be said about both these issues at a general theoretical level, but the fact that schools are continuing institutions where teachers, students and parents have existing beliefs and enthusiasms means that in practice different approaches may be appropriate (or that a common policy will produce different reactions) in different schools. So there is something to be said for some local determination of these matters. The other side of this dilemma, however, is that in relation to equal opportunity for women and girls, the framing of general system-wide policies which are binding on all schools is an important avenue of reform.

Finally, on the matters relating to education as selection and education as learning, and short-term and long-term perspectives, I want to draw attention to an interesting split which I think is found in the theoretical attempts to deal with gender and schooling. Feminist sociologists take as their central focus education's role in producing the perpetual division of labour in society. They do, of course, deal with education as learning, but they see this learning as socialization or, more precisely, as the inculcation of the ideological foundations of the division of labour. Writers like Barrett (1980), Branson and Miller (1979), McDonald (1981), Porter (1983), David (1980), O'Donnell (1984) and others show how schooling inculcates ideology about women's place, though they also might allow that there are contradictions in its processes of doing so (for example, between achievement orientation as compared with domestic ideology) and that these may provide some basis for change. But in these analyses, at most what educationists can do is be critical and resist.

Now there is another group of theorists who focus centrally on education as about learning, who see this as a potential area for creative action, not simply 'resistance', and who are interested in feminine epistemology and working out the basis of a better form of education. These theorists are philosophers like Jane Roland Martin (1982) and Madeleine Grumet (1982) and psychologists like Carol Gilligan (1977). These writers try to look at how institutionalized education has been framed around masculine interests at a deep level, not just in terms of its examples and overt encouragement, and try to suggest alternatives. For example, Gilligan's (1977, 1982) well-known work was trying to show something of the logic, substantiality and difference when knowledge, morality and reasoning were framed in terms of an integrated and embedded standpoint of responsibility and care, as compared with the familiar cause–effect hierarchical reasoning which values general principle over personal relations (see also Gilligan et al., 1990). And Jane Roland Martin (1982) deconstructed the traditional foundation of liberal education, the concept of the 'educated man', to show its genesis in a figure detached or abstracted from all concrete responsibility. She concluded,

> An adequate conception of the educated person must join together what Peters and Hirst have torn asunder: mind and body; thought and action; reason, feeling and emotion. To do this the educational realm must be reconstituted to include the reproductive processes of society (Martin, 1982, p. 147).

But Martin, along with Gilligan, and to a lesser extent Grumet, has almost nothing to say about schooling's involvement in selection.

What I have been trying to say in all this is that a continual dilemma for both practitioners and theorists is trying to negotiate useful and creative approaches, given the complexities of schooling and education as an institution. Some of these complexities which action and theory has to try to deal with are:

1 that schooling is both an allocating institution and a source of under-standings for each generation and that each of these potentially contribute to change in women's situation, though action towards one may undermine action towards the other;
2 that we need to maintain a critique of schooling given its role as an insti-tution of the state, but we also need to work out things to do other than simply critique;
3 that we have to consider both short-term and long-term outcomes;
4 that the processes contributing to the effectiveness of strategies do not necessarily work in the same way in different schools and for different individuals.

Essentialism versus Pluralism

A second issue that has been of much concern both for feminist theory and for practice in education has been that of 'essentialism' versus 'plurality'. The dilemma concerns the extent to which 'women' should be treated as a category or group and sexism or women's inequality understood as founded in some common processes related to all women, and the extent to which feminism is rather a recognizing, being sensitive to, valuing of plurality, and that women's inequality/oppression does not take a common form, but operates differently as one's race, class, country differs.

In Australia, in research, in policy and in the rhetoric on gender and education since 1975, we can see some changes, changes that represent development towards a greater recognition of plurality or diversity but, paradoxically, also signs of development towards a greater essentialism. In the mid-1970s, the problem of the inequality of girls, of women being invisible, of sexism in the processes of schooling, was seen as one common to women as a category, though groups such as migrant girls or working-class girls had some added-on disadvantages which might also be attended to. From the late 1980s, however, we can see some changes. One plank of the 1987 *National Policy for the Education of Girls in Australian Schools* is that, 'Strategies to improve the quality of education for girls should be based on an understanding that girls are not a homogeneous group.' This policy takes examples of Aboriginal girls and girls of non-English-speaking background in its mainstream presentation of how schooling for girls operates, whereas the 1975 report, *Girls' Schools and Society*, had dealt with these groups separately as 'Groups with Special Needs'. Policy-makers and teachers, I think, partly as a result of quite a lot of good Australian research in this area, are also far more sensitive now to class issues in relation to counter-sexist strategies. So in these respects, a pluralist or differentiated understanding of gender as an issue for education has been developing.

On the other hand, some of the work now going on in relation to curriculum development and teaching processes appropriate to girls assumes more strongly than in earlier strategies some view of a common 'women's culture', and that certain curriculum and pedagogical procedures (using discussion, non-competitive assessment, negotiation, focusing on social interests) are commonly appropriate to girls and are to be contrasted with a traditional form of schooling/organization/administration which is tagged as a masculinist one. Yet some of those working in the area of girls of non-English-speaking background are beginning to raise questions about whether some of these pedagogical procedures are in fact related to the preferred styles of women of a particular culture, rather than springing from some essential quality of womanness (Kalantzis and Cope, 1987; see also Walker and O'Loughlin, 1984; Martin, 1982). In recent developments, too, very little attention has been given to the sizeable numbers of girls who do in fact like mathematics and science (currently, at a time when girls' participation in mathematics and science is seen as a big problem, they in fact constitute around 40 per cent of those doing science at university and over 40 per cent of those doing medicine and veterinary science; the falling popularity of science courses at HSC level has been a phenomenon affecting boys, not just girls). Each year in my DipEd elective on 'Girls, School and Society' I find a number of women who have done mathematics and science, who are fervently enthusiastic about these subjects, who recount their early dislike of essay-based discursive subjects, and who object strongly to the idea that mathematics and science have to be transformed into a form of social science before girls will be able to cope with it. Of course, the reasons why these women are then choosing teaching rather than other science-related occupations is another issue.

Yet another aspect of this essentialism–pluralism dilemma is that, although sensitive differentiated understanding is needed, if we are not careful we can differentiate gender as an issue out of existence. Mary O'Brien has coined the term 'commatization' to explain the way enlightened theorists and policy-makers now refer to 'class (comma), gender (comma), ethnicity (comma), youth (comma), and so on (O'Brien, 1984) as a token gesture in an analysis which remains based on one sort of framework, the class one. In Australia, the most widely-read contemporary study of schools and inequality, *Making the Difference* (Connell *et al.*, 1984), took gender as part of its focus. Yet when it came to the crunch, the proposed solution was the 'organic *working-class* school', not a form of schooling that addressed processes relating to gender division. And in Australian policy documents, references to a 'sexually inclusive curriculum' in the early 1980s soon becomes transformed into the more general 'inclusive curriculum'. In at least some of its current government-sponsored forms, the 'inclusive curriculum' has been turned into a flabby, commatized injunction to take account of everyone, with no clear sense of what this would mean, as compared with Jean Blackburn's original discussion of a sexually inclusive curriculum that had a clear framework as to the sort of curriculum transformation that would be required (see discussion, *Curriculum Perspectives* and in particular Suggett, 1987; Yates, 1988). So some 'essentialism', in so far as it means having some heart to the analysis, is not a bad thing.

In relation to the essentialism–pluralism dilemmas for gender studies in education, we need both types of discussion going on and being refined in the light of each other. In order to theorize how the curriculum has excluded women, or how women have been excluded from high positions, or what schooling should be aiming to do for women in terms of learning and preparation for employment, we need to do some 'essentialist' thinking about what women as women tend to do and have done: their involvement in child bearing and rearing; their heavy involvement in unpaid labour; their association with emotional or integrative approaches, and so on. But in order to work out appropriate strategies and pedagogies, as well as to refine our understanding of sexism, we need careful empirical studies of women and girls, so that we see gender in concrete terms which always take class/ethnic/age/national culture forms.

The Conditions and Mood of the Times

In that both feminist theory and educational theory are theories for practice, aimed to produce change and not just armchair critique, the conditions and mood of the times are clearly of concern regarding lines of strategy to develop.[5]

Earlier in this paper I suggested that at times what action in relation to gender in education needs is a better critique, but at other times what is most important is simply the conviction that something can be done and some support for doing this. In the case of class and education, the popular writings of the 1960s (Illich, Freire, Goodman and others) and the critiques of 'new sociology' of the early 1970s, in the conditions of economic boom and reforming optimism of the period, were taken as an inspiration for new ways of tackling the class problem. Since then, conditions have got worse, the critiques have got bigger and better, and in practice the dilemmas of class inequality and education are being treated as a lost cause, at most a possibility for holding operations. There is some danger of the work on gender following the same route, especially if all we can offer to increased pressures in the field of practice is a form of grand theory that says in a highly abstract way that ideology, discourse and critique is all there is.

The dilemma facing gender and education today is this. Just as our experience with twelve years of reforming strategies and research has made clear how difficult and extensive a task it is to produce relatively straightforward change in matters such as girls and mathematics or career success for female teachers, we face a climate of economic restraint and ideological reaction which has little tolerance for 'airy-fairy' programmes of long-term reform and which wants results (and results of a certain type) now! Furthermore, in Victoria, those trying to promote different approaches to curriculum and pedagogy in the interests of girls and women are competing with (they are unfortunately rarely part of) an enormous number of other changes being forced on teachers: the complete overhaul in form and content of the HSC; the 'Frameworks' project, aimed at providing a new structure and coherence to the school curriculum P-10; the dismantling and regionalization of support services, including the Equal Opportunity Unit. In the UK, teachers have to contend with the National Curriculum on the one hand and the radical transformation of the conditions of schools and teachers on the other. In the USA, teachers in many states have to contend with a major reduction in the funding of schools. And in all these countries, just as considerable numbers of female teachers have become fired up about getting promotion, attending' workshops, networking, doing the right things, opportunities for promotion are dwindling, ambitious men are fighting harder than ever for them, and there is the beginning of a backlash against affirmative action under the mistaken impression that it had ever really been in place.

For theory and research, there is plenty of work to do. One issue which deserves careful study, for example, is the nature of the paid work currently available and likely to be available in the future, to get some critical perspective on the 'mathematics and science' problem. But the overall dilemma for research and practice at present is how to continue to find doable things in an era when concern about sex equity is no longer seen as a priority. Equally, there is a problem of how to maintain a critique and a wider perspective on the changes that are needed which does not follow the route of the class analysis of education, which does not split completely into, on the one hand, an analysis which has no practical outcome and, on the other, reformist practices that take as given that a small amelioration rather than altering the overall picture is the aim.

Notes

1 For a more extensive discussion of the issues raised in this chapter, see L. Yates (1990) *Theory/Practice Dilemmas: Gender, Knowledge and Education*, Geelong, Deakin University.

2 These reform projects are taken from the Australian context, but similar projects can be found in other Western countries in this period. See Kelly, G. (Ed.) (1989) *International Handbook on Women and Education*, New York, Greenwood Press.

3 In the UK, the work of Valerie Walkerdine provided another line of valuable enquiry about why such reforms did not simply produce the desired outcomes.

See, for example, Walkerdine, V. (1985) 'On the regulation of speaking and silence: Subjectivity, class and gender in contemporary schooling', in Steedman, C., Urwin, C. and Walkerdine, V. (Eds) (1989) *Language, Gender and Childhood,* London, Routledge; and Walkerdine, V. (1989) *Democracy in the Kitchen: Regulating Mothers and Daughters,* London, Virago.

4 It was one of the few concrete suggestions about ways to change the shape of schooling made in Connell *et al. Making the Difference* (1984) which identified the 'competitive academic curriculum' as at the heart of the problem.

5 In Victoria, I think Ministerial Paper No. 6 will go down in the future as a classic example of a reforming policy out of key with the changes of its time, a promoter of PEP and an ignorer of schooling's relation to the workforce just at the moment when the holes in the process approach to equity and the concern about the economic realities of life were beginning to gather momentum — and I very much hope that the recent *National Policy for the Education of Girls* does not suffer the same fate.

References

Australia, Committee on Social Change and the Education of Women Study Group (1975) *Girls Schools and Society,* Canberra, Schools Commission.

Barrett, M. (1980) *Women's Oppression Today,* London, Verso.

Blackburn, J. (1981) Becoming Equally Human, Address to the Australian Womens Education Conference, Canberra.

Bowles, G. and Duelli Klein, R. (Eds) (1983) *Theories of Women's Studies,* London, Routledge and Kegan Paul.

Branson, J. and Miller, D. (1979) *Class, Sex and Education in Capitalist Society,* Melbourne, Sorrett.

Burns, R. (1984) 'Getting there, staying there, going on', in Burns, R. and Sheehan, B. (Eds) *Women and Education,* Bundoora, La Trobe University.

Cass, B., Dawson, M., Temple, D., Wills, S. and Winkler, A. (1983) *Why So Few?,* Sydney, University of Sydney Press.

Commonwealth Department of Education (1985) *Women in Australian Education II: Educational Attainment and Labour Force Status,* Canberra.

Connell, R.W., Ashenden, D.J., Kessler, S. and Dowsett, G. (1982) *Making the Difference: Schools, Families and Social Division,* Sydney, Allen and Unwin.

David, M. (1980) *The Family, the State and Education,* London, Routledge.

Department of Employment, Education and Training (1987) *The National Policy for the Education of Girls in Australian Schools,* Canberra Australian Government Printing Service.

Eisenstein, Z. (1981) 'Reform and/or revolution: Towards a united women's movement', in Sargent, L. (Ed.) *Women and Revolution,* Boston, South End Press.

Elshtain, J.B. (1981) *Public Man, Private Woman,* Princeton, Princeton University Press.

Ferguson, K.E. (1984) *The Feminist Case Against Bureaucracy,* Philadelphia, Temple University Press.

Fomin, F. (1984) 'The best and the brightest: The selective function of mathematics in the school curriculum', in Johnson, L. and Tyler, D. (Eds) *Cultural Politics* (Melbourne Working Papers Series 5), Melbourne, University of Melbourne Department of Education.

Franzway, S. and Lowe, J. (1978) 'Sex role theory: Political cul-de-sac?', *Refractory Girl,* 16, pp. 14–16.

Frieire, P. (1972) *Pedagogy of the Oppressed,* Penguin, Harmondsworth, Middlesex.

Frieire, P. (1972) *Cultural Action for Freedom,* Penguin, Harmondsworth, Middlesex.

GILLIGAN, C. (1977) 'In a different voice: Women's conception of self and morality', *Harvard Educational Review*, 47(4), pp. 481–517

GILLIGAN, C. (1982) *In a Different Voice: Psychological Theory and Women's Development*, Cambridge, MA., Harvard University Press.

GILLIGAN, C., LYONS, N.P. and HAMMER, T.J. (Eds) (1990) *Making Connections*, Cambridge, MA., Harvard University Press.

GOODMAN, P. (1971) *Growing up Absurd*, Vintage Books, New York.

GRUMET, M. (1988) *Bittermilk: Women and Teaching*, Amherst, University of Massachussetts Press.

ILLICH, I. (1971) *Deschooling Society*, Pelican Harmondsworth, Middlesex.

KALANTZIS, M. and COPE, B. (1987) 'Cultural differences, gender differences: Social literacy and inclusive curriculum', *Curriculum Perspectives*, 7, 1, pp. 64–9.

KELLY, G. (1989) *International Handbook of Women's Education*, New York, Greenwood Press.

McDONALD, M. (1981) 'Schooling and the reproduction of class and gender relations', in DALE, R., ESLAND, G., FERGUSON, R. and McDONALD, M. (Eds) *Education and the State, Vol II*, Lewes, Falmer Press.

MAGAREY, S. (1983) 'Women's Studies in Australia — towards transdisciplinary learning?', *Journal of Educational Thought*, 17, pp. 162–71.

MARTIN, J.R. (1982) 'Excluding women from the educational realm', *Harvard Education Review*, 52, 2.

MOI, T. (Ed.) (1986) *The Kristeva Reader*, Oxford Blackwell.

NEWELL, E. (1985) 'Gender and schooling', in TOWNS, D. (Ed.) *The Responsibility to Educate Girls for a Technologically Oriented Society*, Geelong, Deakin University Press.

O'BRIEN, M. (1981) *The Politics of Reproduction*, Boston, Routledge and Kegan Paul.

O'BRIEN, M. (1984) 'The commatization of women: Patriarchal fetishism in the sociology of women', *Interchange*, 15, 2, pp. 43–60.

O'DONNELL, C. (1984) *The Basis of the Bargain: Gender, Schooling and Jobs*, Sydney, Allen and Unwin.

PORTER, P. (1983) 'Social policy, education and women in Australia', in BALDOCK, C. and CASS, B. (Eds) *Women, Social Welfare and the State*, Sydney, Allen and Unwin.

POWLES, M. (1987) *Women's Participation in Tertiary Education: A Review of Recent Australian Research* (2nd ed.), Melbourne, University of Melbourne Centre for Research into Higher Education.

SHERIDAN, S. (1986) 'From margin to mainstream: Situating women's studies', *Australian Feminist Studies*, 2, pp. 1–14.

SUGGETT, D. (1987) 'Point and counter point', *Curriculum Perspectives*, 7, 1, pp. 69–74.

TYLER, D. (1984) ' "For the good of all students" — the marginalization of gender disadvantage in recent Victorian educational initiatives', in JOHNSON, L. and TYLER, D. (Eds) *Cultural Politics* (Melbourne Working Papers Series 5), Melbourne, University of Melbourne Department of Education.

WALKER, J.C. and O'LOUGHLIN, M.A. (1984) 'The ideal of the educated woman: Jane Roland Martin on education and gender', *Educational Theory*, 34, 4, pp. 327–40.

WALKERDINE, V. (1985) 'On the regulation of speaking and silence', in STEEDMAN, C., IRWIN, C. and WALKERDINE, V. *Language Gender and Childhood*, London, Routledge.

WALKERDINE, V. (1989) *Democracy in the Kitchen*, London, Virago Press.

WHITE, D. (1984) 'Participating in nothing: New moves in education', *Arena*, 68, pp. 79–90.

WHITE, D. (1985) 'Education: Controlling the participants', *Arena*, 72, pp. 63–79.

WILLIAMSON, J. (1981–2) 'Does girl no. 20 understand ideology?', *Screen Education*, 40, pp. 80–2.

YATES, L. (1985) 'Is "girl-friendly" schooling really what girls need?', in WHYTE, J., DEEM, R., KANT, L. and CRUIKSHANK, M. (Eds) *Girl-Friendly Schooling*, London, Methuen.

YATES, L. (1986a) 'Disciplines of enquiry, theories of action and movements of social change: Lessons from education', Unpublished paper presented to the Humanities Research Centre conference on *Feminist Enquiry as a Transdisciplinary Enterprise*, University of Adelaide.

YATES, L. (1986b) 'Theorizing inequality today', *British Journal of Sociology of Education*, 7, 2, pp. 119–34.

YATES, L. (1988) 'Does "all students" include girls? Some reflections on recent educational policy, practice and theory', *Australian Education Researcher*, 15, 1, pp. 41–57.

YATES, L. (1990) *Theory/Practice Dilemmas: Gender, Knowledge and Education*, Geelong, Deakin University Press.

Notes on Contributors

Helen Bannister
Helen has a background in teaching, research and policy, and has tutored and lectured in the Sociology of Education at the University of Melbourne and Rusden. In the area of education policy she has published research on gender issues in school assessment and tertiary selection practices for the Participation and Equity Programme and the Curriculum Development Centre. She has held a policy position in youth affairs and, as a result, was a member of policy working parties of the Youth Ministers Council, the steering committee of the National Youth Affairs Research Scheme. At present, she is lecturer in Sociology at Victoria University of Technology and teaches courses in the Sociology of Health and Social Policy. Her current research is in the area of health policy: in particular, the examination of municipal public health plans as a site for the construction of health needs.

Jill Blackmore
Jill Blackmore works as a senior lecturer in the School of Curriculum and Administrative Studies in the Faculty of Education, Deakin University, Geelong campus. She previously taught educational administration at Monash University for two years, and secondary school maths, general studies and history with the Victorian Ministry for fourteen years. She has published in a wide range of refereed journals and edited collections dealing with feminist theories of administration, policy and history, her doctorate being on vocationalism in Victorian education 1900–60. Her current research interests include developing a critical feminist perspective on educational leadership, the equity implications of the vocationalization and 'managerialist' restructuring of education, the history of the parent movement and teacher unionism in education and the relationship of each to the role of the state in education, and the impact of gender reform policies in schools on women and girls. Her publications include *Assessment and Accountability* (1988) and *Making Educational History: A Feminist Perspective* (1991).

Clare Burton
Clare Burton, with a background in anthropology and sociology, has focused in her research and teaching upon organizational theory, gender equity and, more generally, the study of women and work. She was a senior lecturer in

Administrative Studies at Kuring-gai College of Advanced Education. She has published extensively, her first book being *Subordination: Feminism and Social Theory* (1985), and principal author of *Women's Worth: Pay Equity and Job Evaluation in Australia* (1987). An active member of the feminist and labour movements, she has been a consultant to various government agencies, and written monographs for the Affirmative Action Agency, such as *Redefining Merit* (1988). More recently, she has moved into the area of administration, as Director of Equal Opportunity in Public Employment for the New South Wales government, and currently as the Commissioner for Public Sector Equity in the Premier's Department, Queensland. Her latest book is a critical analysis of the assumptions underlying EO policies, their implementation and effect, titled *The Promise and the Price* (1991).

Hester Eisenstein
Hester Eisenstein is the author of the well-known text, *Contemporary Feminist Thought*. Her publications range across feminist critiques of policy, research methodology, bureaucratic, organizational and state theory. Her academic work, which has been included in significant contemporary Australian feminist collections, has been informed by her experience in bureaucracies and Equal Opportunity. In particular, she served in the Office of the Director of Equal Opportunity in Public Employment of New South Wales 1980–6, as Senior Adviser and then Assistant Director, and was Leader of the Equal Opportunity Employment Unit in the NSW Department of Education 1986–8. She is currently Professor in the Woman's Studies Program in the American Studies Department at the State University of New York at Buffalo. Her most recent book is *Gender Shock: Practising Feminism on Two Continents* (1991), and she is writing a book on the 'gender experience' of Australian femocrats.

Terry Evans
Associate Professor of Distance Education at Deakin University. He has researched and published widely on a variety of education issues including gender and education, sociology of education and distance education. Dr Evans's books include *A Gender Agenda* (Allen and Unwin, 1988); *Critical Reflections on Distance Education* (Falmer Press, 1989, edited with D. Nation) and *Beyond the Text: Contemporary Writing on Distance Education* (Deakin University Press, 1991, edited with Bruce King). He is currently the director of the Master of Distance Education course at Deakin University and is engaged in research into innovation and change within open and distance education.

Shirley Grundy
Shirley Grundy is a Senior Lecturer in the Department of Social, Cultural and Curriculum Studies at the University of New England. She has written extensively in areas relating to curriculum policy and theory, action research and teacher professionalism. From 1989 to 1992 she was head of the department of Social, Cultural and Curriculum Studies. She has also had extensive professional commitments. She serves on the Executives of the Australian Association for Research on Education and the NSW Teacher Education Council, representing this latter body on the Ministerial Council on Teacher Education and the Quality of Teaching. Her book, *Curriculum: Product or Praxis?* has been published in both English and Spanish versions.

Jane Kenway
Jane Kenway works as a senior lecturer in the School of Administrative and Curriculum Studies at Deakin University, Geelong campus. Her research and publications concentrate on the connections between education discourses, social injustice and educational change, and she has published widely on these topics. Her current research includes a post-structuralist empirical study of gender reform programmes in schools and a deconstructive analysis of market metaphors and practices in current education policy. She is an active participant in education debates in academic and professional journals and in a number of public forums organized by teachers and parents. Among her recent publications are *Gender and Educational Policy: A Call for New Directions* (1990) and *Re-visions: Feminist Theories in Education* (1992), and an edited collection with Sue Willis, *Hearts and Minds: Girls, Schooling and Self-esteem* (1989).

Barbara Preston
Canberra-based research consultant, specializing in the teaching profession — its nature and characteristics, future supply and demand, and professional entry standards. She spent ten years as a teacher union research officer with the Victorian Secondary Teachers Association and as Federal Research Officer of the Australian Teachers Union from 1988 to 1991, doing major work on issues such as the relationships between public and private schooling, education funding and administration, curriculum and assessment, teachers' professional training and development, teachers' career and industrial conditions, participation and equity in post-compulsory education implications for women of various industrial strategies, and the nature and role of the public sector. Barbara has an honours degree in Political Science from the University of New South Wales and a Diploma of Education from the University of Newcastle. She has worked overseas and in Australia for government departments, universities and community organizations as well as teacher unions, and has been active in the women's movement and the labour movement.

Kerreen Reiger
Kerreen Reiger taught professional students in health sciences and welfare at Phillip Institute since 1975, and now at La Trobe University since 1989, particularly in the areas of sociology of health and the professions, gender and family, and social policy. Her doctoral research on the Australian family in the first half of the twentieth century traced the historical development of the medicalization of childbirth and the emergence of the domestic economy and infant welfare movements, as strategies aiming at 'modernizing' family life, out of which her first book, *Disenchantment of the Home: The Modernization of the Australian Family 1880–1940* developed. Since then she has received ARC funding for two projects; the first is a study of family and cultural change in the post-war years and includes interviews with women who had children in the 1950s–1970s. The second project focuses more specifically on the politics of reproduction, examining changes in the management of childbirth and infancy since the 1950s. The research is informed by both historical and sociological methodologies and a theoretical framework drawn from critical social theory and contributes to current policy and practice debates.

Deborah Tyler

Deborah Tyler is a Lecturer in Cultural Studies at the Victoria University of Technology. She was a co-editor of the 'History of the present' special issue of *History of Education Review* (Spring 1991), and co-editor with Denise Meredyth of *Child, Citizen and Culture* (forthcoming). Her published work takes a Foucaultian approach to the history of childhood in Australia.

Gaby Weiner

Was a local authority office worker and then a primary teacher before she went into research at the National Foundation for Educational Research (NFER) after completing an MA dissertation on Education and Sex Discrimination in 1976. She has also worked as manager of an inner-city Youth Opportunities Scheme in London and then Project Leader for the Schools Council Sex Differentiation Project. After 1983 she worked at the Open University, first as Course Manager for a number of curriculum courses, then as co-author (with Madeleine Arnot) of the Open University MA module Gender and Education, and finally as a Staff Tutor based in the London region. Since leaving the Open University in 1989, she has taken up the appointment of Principal Lecturer at South Bank Polytechnic (soon to be South Bank University) and is currently Course Director of the MA in Education. She has published widely on gender and education in refereed journals and collections. These publications include a number of research reports and several edited collections (1985, 1987, 1990). Her doctorate was on Harriet Martineau, the nineteenth-century feminist writer (1991). She is currently editor of the *British Educational Research Journal* and Director of the ESRC project Case Studies in the Development of Equitable Staffing Policies in Further and Higher Education (1991–4).

Bruce Wilson

Bruce Wilson is currently the Director of the Union Research Centre on Office Technology, which is a research initiative of the Public Sector Union and the Australian Taxation Office to provide independent advice to the Union on issues associated with the professional and technological modernization of the Taxation Office. He is seconded from the Department of Social and Educational Studies in the Institute of Education at the University of Melbourne, where he has taught extensively in sociology and education and was the Director of the Institute's Youth Research Centre 1988–91. He has co-authored two books, *Confronting School and Work* and *Shaping Futures*, and co-edited a third, *For Your Own Good: Young People and State Intervention in Australia*. His research interests have focused for many years on exploring the character and implications of social division (the intersection of class, gender and ethnic relations) in Australia, and its implications for change, with a specific focus upon the relationship between education and the labour market.

Joanna Wyn

Senior Lecturer in the Department of Social and Educational Studies, Institute of Education at the University of Melbourne, where she is Director of the Youth Research Centre. Her interests focus on the sociology of youth, encompassing the areas of education, the labour market and gender relations.

Lyn Yates

Lyn Yates is Senior Lecturer in the Centre for the Study of Cultural and Educational Practice at La Trobe University. She has written extensively on inequality, feminism and education. Recent publications include *Theory/Practice Dilemmas: Gender, Knowledge and Education* (Deakin University Press) and *Policy, Research and the Question of Gender* (ACER, 1992).

Anna Yeatman

Currently Foundation Professor of Women's Studies at the University of Waikato in New Zealand. Her previous position was as Senior Lecturer in Sociology at Flinders University in South Australia. She is completing a book on feminism and contemporary epistemological politics. Other research interests include restructuring and its implications for the professions and the acquisition/delivery of professional knowledge; and equal opportunity policy in the context of both enterprise bargaining and globalization. An Australian, she has carried out a number of consultancies in public policy and public management areas in Australia, and hopes to acquire similar experience in the New Zealand setting. To some degree this experience will be trans-Tasman in character, and research planning already includes examination of the implications of CER for equal opportunity and related types of policy.

Index